HARRY S. TRUMAN

Fair Dealer and Cold Warrior

TWAYNE'S TWENTIETH-CENTURY AMERICAN BIOGRAPHY SERIES

John Milton Cooper, Jr., General Editor

HARRY S. TRUMAN

Fair Dealer and Cold Warrior

William E. Pemberton

TWAYNE PUBLISHERS • BOSTON
A Division of G.K. Hall & Co.

To my wife, Martha

Copyright 1989 by William E. Pemberton
All rights reserved.
Published by Twayne Publishers
A division of G.K. Hall & Co.
70 Lincoln Street, Boston, Massachusetts 02111

Twayne's Twentieth-Century
American Biography Series No. 9

Copyediting supervised by Barbara Sutton.
Book Production by Janet Zietowski.
Typeset in 11/13 Goudy by Compset, Inc.

Printed on permanent/durable acid-free paper
and bound in the United States of America.

Pemberton, William E., 1940–
Harry S. Truman : fair dealer and cold warrior / William E.
Pemberton.
p.   cm.—(Twayne's twentieth-century American biography
series ; no. 9)
Bibliography: p.
Includes index.
ISBN 0-8057-7767-9 (alk. paper).
ISBN 0-8057-7783-0 (pbk. : alk. paper)
1. Truman, Harry S., 1884–1972.   2. Presidents—United States—
Biography.   3. United States—Politics and government—1945–1953.
4. United States—Foreign relations—1945–1953.   I. Title.
II. Series.
E814.P46 1988
973.918'092'4—dc19   88-16534
                                                                              CIP

CONTENTS

PREFACE

In the 1960s, the American people experienced deep and searing social conflict. The civil rights movement, the rediscovery of poverty, and the controversy over the Vietnam War restored vigorous public discussion to issues long obscured by prosperity for the majority and by a sense of living in a world too dangerous to allow national debate over fundamental matters. Social critics found an audience as they questioned the ability of the regulatory and welfare state apparatus established by the liberal reform movement to solve chronic domestic problems. The Vietnam War sparked particularly trenchant debate over the role of the United States in post–World War II global relations.

Social dissension affected the history profession more than most other academic disciplines. A long-standing interpretive consensus crumbled as historians attempted to provide perspective to questions raised by defenders and critics of U.S. domestic and foreign policy. Controversy among scholars particularly centered on the presidency of Harry S. Truman, an appropriate focus since he forged many of the policies and programs that came under fire in the 1960s.

As they subjected Truman to closer scholarly scrutiny than he had ever received before, many historians found much that they liked. Although his Fair Deal added few social programs, Truman still contributed to reform by placing civil rights and national health care on the liberal agenda and by protecting Franklin D. Roosevelt's New Deal from any important erosion in the face of a conservative counterattack after 1945. The scrappy Missourian stood firm against Republican and Southern Democratic reaction and against the anti-Communist hysteria stirred by Senator Joseph McCarthy and others.

While guarding social gains and civil liberties at home, Truman mobilized the free world in defense against an expansionistic Communist bloc dominated and directed by the Soviet Union. Although new evidence in the 1960s and after convinced many of Truman's admirers that Washington probably overreacted to Soviet activities in the postwar years, they cautioned scholars to recognize that the president could act on only the knowledge available to him at the time.

Truman's personal qualities also proved attractive to these sympathetic historians. His apparent integrity and blunt honesty contrasted with the shoddy public relations gimmicks and lying indulged in by the presidents of the 1960s and 1970s. Many scholars appreciated Truman's modesty and simplicity in an office that did not encourage such qualities. He fulfilled the democratic ideal of the common man rising from obscurity to perform admirably in the nation's highest office. Although he left office with only about a 23 percent approval rating in the polls, soon after his death in 1972, the general public classed him with Washington and Lincoln, and surveys of historians placed him in the "near-great" category.

Revisionist historians, however, found a Truman that differed significantly from the man their colleagues described. They judged his leadership of the New Deal–Fair Deal social reform movement defective because of his political incompetence and lack of personal commitment. Some critics went further, arguing that the mild Roosevelt-Truman reform programs would not, in any case, have overcome such chronic problems as a racist and sexist social structure, a maldistribution of income and wealth, and an oligopolistic economic structure.

Truman's image as a democratic battler for the common man, symbolized by his 1948 presidential election victory, obscured the erosion of democracy in the United States, some revisionists concluded. Democratic dialogue became difficult as the president stirred anti-Communist hysteria with the Truman Doctrine and based policy on such mystical but seemingly unchallengeable concepts as the domino theory and monolithic communism. Liberal politicians who survived at the polls abandoned their leftist allies and joined their moderate brethren at the "vital center." They followed Truman's leadership in implementing containment and condemned alike fascism and communism as equally evil forms of totalitarianism. As they moved toward the center, these cold war liberals counted on maintaining social harmony by repairing flaws in the capitalist system through modest additions to the welfare and regulatory reform programs and by using Keynesian techniques to promote economic growth.

Revisionists studying the origins of the cold war concluded that Americans were not forced to take defensive actions against Communist aggression. Rather, Washington attempted to use its great economic and military power to impose on a war-devastated globe a liberal, capitalist world order. American leaders had long believed that U.S. prosperity, internal stability, and social progress rested on its ability to expand through an open door into a world of free trade. Now they took steps to translate their vision into reality and used the Soviet bogeyman to explain and justify their actions. The Soviet Union had to resist the imposition of American hegemony or subordinate itself into a U.S.-dominated world order.

In the 1970s, most people remembered Truman for his feisty aphorisms— "the buck stops here," "if you can't stand the heat, get out of the kitchen"— and for his dramatic decisions to drop the atomic bombs on Japan, conduct the

Berlin airlift, and intervene in the Korean War. Public memory aside, his most enduring, but less dramatic, legacy was to preside over the creation of the national security state. Under his leadership, Congress created the Central Intelligence Agency, the National Security Council, the Atomic Energy Commission, and the Loyalty Review Board and unified the military into the Department of Defense. By 1953, Truman had demonstrated the magic of "military Keynesianism" in creating economic growth, which fed the rapidly expanding military-corporate-educational complex.

When Truman went home to Independence, his years of anti-Communist rhetoric and actions had convinced most Americans that the world was a dangerous place requiring a powerful presidency and a bipartisan foreign policy based on White House leadership. Truman was a modest and unassuming man and remained so in an office that turned the heads of many of its other occupants. Yet his very modesty allowed him to take major steps toward what came to be called the imperial presidency. He did not feel that he was glorifying the person of Harry Truman, the simple man from Missouri. Rather, he was protecting and institutionalizing the office of president, which he revered and regarded as the essential protector and promoter of national well-being.

Revisionists found little comfort in Truman's battles against McCarthyism. His strident anti-Soviet rhetoric shaped the environment that made a Red scare inevitable. He used anti-Communist fears to put through his foreign policy program and to destroy opponents like Henry A. Wallace. His heroism in fighting McCarthy was betrayed by his toleration of Federal Bureau of Investigation director J. Edgar Hoover, who did in the dark what McCarthy gloried in doing openly.

Controversy among historians moderated somewhat as scholarship on the cold war and other issues moved away from Truman as the focal point of research. Significant shadings exist within the different schools of Truman historiography, and a blurring of the lines between the traditional and revisionist schools perhaps represents a base on which a new consensus will be built. Yet neither the social conflict that surfaced nationally in the 1960s nor the controversy among historians has ended. Historians now rank Truman high as a president but not as high as the American public does. Truman specialists rate him lower than the profession generally, and younger historians place him lower than older ones do. The Truman presidency remains one of the most controversial in American history.

Everyone at the Truman Library in Independence, Missouri, directly or indirectly has helped me in the twenty-five years I have been drawing on its resources. People who aided me particularly on this project were librarian Elizabeth H. Safly, archivists Dennis E. Bilger, Philip D. Lagerquist, and Erwin J. Mueller, and photograph archivist Pauline Testerman.

For years staff members at Murphy Library, University of Wisconsin–La

Crosse have provided me with resources, advice, and the benefits of their time and energy. I feel deep gratitude for their help.

Professors Stanley R. Rolnick and J. Richard Snyder of the UW–La Crosse History Department read the entire manuscript and made valuable suggestions. My teaching partner and friend James R. Parker gave me excellent advice on the chapters relating to foreign policy. Several UW–La Crosse Department of Psychology professors read a brief sketch I wrote of Truman's life and gave me valuable insights into his personality, as well as cautions on some pitfalls to avoid in a biography. They are Clark E. Himmel, Harold D. Hiebert, Harry W. Gardiner, William J. Cerbin, and Robert E. Arthur.

Carol W. Gundersen has been an integral part of my intellectual development for many years. She has used her feminist perspective to challenge and enrich my understanding of history.

Linda L. Jorgenson translated my scribbles into typed script and kept me on schedule. Scott A. Guthrie and Mary K. Viner of the UW–La Crosse Academic Computing Center and Professor Joan R. Yeatman of the UW–La Crosse Department of English introduced me to the mysteries of computing and word processing.

At G.K. Hall Anne Jones gave me invaluable editorial suggestions, and Barbara Sutton and Beverly Miller assisted in the editing of the manuscript. I thank John M. Cooper for inviting me to write a Truman biography for the Twayne American Biography Series.

My wife, Martha Wallace Pemberton, has shared in my research and writing. Only her willingness to assume an unequal share of the burden of managing our lives and to spend additional hours with Truman after her own workday allowed me to complete this work.

I also want to thank my little friend Sage Tsou, who patiently put up with my neglect of her while I was spending time with Harry Truman.

The UW–La Crosse Foundation and the National Endowment for the Humanities provided grants for research at the Truman Library. I thank William R. Gresens, of the UW–La Crosse Grants Office, for his help on these matters.

1

ROOTS

In the late afternoon on 12 April 1945, Vice President Harry S. Truman rushed to answer a summons to the White House. He entered expecting to find President Franklin D. Roosevelt waiting for him. Instead Eleanor Roosevelt quietly told him that her husband had just died and that Truman was now president of the United States. "Maybe it will come out all right," a still-shaken Truman wrote to his mother a few days later.

Truman's assumption of the presidency culminated a lifetime full of changes. Born in rural Missouri, he learned the values and ethics taught rural children for generations past, a code already undermined by an emerging bureaucratic society. The boy who practiced mule-powered agriculture, went to town in buggies, and looked into a sky marred only by simple man-made objects like kites and balloons lived to initiate programs to produce guided missiles carrying hydrogen bombs.

In private notes, Truman often retraced his years, as if trying to convince himself that one man's life could take so many turns. He had lacked money to go to college, fought a losing battle to save a heavily mortgaged farm, failed in mining and oil investments, and gone bankrupt as a retail merchant. He found his life's work finally at age thirty-eight when he entered politics and then seemed destined to remain in the local arena. Even his talent for politics seemed incongruous; the young Baptist brought up with nineteenth-century rural values won success by allying with the notoriously corrupt Pendergast organization that controlled Kansas City and much of the rest of Missouri. The machine put him into the U.S. Senate, where his work persuaded Democratic party leaders to reward him with the vice presidency. As a young man, Truman felt that destiny held something special for him, yet even in his most optimistic moods, he could not see a path leading from a Missouri farm to the White House.

Little in his background pointed to the possibility of unusual achievement. John Anderson Truman and Martha Ellen Young married in December 1881 and moved to Lamar, Missouri, where Harry was born on 8 May 1884. John Truman, an ambitious livestock trader and farmer, moved several times during the next few years looking for better opportunities. In 1887 he agreed to return to Jackson County, the home of both the Trumans and Youngs, to help run the six-hundred-acre Young farm near Grandview, about twenty miles south of Kansas City.

Jackson County was filled with Harry Truman's relatives. Almost always some members of his extended family lived with him, including at one time three of his grandparents. Both the Youngs and Trumans had grown up and married in Shelby County, Kentucky, before moving to Jackson County in the 1840s, where they worked larger-than-average farms and were well connected to the community. Harry Truman credited them with influencing his outlook and habits. They were loving and kind but strong, determined people, who achieved prosperity and stability despite the turmoil of life on the frontier and the disruption of the Civil War. They imparted to Harry his southern heritage, sparked his interest in history with tales of pioneering days and the war, and passed on their Baptist beliefs. Their unquestioning acceptance of the work ethic, their conviction that right and wrong were easily determined, and their view that duty and obligation were binding on the individual deeply impressed young Truman.

In 1890 John and Martha Ellen moved from the farm to Independence, searching for wider business opportunities and better schools for the children: Harry, his brother, Vivian, and his sister, Mary Jane. Independence had once been a center of trade during the westward movement, but its identification with the South had left it in post–Civil War economic lethargy. When the Truman family moved there in 1890, it was a snobbish little town, proud of its southern heritage and prizing its view of itself as a center of culture. Kansas City, a growing, bustling, energetic center only ten miles west, was viewed as a crude, materialistic place tainted by Yankee values. When John Truman's sister found it necessary to board with some Yankees, she found them to be nice people but "their ways abominable." Her nephew Harry obtained a valuable political education by mastering both the southern customs of Grandview and Independence and the northern, urban ways of Kansas City.[1]

Truman also absorbed the racial views of the South. Both sides of his family had owned slaves. Slaves had worked the farms of rural Jackson County, had built many of the buildings and fine homes in Independence, and had been sold at auction in the town square. The census listed 701 blacks in Independence in 1860, 23 of whom were free. In 1910, 1,031 of Independence's 9,859 people were blacks, and they were economically deprived and poorly educated. Truman's sunny and romantic recollections of life in Independence were skewed.

The two most important people shaping Harry Truman's values and attitudes, including his racial views, were his mother and father. Martha Ellen Truman is sometimes portrayed as a colorful character sprung from dirt-farming ancestors, displaying the strength and lack of refinement of that dwindling minority. Actually she attended the Baptist Female College in Lexington, Missouri, more education than most other nineteenth-century rural women could expect. She was hardly bowed with farm work. She never milked a cow or even cooked for the farmhands; rather, she supervised her household help and let Harry and Mary Jane do much of the family cooking. She inherited the 600-acre farm from her family, valued in 1913 at five hundred to a thousand dollars an acre, when the average Missouri farm was 125 acres.

She was an extraordinarily strong woman. She enjoyed the world of music and books, but her frontier roots allowed her to avoid the Victorian-era female trap of being placed so high on a pedestal that she was removed from the rough and tumble of life. She appeared sarcastic and caustic to some people. She had opinions on everything and never hesitated to express them. "She hates her enimies [sic] and makes no bones about it," her son wrote, "and she's for her friends, strictly on emotion in both cases." She was also a charming, fun-loving woman. She was a "lightfoot" Baptist who believed in dancing and never wanted to be considered "overly religious." As a young woman, she and her sister-in-law had a "boss time" fishing, horseback riding, going to the opera, and returning social calls. "Being too good is apt to be uninteresting," she often said. She was unconventional in her farming community as a young woman but sensible. Women should always ride sidesaddle, she said, never wear pants, and stay home with their children.

Harry Truman was a dutiful son who practiced piano and read while other boys, including his brother, went off to play. He cooked, combed his little sister's hair, and sang her to sleep. "Most of the time . . . my father's world revolved around his mother," Margaret Truman wrote. Truman, like many other presidents, was the eldest son of a strong, loving mother who admired achievement and expected high accomplishments from him. Harry was not a "mama's boy" in the sense that he could not, when the chance came, enter into the world of men, nor was his spirit crushed by a domineering mother. Instead she provided the loving psychological nourishment that he drew on for strength as he pursued his career.[2]

Do not overlook my father, Truman told a journalist who asked about his mother: "He was just as great as she was and had every bit as much influence on me." Despite this caution, writers often referred to John Truman only as a speculator whose failure prevented his son from going to college or as a high-tempered street brawler. John died in 1914, and memories of him had dimmed by the time people began examining Harry Truman's roots.

John Truman spent most of his life as a farmer, "always a man of the soil," recalled Vivian: "We were all raised around here—this was our domain—the farm and the land. To be a good farmer in Missouri—that's tops. That's the finest thing you can say about a man. And that's what Father was—a first-rate farmer." He also was ambitious and a bit of a plunger. He used his knowledge of agriculture to move into livestock trading and grain speculating where the potential return was higher than farming but the ground more treacherous.

He was precise in business affairs, partisan in politics, and patriarchal toward women. Any questioning of his personal integrity could set the small but powerful man off in violent explosions of temper. His two-fisted quality, along with his love of farming and livestock trading, also meant that in their early life, Vivian, attracted to rough-and-tumble outdoor activities, was closer to his father than was Harry. By the time Vivian was twelve years old, John had already given him a personal checkbook and brought him into the family business. John Truman was a doer more than a talker; as a politician, Harry Truman was a talker as well as a doer. If John was known for fast use of his fists, Harry was known for the hot flow of his words.

There was another side to both John and Harry, however. Just as Harry later learned to love farming, so John had a more complex personality than many people remembered. His explosive temper cooled quickly. Friends recalled his devotion to his family and his love of life. Harry Truman said John was the happiest man he ever knew. Nor did all the cultural interest in Harry's life come from Martha Ellen. John helped his son save money to buy a set of Plutarch's writings, and they read it aloud, together. Even when the family was in financial difficulty, he urged Harry to quit a part-time job so he would have more time to study. He taught his son rigorous but simple conceptions of right and wrong: "He worked from daylight to dark, all the time," Truman told an interviewer, "and his code was honesty and integrity. His word was good. . . . And he raised my brother and myself to put honor above profit. He was quite a man, my dad was."

The value of hard work, a black-and-white view of the world, the sacred bond established by giving one's word—all of these John and Martha Ellen passed along to their son.[3]

Truman's memories of his youth revolved around his family; aunts, uncles, cousins, and grandparents were a vital part of his life. He played in the fields and pastures and in unpolluted streams with Vivian and other friends. He remembered the smells of fall canning, the taste of fruit pies and preserves, and the excitement of hog butchering time. He went to the county fair with his grandfather and had "the best time a kid ever had." His uncle Harrison Young told him tall tales, and his grandmother Harriet Young recounted stories of the Civil War.

Life in Independence was not very different from that on the Grandview farm. He and his friends easily reached woods and streams. Harry remembered playing with the children of black servants, engaging in innocent pranks, and continuing games into the dusk of warm summer nights. Some of the boys of the neighborhood were bad, but "the girls were all above reproach and decent." It was a very happy time, Truman remembered.

School also enriched Truman's life. He entered the first grade in 1892, at age eight. Dutiful and courteous, he was a favorite of the teachers. Truman met this academic trial like he would all other challenges throughout his life: he worked harder than those around him. By the time he graduated from high school in 1901, he had gained a solid grounding in literature and composition, Latin, history, and arithmetic.

Unfortunately, at about the same time as graduation, his father's finances became "entangled," and Harry had to go to work to keep his brother and sister in school. He had to enter the adult world of work rather than go to college as he had planned. Therefore he never acquired depth in economics, social and physical science, and philosophy. His education did not provide him with an appreciation of ideas or an understanding of intellectuals.[4]

These changes in 1901 became a major dividing line in Truman's memories of his life. As an old man, Truman often turned his thoughts back to that early period before graduation. He usually wrote only of pleasant memories and sketched a childhood seemingly free of pain and tension. Yet there was conflict, for Harry did not entirely fit in with the world of his friends in Independence and Grandview. When he was about five years old, his mother discovered that his eyesight was severely impaired, and a doctor soon fitted him with particularly expensive eyeglasses with heavy, thick lens. Glasses set him off some from his playmates, inhibited his play in most games, and turned him more to the world of books. His playmates sometimes called him "four eyes" and other names. "That's hard on a boy," he later recalled: "It makes him lonely, and it gives him an inferiority complex, and he has a hard time overcoming it." He had not been popular, he told a young boy years later: "The popular boys were the ones who were good at games and had big, tight fists. I was never like that. Without my glasses I was blind as a bat, and to tell the truth, I was kind of a sissy. If there was any danger of getting into a fight, I always ran."[5]

Necessity encouraged Truman to learn to love books, but his life was further enriched by music, an interest that again set him off from his friends. His mother, who had studied music in college, started him with the piano, and he showed talent enough to study with an outstanding teacher in Kansas City. Although Truman quit his lessons at about age seventeen, he retained his love for music throughout life. Mozart and Chopin were his favorites, along with Bach, Beethoven, Mendelssohn, and Liszt. Music provided him a way to dream and to escape the disappointments of everyday life. He wrote to his friend Bess Wallace: "Did you ever sit and listen to an orchestra play a fine overture and imagine that things were as they ought to be and not as they are? Music that I can understand always makes me feel that way."[6]

The Trumans were socially respectable, but this shy boy from the country did not move in the highest social circle, as did Bess Wallace. Although he was neither excluded from play and social activities nor shunned as a withdrawn, lonely bookworm, he received social slights he never forgot or forgave.

Reading filled some of the emptiness that might otherwise have existed and made up somewhat for the limited intellectual life in rural and small-town Missouri. In 1899, the Independence school district created a small library serving the general public, except blacks. Truman later claimed to have read every book in it. He and his parents also saved to build a personal library that included a forty-volume set of Shakespeare. He read the many biographies written by Jacob Abbott; he read and reread Plutarch, loved books by Charles Dickens, and regarded Mark Twain as his "patron saint in literature." His family subscribed to several popular magazines, including some muckraking ones. As president he still carried a poem by Alfred Lord Tennyson that he had first copied in 1901. His speech and writing reflected his immersion in the Bible, which he read several times before he reached adulthood.

Truman owned and loved the four-volume *Great Men and Famous Women,* edited by Charles F. Horne. These volumes, in which "great men" far outnumbered the "famous women," contained essays on military and political leaders, artists, authors, "sages," and such all-purpose heroes as Hercules. They were filled with dramatic and idealized drawings, a captivating set of books for a young boy, and Truman drew from them until the end of his life. How men became great became one of his major intellectual concerns, and the lessons from Horne's books seemed very clear to him. The biographical sketches usually reinforced the conventional moral messages of his parents.[7]

Truman read incessantly, especially history and biography. He believed that it was his study of history that awakened his interest in government. His writing and conversation were filled with historical references, often from the Horne volumes, and his knowledge of the past impressed even many well-educated people. In truth, however, wrote Jonathan W. Daniels, aide to both Roosevelt and Truman, although Truman imagined himself a great historian, he "knew the kind of history that McGuffey would have put in his readers." Historian George E. Mowry found that of all presidents from Warren Harding to John F. Kennedy, Harding and Truman used historical references most inexactly. Truman had a buff's knowledge of isolated events, but he had little historical perspective on his times and gained from his reading little sense of ambiguity, skepticism, or relativism. His study of history actually reinforced his tendency to see reality in simple black-and-white terms.

Perhaps it was the simplicity of his view of the past that inclined him to turn to history to interpret the present. He believed history moved in cycles and that the people in ancient Mesopotamia, Egypt, and Rome had faced the same problems that Americans confronted in the twentieth century. His reading taught him that individuals, not forces, make history: "Ancient History is one of the most interesting of all studies," he wrote to his daughter, Margaret. "By it you find out why a lot of things happen today. But you must study it on the basis of the biographies of the men and women who lived it."[8]

Historical theory aside, Truman learned practical lessons from reading. He, who rose from the obscurity of a Missouri farm to the presidency, denied ambition, claiming that each career advancement was thrust on him, often against his will. But while Truman may never have felt ambition ruling his life, his success was not an accident. Building on the foundation of his reading about the lives of great men and on a work ethic strengthened by his parents and teachers, Truman followed a simple formula for success: whenever he undertook a new task, he tried to work harder and better at it than anyone else ever had. As Truman's competitive arena broadened and he was confronted with better educated, more polished, or wealthier rivals, he became confident that he could succeed through self-discipline.

Thus, Truman did not view himself as a person driven by ambition to advance his career. He simply worked hard at the task before him and then reached out for more work. This work ethic pushed him onward and upward. At the end of his first year in the Senate in 1935, he wrote Bess: "It's a peculiar feeling to have nothing hanging over me. I keep wanting to do something—there's a driving force inside me that makes me get into things[.] I can't sit still and do nothing." He wrote his daughter, Margaret:

> It takes work to do anything well. Most people expect everything and do nothing to get it. That is why some people are leaders in society, in politics, in religion[,] on the stage and elsewhere and some just stand and cry that they haven't been treated fairly.
>
> It just takes work and more work to accomplish anything—and your dad knows it better than anyone. It's been my policy to do every job assigned to me just a little better than anyone else has done it.[9]

Truman's background might easily have produced an inner-directed man possessing executive and professional abilities geared to win success in the private marketplace. As a child and young man, however, he had developed personality traits that contributed to his budding political skills. Shy and awkward, he nevertheless enjoyed other people: "I like people. I like to see them and hear what they have to say," and success in politics, he believed, was based on liking people and being a joiner.

Truman, perhaps because he maintained unusually tight bonds with his mother, possessed, more than most other men, special skills of empathy. In a revealing comment in his memoirs, he wrote:

> When I was growing up it occurred to me to watch the people around me to find out what they thought and what pleased them most. . . . I used to watch my father and mother closely to learn what I could do to please them, just as I did with my schoolteachers and playmates. Because of my efforts to get along with my associates I usually was able to get what I wanted. It was successful on the farm, in school, in the Army, and particularly in the Senate.[10]

Truman could often bring together disparate political elements. Throughout his life, he acted as a peacekeeper, first within his family and later in wider arenas. In Jackson County politics, he worked effectively with the rural and farm population and with the Kansas City machine; in the Senate, he maintained good relations with northern urban liberals and with southern conservatives.

Surrounded later by military and diplomatic advisers and confronting such world leaders as Winston S. Churchill and Joseph Stalin, he could also act as a masculine line drawer. Varying circumstances could pull one part or another of his complex personality into play. Truman's early life had conditioned him in an inner-directed way suitable to run a farm or small business firm of the nineteenth century, while his empathy and sensitivity to the wants and needs of others fitted him to find success within the organizational society of the twentieth century.

In 1901, when Truman graduated from high school barely seventeen years old, he was a hard-working, dutiful young man, skillful in understanding the wants and needs of those around him. He knew from his books that a larger world offered him the opportunity for success, but he did not yet know his place in it. Graduation created a minor crisis in his life and left him without clear direction. His plans to go to college fell apart, and his family lost its home in Independence and moved to Kansas City.

Truman now moved into a largely masculine world of work. After holding several jobs briefly, he took a position in 1902 with the National Bank of Commerce, one of the largest banks in the Midwest. He worked there until May 1905, when he got a better offer at Union National Bank. When he quit banking in 1906, he was making one hundred dollars a month, excellent pay at that time. On his application form at the

National Bank of Commerce, Truman claimed, truthfully no doubt, that he did not smoke, drink liquor, gamble, owe money, or live extravagantly. His recreation included "good plays and gatherings of young people of my own standing." His supervisor at the Commerce Bank recorded the first extended contemporary evaluation of Truman: "He is an exceptionally bright young man and is keeping the work up in the vault better than it has ever been kept. He is a willing worker, almost always here and tries hard to please everybody. We never had a boy in the vault like him before. He watches everything very closely and by his watchfulness, detects many errors which a careless boy would let slip through."[11]

Truman succeeded in his banking jobs, but the world of finance, one of three paths he believed men usually followed to greatness, did not satisfy him. He was ready to try the second, farming. His grandmother, Harriet Louisa Young, was very old, and his uncle Harrison Young, who ran the farm, also wanted to retire. The Youngs persuaded John and Martha Truman to move to Grandview and take over management of the farm. In 1906 Harry joined his family. Although his friends, watching his enjoyment of the social and cultural life of Kansas City, wagered that he would not last two weeks, he stayed ten years. He went to the farm hoping to find new direction in his life: "I thought of Cincinnatus and a lot of other farm boys who had made good and I thought maybe by cussing mules and plowing corn I could perhaps overcome my shyness and amount to something."

"Farm life as an every day affair is not generally exciting," Truman wrote Bess Wallace in 1910, but he found these years satisfying. He worked with his father and established himself as a man of worth in John's eyes, while proving to himself that he could do the physical and mental labor required to run a diverse enterprise of six hundred acres, with several hundred more of rented land. After his father's death in November 1914, he ran the whole operation himself, with the help of farmhands. His self-confidence grew; he toughened physically, and he learned to handle animals, machinery, and farmhands and to make complex decisions about weather, commodity markets, interest rates, and other agrarian imponderables.

Most observers agreed that the Trumans were excellent farmers. Yet Harry wrote, as thousands of other farmers had before and have since, "We never did catch up with our debts. We always owed the bank something—sometimes more[,] sometimes less—but we always owed the bank." After his grandmother Young died in 1909 and left almost her entire large estate to Martha Ellen and Harrison, the other children sued to force a redistribution of its value. The settlement allowed Martha Ellen and Harrison to keep the farm but forced them to put a thirty thousand dollar mortgage on it to provide a cash settlement to their brothers and sisters. When Harrison died in 1916, he left his share of the farm to Martha Ellen and her three children. With poor crops, low prices, weather disasters, John's death, and Harry's leaving the farm for war service, the farm never got out of debt. The holders of the mortgage foreclosed in 1940, but the family regained the farm in 1945 when some friends purchased it and allowed the three Truman children to buy it.[12]

Hardship, however, was not misery. When Truman left the farm in 1917, he was a muscular man, five feet, nine inches tall and 160 pounds in weight. He had improved farm operations and output and had won the respect of most of his neighbors. He also absorbed as a basic part of his idiom the information, language, and mental images that allowed him to identify with common people. He was gregarious and sociable. These qualities helped prepare him for politics. Truman became president of the local Farm Bureau chapter and worked with the 4-H Club. He joined in the parties, box suppers, picnics, and other social activities of rural life. His skill at the piano made him the center of his fun-loving social group, though one doubts that he often played Mozart. He joined friends at the theater, vaudeville, and music concerts in Kansas City and saw with them the most famous entertainers of his day. His enlistment in the National Guard in 1905 provided additional social opportunities.

His religious convictions also matured. At age eighteen, Truman was baptized into the church of his ancestors, though he never cared much about theological questions or ideas generally nor did he like ritual: "I'm a Baptist because I think that sect gives the common man the shortest and most direct approach to God," he wrote in later years. "I've never thought that God gives a damn about pomp and circumstance, gold crowns, jeweled breast plates and ancestral background," he wrote: "Forms and ceremonies impress a lot of people, but I've never thought that the Almighty could be impressed by anything but the heart and soul of the individual. That's why I'm a Baptist, whose church authority starts from the bottom—not the top."

Truman prayed daily, believed that God guided him and answered his prayers, and thought that the Bible contained remedies for all human troubles. He said, however, that he had not been interested in the "religious thing" but in the Bible as a source of moral guidance. Unlike many other Baptists, he almost never used "born again" images of Christ having died to absolve human sins. This focus made him more religiously tolerant than many others of his background. Additionally, he believed many of the world's problems came from conflict over religious interpretations: "It is all so silly and comes of the prima donna complex again." He added: "The Jews claim God Almighty picked 'em out for special privilege. Well I'm sure He had better judgment. Fact is I never thought God picked any favorites. It is my studied opinion that any race, creed or color can be God's favorites if they act the part—and very few of 'em do that." This tolerance, and lack of focus on Christ as Savior, allowed Truman to find a similar moral foundation in all religions. Buddha, Confucius, Muhammad, and Christ all taught the same message, he believed.

Perhaps it was his emphasis on moral codes that attracted Truman to Freemasonry. He overlooked his Baptist devotion to simplicity and mastered the elaborate Masonic ritual. In the early twentieth century, Freemasons still exercised important influence in the political and economic life of rural and small-town communities in the Midwest. Freemasonry provided Truman with a social outlet and a moral code that transcended Christianity. He joined the Freemasons in 1909 and moved through the ranks until he became Grand Master of Missouri in 1940.[13]

Politics provided an important social outlet for the increasingly gregarious young man. His mother and father were fanatical Democrats, hating Republicans as only southerners of the Civil War generation could. Truman's father was active in Jackson County politics, serving as road overseer, a patronage reward for his work with the local party. Harry attended the 1900 Democratic National Convention in Kansas City and heard his hero William Jennings Bryan speak. By 1908 he was serving as a precinct captain in Grandview and later, after John's death, replaced him as road overseer and served for a time as Grandview postmaster. Truman and his father supported that faction of the Democratic party controlled by Thomas J. Pendergast, the Kansas City boss whose organization later served as Truman's own political base. "Politics sure is the ruination of many a good man," he wrote Bess in 1913, but he was already being pulled into the political game.[14]

The greatest joy in Truman's life during his years on the farm came when he reestablished contact with Bess Wallace. Bess had moved in different social circles from the Trumans. Her grandfather George Gates had made a fortune in flour milling, and her mother, Margaret Gates, had been part of the Independence elite. Margaret Gates had married handsome, charming David Wallace over her father's objections; he doubted the young man's ability to support her, and time proved him right. Although David's minor political patronage positions provided a steady income, he found himself unable to support his extravagant wife and their five children. Even with help from his father-in-law, he could not afford to send Bess to college, though her mother retained several servants. David suffered from alcoholism and depression: "I try to look on the bright side of things, but even then it is dark," he wrote. Finally in the early morning of 17 June 1903, with Bess sleeping in a bedroom down the hallway, he went into the bathroom and killed himself with a gun. Humiliated by the social stigma attached to suicide, Mrs. Wallace took her children to Colorado for a year and then returned to live as a recluse until her death in the White House in 1952.

Bess Truman's daughter, Margaret, believed that the year in Colorado had a great impact on her mother's personality. Bess, eighteen when her father committed suicide, was a charming, athletic girl, very popular and witty, with many boyfriends. After her father's death, she became more reserved, private, and pessimistic, even losing her belief in a benevolent God comprehensible to humans. Ultimately she saw that her mother's relationship with David had been destructive. He, following the mores of his time, had protected his wife from the realities of the world. She had not shared his problems and stresses, and he, trying to cope alone, had broken under the strain. Bess resolved that if she married, the union would be a partnership.[15]

Harry Truman first met her—Elizabeth Virginia Wallace—in Sunday school at age six: "I saw a beautiful curly haired girl there. I thought (and still think) she was the most beautiful girl I ever saw. She had tanned skin[,] blond hair;[sic] golden as sunshine, and the most beautiful blue eyes I've ever seen, or ever will see." Although Truman evidently never had any other serious romantic interests, he did not date Bess and lost contact with her after high school. In late 1910, they met again, and Bess now confronted a more muscular, self-confident man than she had known before. Harry's somewhat lower social class, rural background, and Baptist faith probably no longer seemed as important as it had during their school years. The two shared love of reading, plays and vaudeville, walks, and picnics. Truman's frequent letters to her displaying wit, confidence, and the optimism she lacked also revealed his vulnerability. The combination was attractive to Bess, and after first turning him down in 1911, she told him in November 1913 that she would marry him, if she married at all.

Bess now brought focus to Harry's life, and his struggle for financial success on the farm took on a new intensity. He wrote her: "I am so crazy to make things go I can hardly stand it." In 1916, when it seemed clear that the farm would not provide the financial breakthrough that Truman wanted, he invested in and helped run an Oklahoma mining operation. He put thousands of dollars into the mine, as well as time, energy, and boundless hope—and watched it all come to nothing. Still, he admitted, "I don't suppose I'd ever have been real pleased if I hadn't tried just once to get rich quickly." Truman never stayed depressed for long, and, showing a surprisingly erratic streak in a man who later would seem so steady, he at once invested in a new speculative scheme, this time joining an oil company and even getting Bess to invest with him. This company too failed.[16]

In 1917, when the United States entered World War I, Truman was thirty-three years old. Many of those who would later figure prominently in his life—George C. Marshall, Douglas MacArthur, Joseph Stalin, Winston S. Churchill—were already well along in their careers, while Truman still was running a heavily mortgaged farm. The war, however, started a sequence of events that propelled his life in a new direction. Banking and farming, two of the paths he believed most great men had followed, had proved disappointing. Now he turned to the military, the third path. He was always timid, he later recalled, but "he made up his mind that he would be a military man, although he was afraid of a gun and would rather run than fight."

When the war started in Europe it did not at first seem to have a big impact on Truman, but, very much a man of the nineteenth century, he was soon caught up in the romance of battle. With his sentimental view of history, he sympathized especially with the plight of France, believing that the United States owed a debt to one of his many heroes, the marquis de Lafayette. Like many other naive young men, he was stirred "heart and soul" by the messages of Woodrow Wilson. "I wouldn't be left out of the greatest history making epoch the world has ever seen for all there is to live for because there'd be nothing to live for under German control," he wrote Bess on 27 January 1918. He enlisted in the national guard in mid-1917 and was immediately commissioned a first lieutenant. After his artillery battery was drafted into federal service in August 1917, Truman went to Camp Doniphan at Fort Sill, Oklahoma, for training.

Training was tough intellectually and physically, but Truman performed well by working harder than those with better education or more military experience. As the months dragged on, his main worry was that the war would end too soon. In a letter to Bess Wallace in March 1918 from New York ("kike town," he called it), he revealed the lack of depth in his mental world:

> I am crazy to leave because I know that if the British stem this tide there'll not be another and I do want to be in at the death of this "Scourge of God." Just think what he'd [the kaiser] do to our great country and our beautiful women if he only could. That is the reason we must go and must get shot if necessary to keep the Huns from our own fair land. I am getting to hate the sight of a German and I think most of us are the same way. They have no hearts or no souls. They are just machines to do the bidding of the wolf Kaiser.[17]

Truman and his comrades sailed for Europe on 30 March 1918. In France he was subjected to even more intensive training, and in July 1918, Truman gained command of Battery D of the 129th Field Artillery of the 35th Division. This was a disorderly battery of 190 men, composed of many tough, big city boys, often Roman Catholics, from Kansas City. Truman, a rural Baptist and a Mason with barely adequate military training, confronted a group that had already broken several officers. Even after the tumultuous years of the presidency, the day he took command of Battery D still stood out in his mind as the most frightening experience of his life. He hid his fear and subjected the men to tough but fair discipline. He won their respect and even love, and Truman returned their feeling. And he learned lessons that helped him as president; he delegated authority to subordinates and backed them, returned loyalty for loyalty, and mastered the details of his job.

Truman finally got his wish and in September 1918 went into action. He took part in the Saint Mihiel campaign and then in the battle of Meuse-Argonne before moving to Verdun: "I shot out a German battery, shot up his observation post and ruined another battery while it was moving down the road. . . . I saw tanks take towns and everything else that there is to see," he wrote on 6 October 1918, and a few weeks later he wrote: "I am so pleased that I was lucky enough to get in on the drive that made the Boche squeal for peace that I sometimes have to pinch myself to see if I am dreaming or not. It really doesn't seem possible that a common old farmer boy could take a battery in and shoot it on such a drive and I sometimes think I just dreamed it."

When peace came in November 1918, Truman traveled around France but did not see much that impressed him compared to Missouri.

Larger events seemed unimportant: "It's my opinion that we'll stay there until Woodie [Wilson] gets his pet peace plans refused or Ok'ed. For my part, and every AEF [American Expeditionary Force] man feels the same way[,] I don't give a whoop (to put it mildly) whether there's a league of nations or whether Russia has a Red Government or a Purple one." He received his discharge in May 1919.

The war did not lead Truman to engage in deep thought about the meaning of the experience, though he could toss off standard clichés about its horrors. He revealed his shallowness of thought a few years later when he recalled that his mother had not cried when she visited him at Fort Sill: "But she cried all the way home and when I came back from France she gain[ed] ten or fifteen pounds in weight. That's the real horror of war." Wars were fought to protect "our beautiful women" and were horrible because they made women sad.[18]

World War I shaped Truman's life in many ways. He enjoyed a degree of male camaraderie that was not possible on the farm. He demonstrated his physical courage and his ability to lead panic-stricken men under dangerous and terrifying conditions. Truman biographer Jonathan Daniels perceptively noted that his earlier life had made his war service successful: the years of reading about military tactics and the roles of heroic officers that taught him how to conduct himself, the years of working with animals that helped him effectively manage a horse-drawn battery under fire, and the years as a bank clerk that gave him knowledge to manage the details of running an organization. The war service also provided him with a large group of veterans whose help he would call on first as a businessman and then as a politician. It taught him the value of organization and basic management principles that he drew on in his later career. He also developed a great admiration for military men, leading him as president to appoint more military leaders to high positions than any other president in the twentieth century.[19]

2

TRUMAN FINDS HIS CALLING

Truman returned from the army in May 1919 determined to make changes in his life. He wanted a successful business career and talked in vague terms of turning to politics later in life. He went back to the farm but soon sold his share to his family: "When we were discharged I went home but I couldn't sit still or stand still," wrote the man who took pride in his self-discipline.[1]

Some goals had become clear to him. On 28 June 1919, twenty-nine years after deciding she was the only woman for him, he married Bess Wallace. She had always been on a pedestal in Truman's view and remained there until the end of his life. When he entered the rough, masculine world of politics, Bess Truman provided a secure and nurturing home for him. The emotional vitality of the marriage, so evident in Truman's many letters to her, was not one-sided. The intensity of her love matched his, and Bess regarded her relationship with Harry as the most important force in her life.

That he wanted to marry Bess was clear to Truman and quickly accomplished, but earning a living presented more difficulty. While at Camp Doniphan, Truman and Edward Jacobson, a sergeant with some experience in retail business, successfully ran the regimental canteen together and found that they liked and respected each other. Truman took the money he had from the farm sale, borrowed more, and opened a men's clothing store with Jacobson in downtown Kansas City. The store did well at first but failed in 1922 during the postwar depression. Truman lost his investment and went so deeply in debt that he was still paying it off in 1934.

Truman might well have changed careers at that time in any case. His family had long been involved in a minor way in Jackson County politics, loyal to the faction of the Democratic party controlled by Thomas J. Pendergast and his brother Michael J. Pendergast, who handled political affairs outside Kansas City. While in the army, Truman had successfully defended James M. Pendergast, Michael's son, in a court-martial hearing on charges stemming from an accident that killed several men.

In 1922 Tom Pendergast's lieutenants searched for a strong candidate to run for county judge of the eastern district of Jackson County, which included Independence. The machine faced a revolt in its county organization from an ambitious underling, and the heavily Catholic Pendergast organization also feared growing opposition in rural areas from the Ku Klux Klan. James Pendergast convinced his father, Mike, to support Truman. "Captain Harry" was a well-known veteran at a time when that voting bloc was powerful, a Mason and Baptist, as were many klansmen, and had relatives and friends all over the county who could help him in the campaign.

Truman applied his standard rule for success: he worked harder than his four opponents. He visited every township and precinct in the eastern district, promising to bring honest, businesslike administration to county government. He used all of his farm, veteran, family, and religious contacts and even agreed to join the Ku Klux Klan until they asked him to pledge not to hire Catholics. Truman narrowly won the primary race and gained easy victory in the general election.[2]

During Truman's 1923-24 term, he teamed up with western district judge Henry F. McElroy to dominate the three-member court, an administrative body similar to county commissions in many other states. The two Pendergast men overrode the presiding judge, a member of the Democratic faction loyal to Pendergast's chief rival, Joseph B. Shannon. Truman worked hard, supervising operation of county institutions, studying road building needs, and probing the nature of the political power structure. Truman and McElroy's efforts won applause from local business leaders, most journalists, and an independent "good-government" organization, the Kansas City Public Affairs Institute. The Pendergast men brought order to government operations, reduced corruption, and eliminated some nonessential jobs.

In his study of Truman's early career, Richard L. Miller has detected some sleight of hand in these Truman-McElroy activities. The "unessential" jobs that were eliminated were held by followers of Shannon and other Pendergast opponents, who saw their men fired from county positions as the machine tightened its grip on local government. McElroy and Truman won applause for serving the public, but they served the Pendergast organization as well. Before the 1924 election, however, McElroy and Truman overreached themselves and broke a patronage-sharing agreement between Pendergast and Shannon. The election turned into a brawl, with Truman and McElroy losing the general election when the Shannonites joined the Republicans to defeat them.[3]

This was the only election defeat Truman ever suffered in his long political career. But the loss did not subdue his energy or spirit; for the next two years, he remained active and visible. He provided for his family by selling memberships in the Automobile Club of Kansas City. He continued his work in Freemasonry, helped establish the Reserve Officers Association, and engaged in various civic activities. By 1926 the Democratic chiefs in Kansas City had made peace, and Truman was ready to move back into politics. He had spent the previous two years thinking about his experience as the eastern district judge and had realized that despite public acclaim, he had not performed well in office.

In 1926 the machine took control of the county, with Truman elected as presiding judge, and tightened its grip on the city, with the Pendergast majority on the city council making McElroy city manager. Shannon, now at peace with the "Big Boss," Tom Pendergast, received a seat in the U.S. House of Representatives as his reward.

In reentering the tumultuous world of politics, Truman continued to rely on Bess to provide stability in his life. She encouraged her husband to pursue his career, although she did not play a public role herself. She said: "A woman's place in public is to sit beside her husband, be silent, and be sure her hat is on straight." But she mastered political issues and personalities sufficiently to offer him valuable advice, always privately. She believed her function was the traditional one of keeping a stable, comfortable home and caring for their daughter Margaret, born 17 February 1924.[4]

When Truman took up his new responsibilities as presiding judge, he found Jackson County roads, buildings, and finances strained to the limit. The county was growing rapidly, with 470,000 people in 1930. He brought order to public affairs but did not lose sight of political reality. After meeting with Pendergast and Shannon to discuss division of patronage, he announced that all jobs would go to Democrats. Whatever he accomplished, it would have to be through the Pendergast organization. That was the reality that Truman could never escape, nor did he indicate any desire to do so.

With a cigar stuck between his full lips, burly, ham-fisted Tom Pendergast exactly fit the American image of a political boss. He sat in an upstairs room of his office located a few blocks south of downtown Kansas City and dispensed favors to friends and plotted against enemies, the latter being anyone who resisted his domination of public life. Pendergast had emerged from the tough world of saloons and brothels in one of the most wide-open towns in the United States. His brother James started the organization, but Tom took over in 1910 and skillfully built alliances with heads of major business firms. These he could give tax breaks, contracts, deposits of public money, and peaceful labor relations, and they in turn provided jobs for his followers.

Political realists understood that big city machines existed partly because they met the needs of the poor and of ethnic minorities and thus sometimes dismissed corrupt machine operations as "honest graft." Nevertheless, these activities did corrupt the police force, and they resulted in higher taxes and loss of jobs for those not graced by machine support. Machine practice of stealing votes mocked democracy and created a cynical populace. Crushing the opposition sometimes meant kidnapping or even murder. Less violent suppression of opponents was accomplished by threats of punishment inflicted in all the ways open to the organization through its control over public agencies and many private firms.[5]

The Pendergast years added to the color and flavor of the Truman legend. The incongruity of this rural, southern man, a Baptist and a Mason, becoming part of a corrupt big city machine, while providing good progressive government and remaining personally honest, fed the myths that gave Truman near folk hero status in the 1970s. The legend, however, was partly wrong and certainly incomplete. Truman benefited from machine support, and, in turn, it fed off of his successes. It could not have gained the power it did without him. Truman, McElroy, and a transplanted Chicago gangster, John Lazia, composed a triumvirate just below the "Big Boss." Truman and McElroy handled county and city matters, and Lazia enforced machine discipline. Truman bragged that he could deliver eleven thousand honest votes on election day; he controlled over nine hundred patronage jobs and millions of dollars in county purchasing.

Perhaps his most important role was to provide a cover of respectability for a crooked organization. In the 1920s, Pendergast, a master politician, sensing that corruption in the county court had damaged the Democratic party among rural voters, concluded that patronage and honestly fulfilled contracts given to favorites could be more helpful to the machine than graft. He allowed Truman to reduce corruption in county government in return for a more secure hold on patronage. Truman benefited politically, and voters gained the cleanest county government in years, much cleaner than McElroy gave Kansas City. Truman's reputation for providing businesslike, efficient government helped Pendergast cement his alliance with key business interests, providing the foundation of his power.

Truman thus coped with the machine by using his personal assets to demand leeway in carrying out his responsibilities, and Pendergast was astute enough to give it. A perceptive observer of the organization said that Truman wore the "boss collar" more lightly than any other local politician. Still, the collar was there. Truman told municipal reformer Walter Matscheck: "I'll go along with you on this just as far as I can. I can't go as far as you would like to go, but I'll go as far as I can."

Pendergast helped Truman maintain his sense of ethics. Truman always claimed that the boss only talked to him about patronage matters and never pressured him on policy issues or tried to force him to engage in corrupt activities. There was one exception to Pendergast's hands-off policy, Truman admitted. This confrontation, over bond issue money, became a frequently told story of the Truman-Pendergast relationship, meant to show both in the best light. In 1928 the county passed a $7.5 million bond issue after Truman publicly pledged to spend the money honestly. When local contractors complained because Truman kept his pledge, Pendergast arranged a meeting. Truman listened to the contractors argue that as local citizens, they should be given the inside track on bids. Then, according to Truman's account, he stood up to them and told the angry businessmen that he intended to award contracts to the lowest bidder. Pendergast backed the judge and chased the businessmen away: "I told you that he's the contrariest man in the County. Get out of here." Truman used the story to illustrate his own honesty and to demonstrate the steadfast quality of Pendergast's character.

The encounter, however, was a little more complicated. In a private account, Truman revealed that Pendergast's anger was turned against him, not the contractors: "The Boss in his wrath at me because his crooked contractors got no contracts, said I was working to give my consulting engineers a nationwide reputation and that my honor wouldn't be [worth a] pinch of snuff." Truman retained his admiration for Pendergast because the "Big Boss" could have used his control of the other two judges to misuse the bond money. Pendergast stood by his word because his political sense told him of the wisdom of letting Truman spend the money honestly. Voters had had before them twenty-eight million dollars in bond issues and approved only Truman's $7.5 million and another for less than a million. The machine's display of honesty on Truman's issue paid off when, reassured, the voters two years later passed a massive county-city bond issue. Then the Pendergast favorites got their contracts.[6]

Truman won, but the pressures of his job took a terrible toll. In the privacy of a hideaway office that he maintained at the Pickwick Hotel in downtown Kansas City, Truman poured out his despair in a series of documents written in late 1930 or early 1931 and in 1934. In these "Pickwick Notes," he revealed the corruption and squalor of the machine he helped build. Pendergast did let him spend the bond money honestly but with strings attached. Truman wrote: "I had to compromise in order to get the voted road system carried out. . . . I had to let a former saloon keeper and murderer[,] a friend of the Big Boss[,] steal about . . . [illegible] from the general revenues of the County to satisfy . . . [my fellow judge] and to keep the crooks from getting a million or more out of the bond issue. Was I right or did I compound a felony? I don't know." He estimated that he had to let his associates steal a million dollars from the general reserve; otherwise they would have taken half the bond money: "I wonder if I did right to put a lot of no account sons of bitches on the payroll and pay other sons of bitches more money for supplies than they were worth in order to satisfy the political powers and save $3[,]500[,]000[.]00. I believe I did do right. Anyway I'm not a partner of any of them and I'll go out poorer in everyway than when I came into office." The costs to his sense of integrity were high: "Am I an administrator or not? Or am I just a crook to compromise in order to get the job done? You judge, I can't."

Despite the strain on his personal values, Truman helped extend the machine's power, allowing it to spread corruption. He tried to square his Baptist conscience with the reality of contributing to crime by offering the excuse often heard from within other twentieth-century organi-

22

zations: that he could do more to clean up the mess from the inside than by becoming a "yellow dog" and attacking it from outside. He also lessened the tension created by his ethical dilemma by universalizing the problem. The whole society was open to corruption: "We teach our boys to worship the dollar and get it how they can." Personal and public corruption was the result. Truman was contributing to the public good, he believed, by doing less evil than other politicians. But years later, when his secretary of commerce, Henry A. Wallace, voiced this ethic—that at times the end justified the means—Truman was shocked and decided to fire Wallace. "I knew I could not get along with him," Truman wrote. But Wallace simply spoke the ethic that Truman had lived by all of his political life.

Truman narrowed his ethical framework during the Pendergast years. In fact, he could uphold his ethics only because they were narrow and unsophisticated: Tom Pendergast was better than his critics because he kept his word; Truman was honest because he did not personally benefit. He shrugged off the ethical dilemmas, focused on practical problems, and became increasingly impatient with those who raised questions about his and his associates' conduct.

The Pendergast years also made Truman more callous, diminishing his special ability to understand human relationships and to empathize with people's needs. His sensitivity to others now became increasingly a part of his manipulative routine put to practical political uses. He became a fanatical organization man who detested those who ran out on the party, and he stood by the machine even when it was crumbling in the 1930s. As vice president, he braved public criticism to go to Tom Pendergast's funeral: "I was there because I thought I should be. Mr. Pendergast was my friend when I needed one and I have been his." As courageous as this kind of loyalty was, it meant sticking by associates even when they betrayed the public's trust.[7]

The ethical bankruptcy of the Pendergast relationship should not obscure the fact that Truman's popularity stemmed from real and solid achievements that benefited the people of Jackson County. Truman was a progressive in the tradition of those who fought for planning, efficiency, and economy in government. He organized the Regional Plan Association of Kansas City, presided over the Missouri Planning Association, served on the board of directors of the National Conference of City Planning, belonged to the American Civic Association, and published a book, *Results of County Planning*.

Truman's popularity and reputation for fairness stemmed from a massive road program that he put through. He understood that Jackson County "pie crust" roads could not stand up under the traffic that increased month by month during the automobile boom of the 1920s. He responded by building one of the nation's first and most successful metropolitan road systems designed to meet the needs of the automobile age. Despite the need for a good road system Truman had to move carefully; government corruption had caused people in the past decade to reject almost all local bond issues. First, he had two highly respected civil engineers, Nathan T. Veatch and Edward M. Stayton, draw up plans for a $6.5 million system of roads; then he sold the program to local civic leaders and to the voters. When Truman took the two engineers to see Pendergast, the boss assured them he would keep his promise to Truman to leave them alone. "It was always a kind of touch and go, but we were never bothered," Veatch recalled, ". . . and it is one of the miracles that I have been through in my life."

The completed system left everyone in the county within two and one-half miles of a concrete road and connected the county and city roadways. A farm spokesman said that the system would save farmers $275,000 a year in transportation costs. The program paid off politically by adding to Truman's reputation, putting loyal Democrats to work, and giving aid to business, farmers, and other economic groups. Kansas City Jews long remembered that Truman ran a good paved road to an isolated Jewish cemetery.

Truman gained respect from municipal reformer Walter Matscheck and other good-government advocates by promoting tax reform, planning at county, regional, and state levels, and government reorganization. While Truman could not deliver machine support to achieve his reform plans, his attempt was important. Years of work with Matscheck and his own experience on the job shaped his administrative ideas. The need for structural unity and clear lines of responsibility and authority were all goals he later fought for as president. In fact, in terms of ideas, if not practice, his theory of government administration developed little after the county court years.

Truman's achievements won him wide support and easy reelection in 1930. As he continued his building and reform programs during the next four years, his work within the urban machine continued to shape his political outlook. He developed new understanding of black Americans. Truman, a product of southern racial values and views, held and expressed racist beliefs until the end of his life. Pendergast, on the other hand, was more interested in political power than in adhering to outmoded southern mores, and he recognized the importance of Jackson County's twenty thousand blacks. Although the black community was mostly Republican, from the 1890s the Pendergasts had aided and used black leaders to build machine power. Truman and other leaders helped by constructing and improving black institutions, ending police brutality against blacks, and rewarding black political allies. By the time Franklin Roosevelt took power, Kansas City black voters were already solidly Democratic. County institutions remained segregated under Truman, but blacks supported him because they believed he treated them fairly within this Jim Crow framework.[8]

Truman later claimed to be a New Dealer from the start. He had acted in progressive fashion by advocating efficiency, economy, and planning in government. He was innovative and forceful in his fight for administrative reform. His progressivism, nevertheless, was typical of a forward-looking small businessman. He did not display much interest in social reform, and when he did, it was usually to ask for greater economy and efficiency. The Great Depression did little to change his thinking about political economy. It did not provoke an innovative response from him as it did from some other government leaders. Rather, he responded as most other politicians did: by applying business-minded values to achieve retrenchment through reducing government services and firing employees. The economic collapse, however, and the people's political response to it, did prepare him to follow Roosevelt's leadership in 1932.[9]

In 1934 Truman seized an opportunity to work directly with the Democratic administration in Washington. He accepted an offer from Pendergast to back the judge in a race for the U.S. Senate. Before daylight on 14 May 1934, the day he planned to announce his candidacy for the Senate, Truman sat alone in his hideaway office in the Pickwick Hotel and began a forty-page sketch of his life. The bitterness of earlier similar notes describing his corrupt associates was gone: "Tomorrow[,] today rather, it is 4 AM, I am to make the most momentous announcement of my life. I have come to the place where all men strive to be, at my age[,] and I thought two weeks ago that retirement on a virtual pension in some minor County office was all that was in store for me." His thoughts turned immediately to greatness: "In reading the lives of great men, I found that the first victory they won was over themselves and their carnal urges." He then resketched his life, as if making it fit one of the little biographical sketches in Horne's volumes. The squalid corruption that weighed on his mind when he sat alone in the Pickwick writing earlier notes disappeared. He wrote lovingly of his wife and family, of his

25

farm, banking, and business background, of his overcoming the adversity of bankruptcy, and of loyal friends like Pendergast. His revised version of his life had all the ingredients suitable for a political Cincinnatus.[10]

Truman's announcement surprised many Missourians. He was limited to two terms as presiding judge, and his future had been in doubt because of Tom Pendergast's fine balancing of political strategies, rewards, and punishments. After passing over Truman for several positions, Pendergast offered him the Senate, using him as a pawn in a power struggle for control of Missouri. Senator Bennett C. Clark had decided to challenge Pendergast's power by persuading Congressman Jacob L. "Tuck" Milligan to run for the second Senate seat in 1934. If successful, Clark and Milligan could funnel patronage to Pendergast enemies and investigate his activities. To block Milligan, Pendergast turned to Truman. Truman, not well known to the average voter in Missouri, seemed completely overshadowed, especially when the St. Louis Democratic organization put Congressman John J. Cochran into the race. Pendergast put Truman forward because he was confident of machine power to carry the election and because Truman, while not widely known, had a good record in office.

Faced with this challenge from two formidable opponents, Truman relied, once again, on his ability to work harder than others. He gave six to sixteen speeches each day in the wilting heat of the Missouri summer, going from one small, dusty town to the next. In addition to his own effort and Pendergast support, he called on his friends in veteran and reserve officer circles and exploited contacts he had forged with members of the county court judges' association. He had friends and admirers in virtually every courthouse in the state.

In the bitterly fought race, Milligan and Cochran portrayed Truman as an obscure local politico put forward by Pendergast only because he wanted a stooge in Washington. Truman countered by pointing to his own record for honesty, underscored by the support of well-known anti-Pendergast newspapers, and by revealing that Cochran and Milligan also had sought help from Pendergast in their own careers. Truman relied most of all on the popularity of the New Deal. His campaign slogan was: "Back Roosevelt," and he told the people: "I am for the Roosevelt program heart and soul. There is no other way to do the job."

On election day, St. Louis went almost entirely for Cochran and Kansas City for Truman, but Truman was stronger in rural areas. He won the primary by a plurality of forty thousand votes and easily rolled over his conservative Republican opponent in the general election.[11]

Truman arrived in Washington as the 1935 congressional session got underway, two years into Roosevelt's first administration. Truman had campaigned as a New Dealer and in the Senate would vote almost without deviation for Roosevelt-backed bills. Yet those committed ideologically to the president's program remained uneasy with Truman, as he was with them. As senator and later as president, he defined himself as a "modern" Jeffersonian, one who lived in an industrial rather than an agrarian society. Truman argued that small farmers were the foundation of liberty and often proclaimed his opposition to concentrations of power, whether in the hands of corporations or of unions: "Big money has too much power and so have big unions—both are riding to a fall because I like neither." He preached his Jeffersonian message, as transmitted to him through two heroes, Andrew Jackson and Woodrow Wilson, after the war to the head of a great corporation:

> I am sure that right down in your heart you know that the ordinary man is the backbone of any country—particularly is that true in a Republic and what I am trying to eliminate is the fringe at each end of the situation. I think small business, the small farmer, the small corporations are the backbone of any free society and when there are too many people on relief and too few people at the top who control the wealth of the country we must look out.

Truman did not, however, incorporate these generalities into a workable program of action. Economic concentration continued during his years in Washington, and despite his populist-sounding attacks on bigness, he did not propose solutions for the problem of how to "adjust" Jeffersonian principles to a modern United States. To the extent that he acted against big business, he did so with limited legislation to end specific abuses, for, despite his vague generalizations, the reality was that he unquestioningly accepted corporate America. He was nonideological and did not think seriously about the nature of modern society, of how the values and ethics inherited from his rural past fit with the urban-industrial society around him, or even of the meaning of the welfare state that he helped construct after 1935.

Fortunately Truman did not have to formulate a domestic program to fit twentieth-century conditions; he had only to follow Roosevelt. Truman believed in strong presidential leadership, and his preoccupation with the great men of history convinced him that social progress came only through strong leadership. The Democratic party, led by Roosevelt, cued him, and he responded willingly. He could not himself think deeply about fundamental social questions. New Deal reforms, which he could understand from within a Jeffersonian-Wilsonian perspective and which remained within the liberal, capitalistic framework, entailed as much change as Truman could easily accept.[12]

If Truman did not become a political thinker during his Senate years, he did evolve as a politician. As a young man, he had developed a gregarious, sociable disposition that fitted him for politics. He then added political experiences that shaped him for success within the multilayered Democratic party. Raised as a Southern Democrat, he found his political footing in the big city Democratic machine and then supported Roosevelt's liberal New Deal program. His preferred stance as a peacemaker enabled him to add these layers of experience without casting off old ones, and he retained ties with each faction of the party, leaving himself in an enviable position when the Democrats searched for a vice-presidential candidate in 1944.

Truman's senatorial voting record revealed him as a New Dealer from the first but one who became more liberal when the reform coalition began to falter in the late 1930s. Truman moved leftward out of loyalty to the presidential faction of the party rather than from ideological concerns. As Southern Democrats and Republicans railed against the New Deal, Truman stood by Roosevelt. He voted for all the major relief and welfare bills that came up while he was senator: the Social Security Act, the Wagner-Steagall Housing Act, the Emergency Relief Appropriation Act of 1935, and the Fair Labor Standards Act. He voted for the Wealth Tax Act, backed the Tennessee Valley Authority, and took strong liberal positions on civil rights and labor votes, including the Wagner Act. Truman supported Roosevelt on issues involving a strong executive, even standing by the president on the coalition-shattering Supreme Court–packing plan and on his executive reorganization program. His own major legislative accomplishments before World War II, the Civil Aeronautics Act of 1938 and the Railway Transportation Act of 1940, brought the government into new areas of business regulation.

Despite Truman's strong support of Roosevelt's program, the president seemed to regard him as a hack Pendergast politician, and Truman, often wounded by Roosevelt's lack of respect for him, regarded the president as devious and unreliable, so self-centered in his search for glory that he stifled those, like Truman, who could have helped him more. Although Roosevelt infuriated and humiliated him, Truman still believed that the New Deal was good for the country and felt that he might be living in a rare era when the nation benefited from the leadership of a great man: "I think [Roosevelt] would like to be a Monroe, Jackson and Lincoln all in one—and is probably succeeding."[13]

Truman regarded his Senate years as the happiest ten years of his life. Hard work and party regularity won him the respect of many powerful figures. Soon Vice President John Nance Garner, Speaker of the House Samuel T. Rayburn (D–Texas), and Senate Majority Leader Alben W. Barkley (D–Kentucky) took notice of him and included him in the circle of "workhorses" who could be trusted to vote correctly and perform well on committee and other assignments. Outside Congress, Truman turned to such figures as Roosevelt confidant Harry L. Hopkins and Democratic party leader James A. Farley for help with political problems and, infrequently, to Justice Louis D. Brandeis and social critic and capitalist theorist Thurman W. Arnold for intellectual stimulation.

These were also good years for Bess Truman. Although she reluctantly left Independence, Washington proved to be a southern-oriented, hospitable city. Wives of Truman's colleagues quickly pulled her into their social life and made her feel at home, although she spent only half of each year there, returning to Independence to be with her mother for the other half. Truman missed her and resented her leaving, but just as Bess understood she should not prevent Harry from pursuing his career, he carefully avoided forcing her to violate her sense of duty that compelled her to go home. Their marriage remained solid, and their partnership continued. Bess became acquainted with Washington figures and issues and continued to participate in Harry's political life by offering him astute advice and listening to his problems.

Truman had special need for that advice and sympathy as his first term neared an end, for his alliance with Tom Pendergast threatened to bring his Senate career to a premature conclusion. Truman had used his national office to provide federal patronage for the Pendergast machine and had helped organization figures in various ways, though Pendergast seldom asked Truman to take particular positions on legislation. The "Big Boss" did not need to tell Truman how to vote, since they both were excellent politicians responsible to the same set of constituents.

Pendergast also had more serious problems than managing Truman's activities in Washington. His facade of respectability and civic service in Kansas City had become harder to maintain as criminal activities by members of his machine increased and as elections became more corrupt and violent. New Deal programs replaced some of the machine's welfare functions, and the machine became less important to business in stabilizing labor relations after the Wagner Act promoted union organization and militancy. Tom Pendergast also began to break down physically in the mid-1930s, and he became so addicted to gambling that it destroyed his judgment and drove him to riskier ventures in graft.

Truman unintentionally contributed to Pendergast's downfall and almost destroyed his own position. He realized that it was important to elect a sympathetic governor in 1936, fearing that if Senator Bennett Clark placed his man in that position, he would use it to overthrow Pendergast. Truman helped arrange for Clark and Pendergast to agree to support Missouri businessman Lloyd C. Stark for governor. With their support, Stark easily won, but he quickly proved too ambitious to be easily controlled by the entrenched leaders. When federal district attorney Maurice M. Milligan began to investigate the 1936 election in Kansas City, unusually violent and corrupt even by that city's standards, Stark, scenting blood, encouraged Milligan to dig into the activities of the Kansas City organization. Milligan won convictions against 259 Democrats, mainly for election fraud. Over Truman's objection, Roosevelt reappointed Milligan in 1938, and Milligan and Stark then went after Tom Pendergast himself. In 1939, Pendergast pleaded guilty to two counts of income tax evasion and went to prison, as did some of his major allies.

Truman watched his associates go to jail and his own political position erode. He had worked hard for six years to master his job and to make powerful friends in Congress. He felt that a second term would allow him to achieve important legislative goals, but now Stark seemed ready to take away his chance for major accomplishment. The wealthy and popular governor decided to run for Truman's Senate seat, perhaps as a stepping-stone to the presidency. Truman hated Stark with a special intensity that he reserved for a select few he felt had double-crossed him. Stark was "a self made S.O.B.," Truman wrote Bess, unfit to be "dog catcher in a Phillipine [sic] village."

In 1940, Truman's organizational base was in shambles, once-friendly newspapers classed him a machine politico, campaign money was nonexistent, and Roosevelt catered to Stark, the powerful heir apparent in Missouri. But Truman campaigned vigorously, the only way he knew, and slowly his political situation improved. Maurice Milligan entered the race, hurting Stark much more than Truman. Stark's unrestrained ambition had also angered and frightened Senator Bennett Clark and other professional politicians, who came to Truman's side. Even Roosevelt began to find the governor obnoxious, and Robert E. Hannegan, a powerful member of the St. Louis machine, brought that organization over to Truman. Personal friends like John W. Snyder and Harry H. Vaughan joined the campaign. Vaughan, with $3.25 in his own bank account, became Truman's finance chairman. Truman had his veteran and Masonic connections and continued support from labor and blacks, who kept track of his Senate record. Most political experts, nevertheless, remained sure Truman would lose. But he carried both St. Louis and Kansas City and increased his vote outside the cities over 1934, easily winning the election.[14]

"I have had enough trouble in the last year to last me the rest of my life," Truman said referring to the 1940 campaign. That victory left him badly scarred: "I've spent my life pleasing people, doing things for 'em and putting myself in embarrassing positions to save the party and the other fellow, now I've quit. To hell with 'em all." Truman had suffered vicious attacks, and winning did not heal the wounds: "When they stand up and call you names, it always hurts some, and I don't care how old or how young you are, what age you are." "But mommy," he wrote Bess in 1942, "I've wanted so badly to make good in the Senate so you and my sweet baby wouldn't be ashamed of me."

Truman's pride had been wounded often from his early childhood. He only pretended to forget social slights and humiliations that he suffered in grade school, he told Margaret. Forced to mortgage the farm before World War I, he had later failed in business, and suffered through years of social and political slights and sneers. No success ever entirely covered the hurts. The scars were there; his self-esteem was fragile; every campaign made him a little more bitter against those, like journalists, who lacerated the wounds.

Fortunately Truman was not a mean man. Essentially happy and optimistic, he seldom used his power to repay enemies, although he often withheld favors from them. He did find an outlet for his suppressed anger by letting fly with hot words in his speeches and sometimes in the form of letters never sent. He reported many angry private confrontations with enemies, but usually these conflicts occurred only in his imagination. "On most occasions Mr. Truman's report of his bark vastly exaggerated it," his friend Dean G. Acheson noted.[15]

While Truman was fighting for his political life in 1939 and 1940, Europe was engulfed by war. Truman considered himself a Wilsonian internationalist, but foreign policy issues did not greatly concern him. In

1935 and 1936, he fell in the middle on an isolationist-internationalist continuum, and in 1937 he voted for neutrality legislation. As Roosevelt moved in an internationalist direction, however, and searched for ways to aid the Allies against Hitler's Germany, Truman followed the president's leadership.

Truman, aware that the United States was poorly prepared for war against Germany, saw no room for waste of time, materials, or money in war preparations. Since he was too old to command a battery of artillery, he decided he could best serve his country by acting as Senate watchdog over the defense effort. His constituents also complained to him about waste and favoritism in defense projects and about big business exclusion of small firms from military contracts. In 1940, with unfailing energy and interest in details, Truman drove thirty thousand miles visiting military bases and projects. Concluding that the complaints he heard were accurate, on 10 February 1941 he described to his colleagues what he had uncovered in his personal investigation. This was a "fateful" speech, Truman wrote, one that changed the course of his life.[16]

The Senate established a special investigating committee, known as the Truman Committee, and granted it extraordinary authority to examine all aspects of war production. Truman moved carefully, anxious to show that his work would not hurt the war effort or politically damage the administration. He first investigated army camp construction, uncovering in August 1941 evidence of one hundred million dollars in waste out of one billion spent. In changing its procedures, the army saved several hundreds of millions of dollars, and after this the Senate routinely gave Truman the money and staff members he requested. He chose his targets well, stood up to pressure from government and private industry, and revealed to the public findings of gross mismanagement, waste, and corruption.

Truman focused attention on the need for strong, centralized administrative authority over the war effort. While most congressional committees tried to splinter executive power, Truman, with his military background and years of frustrating work in a weak executive structure in Jackson County, fought for centralized organization. Bureaucratic red tape slowed the war effort and killed U.S. soldiers; conflicting departmental jurisdiction led to a "fumbling approach" in airplane production; duplication of activity and petty jealousies hindered construction of defense housing; lack of "centralized and sole responsibility" in a supervising agency crippled the synthetic rubber program; barge and farm machinery production lagged because of ineffective use of government authority to get action. "The influence from above must be always toward unity," Truman said.

Despite its criticisms, the Truman Committee won the trust of key people in the war effort. In 1944 newsmen chose Truman as one of the top ten most valuable men in Washington, the only congressman on the list, and his work finally removed the Pendergast label from his name.[17]

The wartime committee opened the vice presidency to Truman. He was not eager for the nomination. He loved the Senate and with his new prestige and added seniority expected to be a real power there. He had, however, one thing in common with those who plotted to make him vice president: neither he nor they wanted Vice President Henry A. Wallace to be renominated to run with Roosevelt in 1944. Wallace was too farsighted, liberal, and independent for narrow, party-bound, conventional politicians; he never fit well with the inner circle of party regulars, some of whom believed Roosevelt would not survive a fourth term. Democratic factions jockeyed for position as World War II neared an end. The conservative and moderate leaders had steadily increased their power after 1936, and since Wallace, more than anyone else except Roosevelt, symbolized New Deal liberalism, they were determined to dump the vice president.[18]

The anti-Wallace group included chairman of the Democratic National Committee (DNC) Robert E. Hannegan, DNC treasurer Edwin W. Pauley, DNC secretary George E. Allen, Postmaster General Frank C. Walker, Chicago boss Edward J. Kelly, and Bronx boss Edward J. Flynn. Pauley later recalled that he mobilized these men against Wallace using the slogan: "You are not nominating a Vice President of the United States, but a President." Roosevelt's advisers convinced him that Wallace's presence on the ticket would not help and might hurt him. Wallace, sensing the threat, demanded a meeting with the president. Roosevelt told him that he remained his personal choice but that Wallace probably could not be nominated and would be humiliated at the convention. Wallace heard only the first part, while Roosevelt wanted him to hear the second.

When party bosses met with Roosevelt at the White House on 11 July 1944 to discuss possible candidates, a consensus developed behind Truman. His defense investigation had won him public acclaim among those who followed national affairs, and he seemed noncontroversial, with solid ties to all wings of the party. He was at least an acceptable second choice to all. Clinton P. Anderson, later Truman's secretary of agriculture, called him the lowest common denominator.

Roosevelt suggested Supreme Court Justice William O. Douglas, but the others greeted his name with silence. Roosevelt gave in and wrote Hannegan a note, which he dated 19 July 1944 to coincide with the opening of the convention: "You have written me about Harry Truman and Bill Douglas[.] I should of course be very glad to run with either of them and believe that either one of them would bring real strength to the ticket." The next day, Hannegan had the handwritten note retyped at the White House, with some punctuation changes, and then Roosevelt signed it. Hannegan carried the note from leader to leader in Chicago, pushing Truman's name.

In the meantime, Roosevelt led Office of War Mobilization and Reconversion director James F. Byrnes to believe that the president wanted him to enter the vice-presidential race. Confusion again ensued when Walker and Hannegan told Byrnes that Roosevelt favored Truman. Byrnes confronted Roosevelt, who said he had told the party leaders that he would not object to Truman but that he would express no preference. Byrnes, believing that he had Roosevelt's support, asked Truman to nominate him. Truman agreed and went to the Chicago convention to work for him.[19]

When Truman arrived in Chicago, political leaders hovered around, urging him to agree to accept the vice presidency. Labor leaders told him that he was the only person they would support other than Wallace, their first choice. Truman reported such conversations to Byrnes, who continued to maintain that Roosevelt wanted him. Hannegan finally had Truman meet with a number of political and labor leaders, who told him that party unity depended on his accepting the nomination and that he was Roosevelt's choice. In an early recounting of this conference, Truman made no mention of a telephone call from Roosevelt during the meeting, but later versions had Hannegan calling the president who, finding Truman not yet in agreement, said loudly enough for Truman to hear that if the senator wanted to divide the party in the midst of war, that was his responsibility. Truman agreed to run and won the nomination on the second ballot.[20]

The campaign against the Republican nominee, New York governor Thomas E. Dewey, was the easiest in Truman's career. He made a few mistakes but none that hurt him or Roosevelt. As usual, Truman worked hard, but it soon became apparent that the American people did not intend to change leadership during the war. Truman wrote Margaret: "You must remember that I never wanted or went after the nomination—

but now we have it, (to save the Democratic Party—so the Southerners and A.F. of L. and R.R. Labor say) we must win and make 'em like it. Maybe your dad can make a job of the fifth wheel office."

After his inauguration, Truman set out in his usual fashion to master his new job. If Roosevelt had lived, Truman might very well have made the vice presidency a more important office than it had been in the past. But time was short; Truman was vice president for only eighty-two days, and Roosevelt was in Washington for only about thirty of those. Both focused their attention on the upcoming transition from war to peace; neither anticipated the more immediate crisis that came with Roosevelt's unexpected death.[21]

3

"IT HARDLY SEEMS REAL"

When Eleanor Roosevelt told Truman in the late afternoon on 12 April 1945 that her husband had died a few hours earlier, Truman was stunned. As he groped for the implications of her softly spoken words, press secretary Stephen T. Early and Secretary of State Edward R. Stettinius moved in to help. They summoned others, including Bess and Margaret, Speaker of the House Sam Rayburn, Chief of Staff Admiral William D. Leahy, and most cabinet members. Chief Justice Harlan Fiske Stone administered the oath of office to Truman, which he finished at 7:09 P.M.

Truman then held a brief cabinet meeting during which he asked all members to stay on with him, pledged to carry on Roosevelt's foreign and domestic policies, and decided that the San Francisco Conference called to write the United Nations charter should proceed as scheduled. Although Stettinius, observing the new president closely, saw no sign of bewilderment or weakness, underneath Truman was worried. He did not know how the nation and the armed forces would react to the death of the most imposing American figure of the twentieth century. Truman had little knowledge of foreign affairs and no detailed information on Roosevelt's wartime conferences, yet he would now have to deal face to face with Winston Churchill and Joseph Stalin, contemporary great men, rather than the long-dead figures he had so often read about in Horne's volumes on historic individuals.[1]

On Friday 13 April Truman began the struggle to get control of the machinery of government, a bureaucracy that continued its operation uninterrupted by Roosevelt's death. The flow of information that came to him through briefings and memoranda seemed unending. He had neither the luxury of testing his staff nor time to set up transition task forces. Truman had to learn the presidency on the run, and both he and the country suffered.

Tension was high around the White House as Truman began his first day. Men—no women would find a place in the inner circle—crowded around, wanting to shape the president's thinking, to interest him in a favorite program, or to sell themselves to him as he filled positions. Roosevelt's men and Truman's newcomers, like Matthew J. Connelly and Hugh Fulton, suspiciously watched one another, unsure of their future. At 11 A.M. military and diplomatic officials briefed Truman on the progress of the war. He met congressional leaders and arranged to address Congress and the nation on the following Monday. After lunch he talked to James Byrnes, one of the nation's shrewdest politicians. They discussed Roosevelt's wartime conferences at Tehran and Yalta "and everything under the sun," Truman noted in a diary entry. He was already thinking of replacing Stettinius with Byrnes.

The next few days followed a similar pattern: listening to briefings, reading stacks of memoranda, and finding positions for trusted friends. When he spoke to Congress on 16 April, he paid homage to Roosevelt and pledged to follow his policies. He reaffirmed the Allied military policy of unconditional surrender and held out a vision of future peace achieved through the United Nations and through continued cooperation among the Allies. He held his first press conference on 17 April and again affirmed his commitment to Roosevelt's policy.

Methodically he went from task to task. At the end of the first week, with his initial public appearances behind him, he felt things were beginning to click. The days went by in a blur, and at the end of two months he felt settled into office. During that brief time Germany had surrendered; serious questions had arisen about the stability of the Soviet-American alliance; he had endorsed major parts of Roosevelt's program such as the Bretton Woods agreement, extension of price controls, and a full employment bill; he also had made several cabinet changes. Within that two-month period, he wrote Bess, "things have changed so much it hardly seems real."[2]

For twelve years, Roosevelt had led the nation through depression and war crises, and he had done so with dramatic and personal leadership. The American people, eager to see that Truman could govern effectively, endorsed his first six weeks with an 87 percent approval rating, with only 3 percent disapproving, figures never achieved by any other president. Americans were cheered to see this largely unknown figure rise to the challenge of the office, just as the democratic ideology of the common man had envisioned.

Some tasks Truman turned to eagerly. He felt superior to Roosevelt as an administrator, convinced that his study of history allowed him to understand the presidency and that his political experience made him a master decision maker. Although Truman displayed an attractive degree of humility and personal simplicity, he accelerated the trend toward making the presidency the center of national life and moved his office far toward what would later be called the imperial presidency. Truman believed that progress depended on guidance of great men; without them, society entered into "dark ages." He had an almost mystical faith in strong leadership, and his conception of the office, glorified to begin with, became unrestrained by constitutional limits as he became concerned with national security during the cold war. He wrote: "Our people looked to him [the president] for leadership and not for passive submission to the rigid limits of a written document. Every hope and every fear of his fellow citizens, almost every aspect of their welfare and activity, falls within the scope of his concern—indeed, within the scope of his duty."[3]

He believed that the president had to guard constantly against congressional invasion of the executive sphere, and as secrecy became increasingly routine, Truman regarded even normal questioning and examination of his activity by Congress or the press, once considered a necessary foundation of democratic government, as invasions of executive prerogatives. Leadership should not follow public opinion; rather, the president should act and then shape opinion to support him. The gap between his glorified conception of the office and the practical limitations on his power deeply frustrated him. He vented his anger against the press, opposing politicians, and anyone else who disputed his role as the only representative of all the people and the guardian of the national security.

Truman conceived the presidency largely in terms of decision making, but despite his pride in his ability to make decisions easily and rapidly, his rush resulted in mistakes, some with serious long-term consequences. Henry Wallace noted a key Truman characteristic when he visited the president on 27 April 1945: "Truman was exceedingly eager to agree with everything I said. He also seemed eager to make decisions of every kind with the greatest promptness. Everything he said was decisive. It almost seemed as though he was eager to decide in advance of thinking." Truman's eagerness to decide reflected a deep need within him, for it connected him with the heroic figures of the past. By being decisive, Truman, who as a little boy had not quite fit into the hard-fisted, masculine world of his brother and father or into the world of the well-educated or social elite, could gain respect and admiration from men of power, education, and wealth.

Henry Wallace caught another, almost contradictory element in Truman's decision making. "It is more and more evident," he wrote in December 1945, "that the President arrives at his decisions on the spur of the moment on the basis of partial evidence. He does *so* like to agree with whoever is with him at the moment." Wallace sensed that Truman's decisiveness stemmed from a feeling of powerlessness rather than strength, for despite continued references to his decision-making ability, Truman's life had been marked by indecision—in choosing a career, in marrying Bess, and in acting on political opportunities. Journalist Samuel Lubell saw the "essential drama" of Truman's presidency in his "fighting stubbornly and, yes, courageously, to avoid decision." Lubell wrote: "When he [Truman] takes vigorous action in one direction it is axiomatic that he will contrive soon afterward to move in the conflicting direction. In the end he manages to work himself back close to the center spot of indecision from which he started."[4]

Despite Truman's self-image of being a forceful mover of men through his willingness to make courageous decisions, to accept the buck stopping with him, he actually was often easily manipulated by his subordinates. He was less subtle in his decision-making process than Roosevelt, and his associates found ways to guide him. Dean Acheson, for example, understood Truman's self-concept and could choose language and images that moved the president in directions Acheson wanted. Those who knew him well could appeal to his numerous prejudices on issues and individuals and his concern for the dignity of the presidency to shape his decisions. They understood that he viewed himself as an impartial judge, searching for the relevant facts to decide questions on the basis of the national good, never in his personal interest, and they carefully presented issues to him in those terms. Truman pictured himself as the president-judge sitting at the top of a pyramidal executive branch with facts flowing to him through orderly lines of communication. Roosevelt, with a surer ability to grasp power, realizing such formalistic structures would make him captive of subordinates controlling the lines of communication, had deliberately short-circuited the system by assigning overlapping responsibilities to individuals and agencies.[5]

Truman believed that a successful president chose trustworthy subordinates and then delegated authority to them. For his personal staff, he kept some of Roosevelt's men, including Samuel I. Rosenman and Admiral Leahy. Truman brought two important staff members to the White House with him. Matthew J. Connelly, a member of the Truman Committee staff, became White House appointments secretary and monitored the constant flow of political requests and intelligence from party officials across the country. Charles G. Ross, a schoolmate from Independence and Pulitzer prize–winning journalist, became press secretary and intimate adviser to the president. There was no leader among these staff members who provided direction, as Clark M. Clifford, John R. Steelman, and Charles S. Murphy would later. Truman's early staff had a reputation for being loaded with mediocre cronies, excluding the men mentioned. There was indeed a number of "little fellows," as Henry Wallace called them, crowding around the president in the early months. Truman soon eased most of them into other jobs or sent them back home, but the image of cronyism remained, to be reinforced when scandals surfaced late in his presidency.[6]

For his cabinet positions, Truman intended to choose competent, loyal people and to delegate responsibility to them. Many of Roosevelt's people were ready to leave, disheartened by their leader's death and tired after years of service during the tumult of depression and war. By the end of May, Truman had announced four new cabinet members: Postmaster General Robert E. Hannegan, Secretary of Labor Lewis B. Schwellenbach, Secretary of Agriculture Clinton P. Anderson, and Attorney General Tom C. Clark. During the next six weeks, two more followed: James F. Byrnes replaced Secretary of State Edward R. Stettinius, and Fred M. Vinson replaced Secretary of the Treasury Henry Morgenthau, Jr. Four Roosevelt men stayed on: Secretary of the Interior Harold L. Ickes, Secretary of War Henry L. Stimson, Secretary of Commerce Henry A. Wallace, and Secretary of the Navy James V. Forrestal, but only Forrestal lasted beyond 1946. The changes did not result in readily apparent improvement over the "mudhole" of a cabinet Truman said he inherited from Roosevelt; some of the new men were very capable, and some were not. He also deliberately excluded women from his inner circle, since he never felt comfortable working with them and thought their presence inhibited free discussion.[7]

Truman entered office with clear views on presidential administration, but he was unprepared on foreign policy. The memoranda flowing to him revealed the immense problems that the peoples of the world faced as the European war ended in early May 1945, followed by peace in Asia in mid-August. During the six years of hostilities, combat destroyed lives and property on three continents and in Oceania. Fifty-seven nations entered the global conflagration, and fifty million people died, more of them civilians than soldiers. Hundreds of cities and towns lay in ruins, thinly populated by slowly starving people. War destroyed the industrial and transportation systems of many nations, disrupted agriculture, and left a barely functioning financial and trading structure. Germany and Japan, the energizing centers of the European and Asian economies, totally defeated, faced complete social, economic, and political reconstruction.

The consequences of the war went far beyond material destruction and disruption. The horrors that people inflicted on one another tested the meaning of civilization and raised such fundamental questions about human nature that to some the task of reconstructing societies seemed a sham, a doomed attempt to hide barbarism behind a meaningless facade of enlightenment. The planned fire storms the allies created in the cities of Dresden, Hamburg, and Tokyo and the atomic bomb attacks on the populations of Hiroshima and Nagasaki were overshadowed by the even more horrible crimes against humanity that occurred when millions of people were judged racially unacceptable and systematically exterminated.

War compounded the misery that millions of European and Asian peasants and workers experienced in the normal course of their lives. Revolutionary currents stirred as the poor and powerless in Western and Eastern Europe and Asia prepared to exploit the opportunity offered them by the disruption of the class structure that had oppressed them. In Asia especially, nationalist leaders pledged resistance to reestablishment of the European empires.

Among the great powers, Germany and Japan were occupied by the victorious allies. China faced renewed civil war. Eastern Europe, long subject to internal conflict and international intrigue, was pacified by the Soviet Union. Great Britain, drained by years of war, with its empire disintegrating, tried to continue its global role, but Churchill ultimately had to content himself with trying to educate Roosevelt and Truman to

41

the need to counter Soviet power in Europe and the Middle East. A battered France groped for internal unity after being defeated by the Germans and then experiencing years of shattering internal division over the proper role to assume in relation to the conquerors.

Above all else, the problem of future relations with the Soviet Union loomed before Truman in April 1945. Russia had been an enigma for American leaders since before the start of the century. Millions of people had migrated to the United States from the old czarist empire, and long before the Bolshevik revolution, Americans had come to regard Russia as an undemocratic police state. This concept of czarist autocracy easily evolved into similar fears of a Kremlin-directed, Marxist-Leninist totalitarianism. Western policies were never informed or compassionate toward Soviet leaders as they struggled to form a new social order.

After the United States and other nations had failed to destroy the Soviet government in its first few years, they maintained a policy of excluding it from the family of nations. Not until 1933 did the United States recognize Moscow, and relations between the two nations remained difficult. The wartime alliance was aberrational and did not overcome the suspicion that existed on both sides. In fact war added new strains. Americans expected gratitude and friendship as they sent lend-lease supplies to their new ally. Instead they often found hostility and suspicion. Americans recoiled from the reality of a closed society and even experienced considerable difficulty in working out joint military plans against the common enemy. On the other hand, while Americans preened themselves on their generosity, the supplies the Soviet Union received, while welcomed, were meager in relation to its expenditure of material. The Red army destroyed German military power with little help from the West. The West delayed for two years relieving German pressure on the Soviet Union by opening a second front. The Soviet army lost an average of ten thousand men each day for fourteen hundred days. Many Soviets suspected this was a continuation of the Western plan to rid the world of communism. Premier Nikita Khrushchev later speculated that perhaps the Allies had needed more time for preparation to open the second front, as they claimed, "but I think they were mostly dictated by their desire to bleed us dry so that they could come in at the last stages and determine the fate of the world."

By the end of the war, the Red army had achieved its greatest strength, and Truman, as he gave the order to atomize the Japanese cities, now faced a Soviet Union whose power controlled Eastern Europe and potentially the Persian Gulf and eastern Mediterranean. Soon what Washington assumed to be Kremlin-directed Communist movements gained force in China and Indochina. The expected Western prize, a Wilsonian global order imposed by the United States for, it believed, the benefit of the rest of the world, seemed threatened even as American leaders directed an economy whose productive capacity was unequaled in the history of the world and a military that possessed an atomic weapon whose explosion in July in a New Mexico desert moved physicist J. Robert Oppenheimer to remember a line from the *Bhagavad-Gita:* "Now I am become Death, the destroyer of worlds."[8]

Truman struggled to evaluate the flood of information cascading in on him. The European crisis of the late 1930s had convinced him that Wilson's international program built around a strong League of Nations could have prevented the impending war; yet Truman did not think deeply or critically about American policy. History had taught him clear lessons about the world. He was convinced of the moral superiority of the United States and assumed that right-thinking people everywhere would support an American-imposed world order.

Truman's views on the Soviet Union were equally culture bound. History had taught him that there was no difference between fascism and communism, between Nazi Germany and the Soviet Union, or between Hitler and Stalin, although he often believed Stalin was better at heart than the Politburo allowed him to be. Since experience taught him what to expect from Hitler and the Nazis, the 1930s, he thought, provided him with a guidebook to predict Kremlin actions after 1945. When he found Soviet behavior matching his predictions, he did not ask if U.S. expectations partly accounted for that result.[9]

Truman could not educate the American public in a realistic view of the world because his own experience and knowledge were limited. Mexico did not have a "real government," he instructed Tom Pendergast in 1935: "It is a sort of Bolshevik organization just like Russia." In 1941, after Germany attacked the Soviet Union, he made his famous statement to the *New York Times* suggesting that the United States should help whichever side was losing: "If we see that Germany is winning we ought to help Russia and if Russia is winning we ought to help Germany and that way let them kill as many as possible, although I don't want to see Hitler victorious under any circumstances. Neither of them think anything of their pledged word." This statement, reprinted in the Soviet Union after he became president, surely gave Stalin pause as he watched the new president consolidate his power. Although Truman publicly accepted the Soviet Union as a U.S. ally, privately he still regarded the "Russian question" as one to be "settled" after the war.[10]

Truman believed that the Americans, morally, technologically, and economically superior, had a duty to lead the world toward peaceful prosperity. The Soviets were incapable of such leadership. As late as 1957 he did not believe the Soviets had an atomic bomb: "After all, they're Russians," he told former aide Richard E. Neustadt: "They're basically peasants. They're not Americans. They can't hope to achieve the technology we've achieved."

In dealing with these backward people and their totalitarian government, which could be expected to act as the Nazis had acted in the 1930s, Truman held two beliefs he thought were clear. First, he entered the White House believing Kremlin leaders were untrustworthy and would not keep agreements. He quickly began to compile evidence to confirm this judgment while ignoring many Soviet actions that contradicted it. Second, he thought the Soviet Union would respond only to power: "The impression became fixed in my mind that force was the only language the Russians understood." On his first day in office, he told Stettinius that Washington had to be tough with the Soviets. A few weeks later in a meeting with a group of liberals, he banged the table with his fist and proclaimed: "We have got to get tough with the Russians. . . . We've got to teach them how to behave." Truman never swayed from this fundamental belief despite the failure of his policy based on force to cause the Soviets to submit to his direction.[11]

Truman did not have long to sort out his thoughts. When Soviet Foreign Minister V. M. Molotov came to Washington to meet Truman on 22 and 23 April, the president quickly displayed his inability to match Roosevelt's skillful maneuvering. Roosevelt had followed a policy of dual diplomacy. He built a Wilsonian internationalist facade for public consumption while carrying out behind the scenes a program of practical power politics based on a recognition of the legitimacy of a Soviet sphere of influence in Eastern Europe, in return for Soviet recognition of U.S. interests elsewhere. Roosevelt regarded the Soviet Union as a power to be dealt with in a traditional way rather than as an evil, ideologically driven empire bent on world domination, with which negotiations were futile and perhaps dangerous. Truman had always regarded great power diplomacy as immoral; he did not understand the subtleties of Roosevelt's approach and would not have liked it if he had. Truman also found it difficult to follow Roosevelt's policy because the former president's advisers were divided. A majority wanted to take a hard-line position, while others urged caution and pointed out that the Soviets, who understandably feared Western intentions, had legitimate security interests, which should be respected. Truman's instincts and personality inclined him toward the hard-liners, but he also respected some of the moderates— Harry L. Hopkins, Joseph E. Davies, and Henry Stimson. Throughout 1945, despite his apparent decisiveness, Truman wavered on which approach to take.[12]

Truman began to pick up the threads of U.S.-Soviet relations in the aftermath of the March 1945 Yalta Conference. Although the results of that meeting had pleased both Roosevelt and Stalin, within weeks, relations between the two nations had taken a nasty turn, especially over issues relating to Poland. Poland had been a source of contention in Europe for centuries and had often been a corridor through which Western armies attacked Russia. Following the German-Soviet partition in 1939, many Poles fled to London, forming a government in exile, dependent on the Western allies. The London Poles' hopes of regaining their former role in Polish life faded as the Soviet Union broke the German offensive and then pushed Hitler's troops back through Eastern Europe. Moscow then recognized another set of Polish leaders, the Lublin group, as the legitimate government. Thus, two Polish governments claimed legitimacy and received the backing of different Allied countries. At Yalta Roosevelt, accepting the Soviet position, agreed that Poland's eastern border would be the Curzon Line, first drawn as a proposed boundary settlement after World War I. Poland would be compensated for this loss of territory by receiving German land on its western frontier. Roosevelt accepted the Lublin government as the basis of an interim authority in Poland, with the understanding that its base would be broadened to include representatives from within Poland and from the London group, with free elections to follow this restructuring. Western acceptance of this boundary and of the Lublin group as the kernel of a new government were major concessions to Stalin, based on power relationships in Eastern Europe and on Roosevelt's recognition of the Soviet Union's legitimate security interests.

The glow of good feeling following Yalta burned out quickly in Poland, with both sides stretching the vague provisions to fit their interests. Truman could not see the subtly varying legitimate interpretations, and on his first day in office he concluded that the Soviets had broken the Yalta agreements.[13]

W. Averell Harriman, U.S. ambassador to the Soviet Union, reinforced these views. After Roosevelt's death, he rushed home, where to his surprise he found that Truman had read his dispatches from Moscow and eagerly awaited his advice. Harriman, who once had been optimistic about the future of Soviet-U.S. relations, now regarded the Polish issue as the key to understanding Moscow's intentions toward its wartime allies. Poland was not a vital American interest, Harriman wrote on 20 September 1944, yet it was important because it revealed a pattern of Soviet behavior. Raising the specter of falling dominos that haunted American policymakers for the next two generations, he said: "If the policy is accepted that the Soviet Union has a right to penetrate her immediate neighbors for security, penetration of the next immediate neighbors becomes at a certain time equally logical." He returned to Washington with a message of alarm. He told Forrestal on 19 April that the "outward thrust of Communism was not dead and that we might well have to face an ideological warfare just as vigorous and dangerous as Fascism or Nazism."[14]

When he met with Truman on 20 April, with the president preparing for his meeting with Molotov, Harriman warned that the West confronted a "barbarian invasion of Europe." He believed that the Kremlin interpreted U.S. wartime policy of generosity and friendship as weakness, but he did not think that Stalin wanted to break with the United States and argued that a policy of firmness could establish grounds for accommodation. Truman responded "that he was not in any sense afraid of the Russians and that he intended to be firm but fair since in his opinion the Soviet Union needed us more than we needed them." In a revealing statement on what American leaders considered to be fair grounds for accommodation with the Kremlin, Truman said "that we could not, of course, expect to get 100 percent of what we wanted but that on important matters he felt that we should be able to get 85 percent."

Truman then decided, only a few days after taking the presidency, that he would bluntly lay the American position before Molotov. His temper intensified as he proceeded from meeting to meeting in preparation for Molotov's visit. He found he could win approval from his advisers, often men of wealth, power, and education, by making rapid decisions and using blunt language. He got so carried away that he alarmed Harriman, who cautioned him against appearing to change Roosevelt's policy.

On 23 April just before he saw Molotov, Truman met with Stettinius, Stimson, Forrestal, Leahy, Army Chief of Staff George C. Marshall,

Harriman, State Department Soviet expert Charles E. Bohlen, and others. Truman said "that he felt our agreements with the Soviet Union so far had been a one way street and that could not continue; it was now or never. He intended to go on with the plans for San Francisco and if the Russians did not wish to join us they could go to hell." Stimson dissented from Truman's hard-line position. He pointed out that the Soviets had kept their word on the big military matters and that it was important to understand what they wanted. He cautioned "that without fully understanding how seriously the Russians took this Polish question we might be heading into very dangerous water." Later in the meeting, he added "that the Russians perhaps were being more realistic than we were in regard to their own security." Both Marshall and Leahy urged caution, and the admiral suggested that the Yalta agreement was open to two interpretations.[15]

Despite the moderation of his military leaders, Truman told Molotov that the United States could not be party to creation of a Polish government that was not representative of all democratic elements in Poland. He said Soviet failure to carry out the Yalta agreement cast doubt on the unity of purpose of the Allies and endangered the ability of the United States to provide postwar loans to the Soviet Union. After several exchanges, Truman told Molotov that the United States wanted to be friends with the Soviets but that this relationship could not be one way. According to Truman's memoirs, Molotov then said, "I have never been talked to like that in my life," and Truman answered: "Carry out your agreements and you won't get talked to like that." This exchange, now part of the Truman folklore, was not included in Bohlen's transcript of the meeting, however, and Bohlen told journalist Robert J. Donovan it did not occur. Truman often described harsh verbal exchanges that in fact did not take place. Still it had been a blunt session.[16]

Truman's initial venture into toughness accomplished little more than to increase Kremlin suspicion that the West wanted good relations with the Soviet Union only in order to use it as a battering ram against Germany. In response to Truman's comments to Molotov, Stalin rejected the president's interpretation of the Yalta agreement on Poland and pointed out that the nature of the Polish government was a security matter for his nation. He promised to try for harmony: "But you demand too much of me. In other words, you demand that I renounce the interests of security of the Soviet Union, but I cannot turn against my country." Truman found this a "revealing" response, but to him it only revealed Kremlin arrogance; it did not teach him that the Soviets responded to toughness with toughness. In fact, after the German surrender on 8 May, Truman took another slap at the Kremlin by immediately cutting off lend-lease. Stalin warned that if this were an attempt to pressure the Soviet Union, it was a mistake; compromise could be reached through friendly approaches but not through pressure.[17]

Harriman, despite his generally hard-line position, believed Truman had been too aggressive in his dealing with the Soviets. To ease tension, Truman decided, at the suggestion of Harriman and Bohlen, to send Harry Hopkins, liked by both Truman and Stalin, as a personal emissary to Moscow. On 19 May Truman talked to Hopkins and told him to tell the Soviet leader that he intended no change in Roosevelt's policy and to "tell him [Stalin] just exactly what we intended to have in the way of carrying out the agreements, purported to have been made at Yalta— that I was anxious to have a fair understanding with the Russian Government—that we never made commitments which we did not expect to carry out to the letter—we expected him to carry his agreement out to the letter and we intended to see that he did." One can see Truman divided in his own mind as he instructed Hopkins: "I told Harry [Hopkins] he could use diplomatic language, or he could use a baseball bat if he thought that was [the] proper approach to Mr. Stalin." Another more cynical note offers insight into Truman's thinking: he told Hopkins to make it clear to Stalin that the only goal of the United States was peace for at least ninety years and that Eastern Europe did not affect American interests but that Poland should have free elections, "at least as free as [Frank] Hague, Tom Pendergast[,] Joe Martin or [Robert] Taft would allow in their respective bailywike [sic]. Uncle Joe [Stalin] should make some sort of gesture—whether he means it or not [—] to keep it before our public that he intends to keep his word. Any smart political boss will do that."

In the meetings starting on 26 May 1945, Hopkins and Stalin spoke frankly. Hopkins assured Stalin that the United States opposed establishing a cordon sanitaire in Eastern Europe and wanted governments friendly to Moscow there. Stalin said there should be no major problem between Moscow and Washington on Poland. He suggested expanding the existing government by bringing into it four or five people acceptable to both the West and the Soviet Union. Hopkins and Stalin, with Washington's concurrence, worked out a list of names during the next few days. Stalin reconfirmed his intention of entering the war against Japan, agreed to back Chiang Kai-shek (Jiang Jieshi) in the Chinese civil war against the Communists, and made concessions that broke the deadlock over membership, voting, and other procedural matters at the United Nations meeting in San Francisco.

The results pleased Truman. Over the next few weeks, the United States recognized the new Polish government, and the San Francisco Conference successfully concluded its work. Truman sent the U.N. charter to the Senate, where it was overwhelmingly ratified.[18]

On 7 July 1945 Truman left for Potsdam, a site near Berlin, to meet with Allied leaders. The Big Three—Great Britain, the Soviet Union, and the United States—met to resolve various problems, like reparations and boundaries, as World War II neared an end. "How I hate this trip!" he wrote. Intimidated by having to meet face to face with two legendary figures, Churchill and Stalin, and irritated by protocol-dominated ritual and ceremony, he considered himself the "new kid on the block." Yet he was not at a total disadvantage. Both Churchill and Stalin were tired after their harrowing years of wartime leadership, and before the conference ended, the British voters gave a majority of seats in Parliament to Labour, thereby replacing Churchill with Clement R. Attlee. Ernest Bevin took Anthony Eden's position as foreign minister. Although some anticipated that the Labour government might be softer toward the Soviets, Attlee and Bevin's foreign policy differed little from that of their predecessors.

Truman immediately liked Stalin. Responding positively to the Soviet premier's frank, friendly manner and regarding him as a political boss similar to Tom Pendergast, Truman believed that Stalin was a man who understood political realities and could be trusted to keep his word.

Observers at Potsdam regarded Truman as self-confident and decisive. Lord Moran, Churchill's physician, said: "His method is not to deploy an argument but to state his conclusions." "He takes no notice of delicate ground," said Churchill, "he just plants his foot down firmly on it." But one British observer noticed another quality of Truman's decision making: he would emphatically take a position one day and then next day quietly recede from it. His blunt manner often obscured his vacillation in both domestic and foreign affairs.[19]

The sessions started on 17 July and ended on 1 August. After Stalin and Churchill made Truman chairman, he moved his colleagues rapidly through the agenda, pushing for quick decisions, whether, he told Eden, they were right or wrong. On the first day, he told them that he wanted not extended discussion but decisions. Already on the second day, he was tired of the conference: "I felt that some progress had been made, but I was beginning to grow impatient for more action and fewer words."

Of the third session he wrote: "I said that if they did not get to the main issues I was going to pack up and go home. I meant just that." Truman needed decisions to prove his worth in his own eyes and in the eyes of others. His impatience caused him to miss opportunities to learn other points of view or to spot not-so-apparent paths toward continued harmony among the Allies. He emphasized surface issues and practical proposals that could be dealt with in conventional ways.[20]

Truman got what was most important to him when on 17 July Stalin told him that the Soviet Union would join the war against Japan by 15 August: "Fini Japs when that comes about," Truman wrote. The toughest bargaining centered on the questions of war reparations, the future of Germany, and Polish issues, especially the western boundary of Poland. The Americans intended to make sure that Germany was not so stripped by reparations that the United States would wind up subsidizing that defeated nation to keep the people from starving. When Truman resisted the Soviet demand for fixed reparations of around twenty billion dollars, Stalin agreed on an American formula to let each power remove goods from its own zone, with the Soviets receiving a certain additional amount from the other zones, monitored by each zone's occupying government. This agreement became meaningless as the alliance broke down since the West stopped the flow from its zones to the Soviet Union. Meanwhile, the Soviets had given Poland part of their German zone to administer, in effect establishing the Oder and Western Neisse rivers as the Polish-German border. The two sides agreed to accept this boundary solution until a final peace conference, which was never held. They also agreed to establish a Council of Foreign Ministers to draft peace treaties with the Axis satellite nations.

Other issues remained unsettled, though Stalin seemed willing to stay as long as necessary to resolve them. Truman, however, was impatient to leave and missed an opportunity to settle details of such questions as joint occupation of Germany and Korea and many other problems that soon arose to vex the Allies. He expected to have future meetings with Stalin, but the two men never met again.[21]

One force operating during the Potsdam Conference was the existence of a new weapon, the atomic bomb. Before he left Potsdam, Truman issued orders to drop the bomb on Japan. For many years historians accepted Truman's version of that decision: that the need to save lives forced him to compel Japan to surrender before he had to order a land invasion of the Japanese home islands. But in 1965, historian Gar Alperovitz concluded that Truman dropped the bombs to intimate the So-

50

viet leaders, forcing them to accept an American-imposed world order. Critics of Truman's decision had made such arguments in the past, but Alperovitz's interpretation took added force because of his access to newly opened archival material. Although other historians have modified aspects of Alperovitz's argument, the emerging story remains closer to his interpretation than to Truman's.[22]

The successful explosion of the atomic bombs in 1945 culminated the 1938 discovery of nuclear fission. In 1938, some scientists, especially those fleeing nazism, had recognized the implication of nuclear fission and feared that Germany might develop an atomic bomb. Thus in October 1941 they and such political allies as Henry Wallace persuaded Roosevelt to put a high-level group to work to develop nuclear fission research policy. He soon authorized the Manhattan Project headed by General Leslie R. Groves, with physicist J. Robert Oppenheimer in charge of the crucial work at Los Alamos Laboratories in New Mexico. As early as 1942, Roosevelt began to realize the potential of the bomb for postwar diplomacy, and he reached agreement with Churchill for British-American cooperation in research. They made the fateful decision to keep the project secret from their ally, the Soviet Union.[23]

Truman first learned of the bomb on the evening he took office. Both his use of the weapon against Japan and his practice of atomic diplomacy to manage the Soviet Union were extensions of Roosevelt's policy. To change that policy would have required enormous self-confidence to oppose an array of experienced policymakers who assumed the bomb would be used, courage to face investigations into the expenditure of two billion dollars and the deaths of American soldiers if the weapon had not been dropped, wisdom enough to understand the meaning of atomic energy for the future of the world, and imagination sufficient to work out innovative plans for international cooperation. It would have taken a different president from Truman. He never seriously considered changing the direction of the government's atomic weapons policy.

More than most other American officials, Secretary of War Stimson understood some of the implications of the bomb for the future of civilization. Vannevar Bush and James B. Conant, who administered government science programs, worked closely with him, explaining the magnitude of the explosion that might be expected, even warning that a "super" or hydrogen bomb would soon be developed. They predicted that other nations could have the atomic bomb within three or four years and urged the necessity of developing international controls before the bomb was used to avoid frightening other nations into a race to develop their own weapons. They also suggested the possibility of a demonstration explosion to show Japanese leaders what they confronted rather than dropping it on cities.

By the fall of 1944, Stimson was clearly sensitive to the potentially destructive impact of the bomb on international relations, while Harriman's reports raised his fear of a breakdown of the alliance with the Soviets. After mentioning the bomb project to Truman on 12 April, Stimson met the president for a full discussion on 25 April. Byrnes had already told Truman that the bomb might allow the United States "to dictate our own terms at the end of the war," but Stimson now warned that the United States could not maintain its monopoly indefinitely and that a nuclear arms race would threaten all civilization. At his suggestion, Truman set up the Interim Committee to advise on nuclear policy.[24]

Although many nuclear scientists had developed concerns about the future of civilization in an atomic age, Secretary of State Byrnes dismissed Leo Szilard, Niels H. Bohr, and other physicists as naive professors who did not understand political realities. Yet those "dreamers" correctly anticipated that the United States could not maintain its monopoly for more than four or five years, that there would soon be a hydrogen bomb, that an arms race would result if the Soviet Union was not brought into a cooperative effort to control atomic energy before the bomb was used, and that there were alternatives to its use. Despite opposition from within the scientific community to using the weapon, the Interim Committee on 1 June 1945 recommended to Truman that the United States drop the bomb on Japan as quickly as possible and without warning.[25]

In the meantime, the military drew up plans for the invasion of Japan, landing first on Kyushu on 1 November and then on the Tokyo plain on 1 March 1946. Truman gave various figures of the cost in Americans killed and wounded during this projected invasion, often using wildly inflated numbers, ranging from 250,000 to 1 million deaths. No Pentagon planners in 1945, however, estimated that invasion would cost over 200,000 American lives, and most military men estimated 20,000 to 46,000 deaths. In any case, not even the first phase of the invasion was scheduled before November 1, three months after Truman ordered the bombs dropped. Many high military leaders, including General Dwight D. Eisenhower, opposed using the bomb, but most did not regard it as their duty to offer advice on the matter. Chief of Staff Leahy, who regarded the atomic bomb as an immoral device for killing women and children, opposed its use so vehemently that he undermined his credibility.[26]

Leahy predicted, and hoped, that the bomb would not work. But on 16 July, Truman received word in a cryptic message that the New Mexico test explosion was successful, and General Groves brought word a few days later that the results exceeded the most optimistic expectations of the scientists. American policymakers listened as he described how the bomb light equaled the intensity of several suns at midday, with force sufficient to be heard and even break windows over one hundred miles away from the site. Truman had delayed the Potsdam Conference to have it coincide with the test; if it worked, he would have an "ace in the hole" or "hammer," he said, in dealing with the Soviets, whose massive land-based military power would no longer be so awesome. As he evaluated the test results, observers noticed that he appeared "pepped up." Possession of this power manifested itself immediately. Churchill, sharing the American mood, told Lord Moran that the Anglo-Americans now had to "fix things up" before the Soviets got the bomb. Lord Moran, quickly grasping the bomb's meaning, wandered that night through the empty rooms where the British delegation stayed. "I once slept in a house where there had been a murder. I feel like that here," he noted in his diary.[27]

Truman went to Potsdam with the purpose of getting Stalin's final agreement to enter the war against Japan. Stalin had told Hopkins that the Soviet Union would enter the war before 15 August, and he confirmed that at Potsdam, although final agreements first had to be reached between his government and that of China regarding concessions the Soviets wanted from the Chinese. After word of the successful test arrived, some U.S. officials no longer felt Soviet entry was necessary or desirable. Truman and Byrnes now encouraged the Chinese to resist making concessions. Although the Americans realized that the Soviets would enter the war in any case, they wanted to delay entry in order to minimize extension of the Kremlin's power into the Asian arena.

Rather than wait to see if the Soviet declaration of war would, as some believed, shock Japan into surrender, the United States hurried to drop the first bomb in early August. Truman rushed ahead though the American invasion of Japan was not scheduled until 1 November and though the Americans knew the Japanese were putting out peace feelers. Truman wanted to speed the Japanese surrender and to impress the Soviet Union with the power of the atomic bomb.

Although the Interim Committee had recommended to Truman that he tell Stalin about the atomic bomb before the president ordered it dropped, on 24 July Truman "casually mentioned" to the Soviet premier that the United States had developed a powerful new explosive. He did not explain that it was an atomic bomb, nor did he, as the committee had urged, assure his ally of his desire to discuss international control. Stalin showed no special interest in Truman's remarks, and American observers of the brief encounter felt he did not understood the implications of Truman's disclosure. Actually the Soviets had begun nuclear research in the early 1930s, and in 1942 Stalin's advisers had told him that the Americans and Germans undoubtedly had atomic weapons programs underway. After he left Truman, Stalin told Molotov of the president's remark, and Molotov said they would immediately speed up their own program. Perhaps the nuclear arms race began that evening.[28]

In 1947 James Forrestal raised the question of whether the United States should have dropped the atomic bomb on Japanese cities. Because Washington long before had deciphered the Japanese military and diplomatic secret code, allowing the Americans to follow cable traffic, Truman knew that Japan was helpless and near surrender. Unfortunately for hundreds of thousands of people at Hiroshima and Nagasaki, American officials were not sure just how close collapse was, and the Japanese leaders did not realize how little time for maneuver they had. Both sides misread the other and failed to take direct action to end the war because such action might appear as a weakness. At Potsdam on 26 July, the United States, Great Britain, and China issued a proclamation that called on the Japanese to surrender or face destruction of its armed forces. It said that the Allies did not intend to enslave Japan or destroy it as a national entity, a statement intended to indicate flexibility on the question of allowing the Japanese emperor to remain and willingness to modify the unconditional surrender formula. The alternatives, it threatened, were prompt and utter destruction. Thus, the message hinted at the atomic bomb but in such an obscure way that even Assistant Secretary of State Dean Acheson, reading it in Washington, did not understand the reference. Some Japanese leaders did catch the hint of flexibility and saw the proclamation as an opening for an acceptable basis of peace, but they moved too slowly and ambiguously to seize the opportunity to end the war.[29]

On 22 July, Churchill and Truman decided to drop the bomb unless Japan accepted the Potsdam Proclamation. The bomb was to be dropped on a "purely" military target, not on women and children, Truman wrote, although how they were to be avoided he did not say. He ordered it to be dropped after 3 August, with the exact time depending on weather, on one of several cities, including Hiroshima or Nagasaki.

The first bomb hit Hiroshima in early morning on 6 August. Recent estimates are that it killed 130,000 people, including thousands of women and children and a few American prisoners of war; by 1950, 70,000 more Japanese had died of its effects. Assuming that this bomb was needed to force Japan to surrender, a doubtful assumption, logic would have at least indicated that Washington should have given the Japanese leaders time to absorb its meaning, especially since on 8 August the Soviets declared war, an event perhaps more shocking to Tokyo than the Hiroshima bombing. But instead of waiting, on 9 August the Americans dropped a nuclear bomb on Nagasaki, with 70,000 killed at once and 70,000 more dying by 1950. Japan then surrendered with the condition that the emperor would continue in his position. On 14 August 1945, the war ended.[30]

"This is the greatest thing in history," Truman said when told of the explosion over Hiroshima. Most Americans fully approved of its use on the Japanese cities. Some did not. A woman, after reading a statement by Truman thanking God that He gave the United States rather than its enemies this weapon, wrote two days after the Nagasaki bombing: "Let us not try to throw a halo around this deed now that it is done. The use of this bomb was not necessary. Already the Japs were practically on their knees and only needed Russia to come in and frighten them into complete surrender. And you knew that Russia was to enter the war." She added: "How very inconsistent we are to break an international rule of warfare and then expect God to make us the special trustees for this terrible weapon."[31]

4

THE TRUMAN
MERRY-GO-ROUND

Americans have faced tragic, dangerous, and frightening years in the twentieth century but none more confusing than late summer 1945 to winter 1946. As Truman reconstructed relations with the Soviet Union and other wartime allies, he also had to reconvert the economy to peacetime operation, guide demobilization of the armed forces, fend off a Congress that wanted to regain powers given to the executive during the war, revitalize New Deal reform, and face the political warfare that followed when he announced on 16 August 1945 that with Japan's surrender, "politics is open and free now."[1]

Reconversion exceeded even the most gifted political leader's ability to manage effectively, and Truman hardly had a chance to cope successfully. His approval rating in the Gallup poll dropped from 87 percent when he first took office to 50 percent in April 1946 and then to 32 percent before the November 1946 election. As problems mounted and people missed Roosevelt's reassuring presence, Truman's lack of style and dignity became an issue. Exaggerated stories spread of his swilling bourbon at poker parties with his Missouri cronies, bringing back memories of the Warren Harding administration. His verbal mistakes at press conferences or in impromptu settings were no longer dismissed as pleasantly amusing examples of a peppery ex-farmer doing his damnedest as president.

Truman's limitations, compounded by challenges to his reconversion policy and his attempt to renew the New Deal, converted his brief honeymoon into political disaster. Strong advisers could lead him in bold, new directions, as happened in the foreign and military field, but in 1945 and 1946, Truman turned to men with conventional views on domestic affairs. Frederick M. Vinson, one of the most important of these advisers, served first as head of the Office of War Mobilization and Reconversion (OWMR) and then as secretary of treasury starting in July 1945; he became the chief justice of the Supreme Court a year later. John W. Snyder, who followed Vinson first to OWMR and then to head the Department of Treasury, was Truman's oldest and closest friend. He was the most conservative Truman insider, and he lacked the strengths to offset the president's weaknesses. When by October 1945 Secretary of Labor Lewis B. Schwellenbach proved unable to cope effectively with reconversion, Truman brought John R. Steelman to the White House as a special assistant. He was a hard-working expert in labor-management relations, who largely took over these operations from Schwellenbach and remained a key staff member until Truman left office in 1953. Steelman, like Vinson, was competent but entirely conventional in his thought and operations.

There were others Truman could have turned to for advice. Chester Bowles, although a self-made millionaire, was a New Dealer with a deep commitment to social reform and to government regulation of the marketplace. As head of the Office of Price Administration, he had directed extensive wartime controls over the economy and wanted to retain price controls until 1947 to prevent inflation. His power eroded, however, as Truman began to place him in the "crackpot" liberal category of New Dealers with whom the president had difficulty dealing.[2]

Bowles, Snyder, Vinson, and other advisers on reconversion matters failed to predict accurately economic conditions in the immediate postwar months. They, like most other experts, expected that World War II would be followed by economic collapse and renewed depression. Months passed before they realized that inflation, not deflation, was the major threat. Many politicians, who had thrived in a depression environment by handing out government benefits to powerful interest groups, found it much more difficult to adjust to the politics of inflation, which called for holding the line on wages and prices and denying benefits to all groups with an even hand. Truman therefore faced not just the confusion of whether to follow an antidepression or anti-inflation program but had to cope as well with tremendous, often conflicting, pressure from the most powerful organized interests in the country.

There was in place a mechanism with which to fight inflation, the Office of Price Administration (OPA). During the war, an elaborate economic stabilization system had effectively maintained controls on prices and wages and had allocated supplies and production. The OPA was one of the keys to the system, and now it bore the brunt of resisting inflationary pressures. Under Chester Bowles, it had also become a stronghold for New Deal reformers who used the agency to protect consumers and other weakly organized groups. On their behalf, it had successfully resisted pressures during the war from organized business, labor, and farmers, but with Japan's surrender, it could not rely on crisis to give force to its orders.[3]

Much of the reconversion turmoil took the form of labor-management conflicts, which became so severe that they threatened economic stability and destroyed Truman's early image as a courageous, competent leader. As the war ended, many union leaders, expecting mass unemployment, believed they had to move rapidly to cement wartime gains before their bargaining power eroded. By October 1945, 275 strikes were under way, involving 400,000 workers, and the National Labor Relations Board had received notice of 416 more strike votes. By late January 1946, 1.3 million workers were on strike, and by the end of the year, 5,000 disruptions had put 4.6 million workers on the picket lines, a record year for labor conflict. This activity stirred the public's ingrained hostility to labor. Many conservative Democrats and Republicans thought it was time to reign in the labor colossus that antiunion propaganda portrayed as dominating the economy and threatening to take over the political system. Actually only 23.6 percent of the total civilian labor force belonged to unions in 1945.

There were good reasons for labor unrest. Workers' prosperity in 1945 was generally overstated. A group headed by economist Walter Heller estimated that in late 1945, an urban family of four needed $2,700, about $50 a week, for a decent living standard; the Bureau of Labor Statistics found that the average factory worker got only $40.98 per week. In that year, regarded as one of exceptional prosperity, about 20 percent of city families had incomes less than $1,500. Thus unrest did not come from just a handful of spoiled workers hoping to continue the fat times of the war years but from many Americans trying to achieve an acceptable living standard.[4]

Truman regarded himself as prolabor. Unions had supported him when he was in the Senate and had been a crucial force in his vice-presidential nomination in 1944. From his small businessman's point of view, however, labor seemed to have achieved equality within the system and now was pushing too far. He came to regard strikes as unpatriotic affronts to the presidency. He added to the confusion within his divided administration by calling on workers to "cut out the foolishness" and by explaining that the strikes occurred because workers wanted to get a little rest.[5]

When negotiations broke down in the automobile, oil, electrical goods, meat packing, and steel industries, Truman seized many companies to prevent shutdowns of essential supplies. Bowles saw the steel strike, which began in January 1946, as the crucial test for stabilization policy. If the administration allowed the steel companies to offset a wage increase with a price rise, then the OPA's ability to hold the line would be damaged or destroyed. Snyder pushed for just such a settlement, and Truman supported him. Bowles submitted his resignation, but Truman persuaded him to head a new unit, the Office of Economic Stabilization. After the steel strike was settled, journalist I. F. Stone estimated that the price rise brought the steel companies $325 million in revenue increases, while the wage outlay totaled $185 million. This settlement encouraged other groups to demand exceptions in their ceiling prices, with labor gaining bigger paychecks, business receiving price increases, and consumers facing higher costs.[6]

In late spring 1946, a threatened railroad shutdown overshadowed all other conflicts. After negotiations between the companies and rail unions broke down, the unions scheduled a strike for 18 May. On 17 May, Truman seized the railroads. He persuaded the key union leaders to delay action for a few days, but on 23 May 1946, the strike began, bringing the total number of workers off the job to 960,000.

Truman increasingly saw these economically hard-pressed American workers as dangerous men attacking the president and, therefore, in his mind, the nation. On 24 May he drafted a speech proclaiming a national emergency. Americans had just fought a war to defend the Constitution, Truman wrote, and while American soldiers were sacrificing themselves on the battlefields, some union leaders at home were sabotaging the effort: "John Lewis called two strikes in War Time to satisfy his ego. Two strikes which were worse than bullets in the back to our soldiers. He held a gun at the head of the Government. The Rail Unions did exactly the same thing." As he ended his draft speech, his anger was out of control. He called on veterans to join him in hanging a few "traitors" and eliminating the "Russian" senators and congressmen.

Fortunately, the president's aides rewrote and modified the speech, although it remained tough and inflammatory when he delivered it on 24 May on radio. On the next day, he addressed a joint session of Congress and repeated that the railroad shutdown was a strike against the government and could not be tolerated. He called for quick action to provide for temporary emergency legislation that would allow him to draft into the army workers who continued striking in industries taken over by the government. As he reached this point in his address, he received word that the rail strike had been settled, but he finished his speech nevertheless and called for quick action. Although the House immediately passed by 306 votes to 13 legislation to carry out Truman's plan to draft workers, Republican leader Robert A. Taft courageously blocked action in the Senate, pointing out that it violated American conceptions of jurisprudence.

The administration's stabilization machinery was disintegrating under the pressures of labor-management conflicts, as well as crises in agriculture and housing. Bowles resigned when in late June Congress extended the stabilization program in greatly weakened form. Truman vetoed it on 29 June. When prices shot up and Congress passed another price control bill, still relatively weak, Truman signed it on 25 July 1946.[7]

Strikes overshadowed agricultural policy in 1945 and early 1946, but by the latter half of 1946, farm problems often dominated newspaper headlines. Bowles and other stabilization administrators found Secretary of Agriculture Clinton P. Anderson to be an opponent as intransigent and as protective of farmers as Snyder was of businessmen but much more subtle and politically skillful. Bowles fought to maintain food rationing and farm price controls in order to restrain inflation and to free American food supplies to send overseas to war-devastated regions. Anderson and many other administration officials who believed that impending food surpluses threatened farmers wanted controls lifted rapidly.

After Truman allowed the rationing machinery to be dismantled, Americans began consuming vast quantities of meat, which diverted grain to animal production rather than to foreign needs. Not until January 1946 did the administration recognize that millions of Europeans and Asians were on slow-starvation diets. The administration bounced back and forth among policies, which resulted first in a great rise in food prices and then in a farm "strike" in early fall 1946 when the administration tried to reimpose controls on meat. A meat shortage hit as farmers withheld their animals from the market or diverted them to black market packers. With the election coming up in November, Democratic party workers reported voters saying: "No meat—no votes." Finally, as so often before in 1946, Truman, under pressure, switched ground and on 14 October 1946 announced that he was lifting the meat controls. By this time, stabilization machinery was in shambles, and both farmers and consumers were angry at Truman's weak and indecisive leadership.[8]

If the meat shortages deprived prosperous Americans of a luxury item, a housing shortage produced real hardships and further damaged Truman's popularity. A housing shortage had been in the making for years, with construction lagging first because of the depression and then because of lack of building materials during World War II. The war ended, leaving people with hundreds of millions in savings that they could use to fulfill a new American dream of owning a home. By the end of 1946, Americans needed 3.5 million more units, especially of middle- and low-priced housing. Three million married couples shared dwellings with other families, a condition increasingly unacceptable to twentieth-century Americans. Newspapers carried stories of veterans living in automobiles, under bridges, and in parks.

The unavoidable shortage worsened when Snyder and others convinced Truman, over Bowles's advice, to lift controls on construction materials. On 15 October 1945, Truman complied, and as Bowles predicted, prices shot upward, with some builders doubling their charges. In early December, Truman admitted to his cabinet that he had made a mistake in lifting controls. He reimposed them and announced an emergency housing program headed by former Louisville, Kentucky, Mayor Wilson W. Wyatt.

In the meantime, on 6 September 1945, Truman had made housing part of his domestic reform program. Senators Robert F. Wagner (D.–New York), Allen J. Ellender (D.–Louisiana), and Robert Taft added Truman's proposals to their own bill, already before Congress, to provide for public housing, slum redevelopment, and various loan and subsidy programs designed to produce decent housing for all Americans. The passage of a housing bill in 1949 gave Truman his greatest domestic reform success.

But it was Wyatt who had to deal with the immediate crisis. He set out to develop a crash program to meet emergency needs and a reform package to provide modest units for low-income people, but ran into resistance from the housing industry, which termed his program social-istic, and from administration officials, often such close Truman friends as John Snyder, who placed bureaucratic roadblocks in his path. In ad-dition, the program depended on the continued existence of the wartime control mechanism, which the administration began to dismantle. Wyatt's position became increasingly untenable, and in early December 1946, feeling he lacked Truman's support, he resigned, casting further doubts on Truman's leadership ability. With Wyatt gone and Congress bottling up the Wagner-Ellender-Taft bill, the nation had to cope with inadequate housing for years in the future.[9]

If Truman's programs were not sabotaged by his own subordinates, they often met resistance from a balky Congress. After the extraordinary Roosevelt years, many legislators felt that Congress had given up too much of its power to the executive branch, and many Southern Demo-crats felt the New Deal had unleashed forces that endangered their val-ues. As president, Truman set out to establish good relations with Congress and to heal splits within his own party. The day after Roosevelt died, Truman went to Capitol Hill and had lunch with a number of his old colleagues. The powerful Republican Senator Arthur H. Vandenberg (Michigan), who would be a key to many of Truman's most important victories in foreign affairs, noted in his diary: "It shattered all tradition. But it was both wise and smart. It means that the days of executive contempt for Congress are ended; that we are returning to a government in which Congress will take its rightful place." Southern Democrats and Republicans rallied behind their former colleague, as a gesture of unity in a difficult time and because they believed that he was at least a polit-ical moderate, if not a conservative.

This extraordinary honeymoon could not last, even if Truman had been what they believed. Congressmen, as individuals and as party mem-bers, had their own needs and priorities. They would make an extra effort to help the president through a difficult transition but eventually had to look to their own interests. Perhaps, too, Truman had changed. If as a legislator he had seen his success depending on his ability to mediate among different factions, as chief executive, his study of presidential bio-graphies and of great men in history taught him that success in such positions depended on strong leadership, not mediation. Perhaps one reason Truman was often so indecisive was that he was torn between his inner penchant for compromise and maintaining relationships and his intellectual conviction that he should lead. He also enjoyed praise from his masculine associates for his strong, decisive leadership.[10]

The already-strained honeymoon period ended on 6 September 1945 when Truman laid out in his Twenty-one Point Address the basic elements of his domestic reform program, later termed the Fair Deal. Samuel Rosenman had begun working on the speech on the way back from Potsdam in early August. Rosenman, a liberal, enthusiastically threw himself into the work as he realized that Truman intended to push for revival and extension of the New Deal. Rosenman fought hard in the next month to keep Truman's original conception. He drew on support from Charles Ross and others but faced opposition from several Truman friends, especially John Snyder, who blinked back tears in the final meeting when Truman approved the speech. Looking back years later, Rosenman believed fighting to retain the reform emphasis in the document may have been his greatest service to the country, and Snyder, as a very old man, still expressed satisfaction that he won the final battle, when Congress blocked Truman's program.

Truman called for raising unemployment compensation payments and extending coverage to new workers, raising the minimum wage level, making permanent the Fair Employment Practices Commission to protect the rights of blacks and other minorities, passing an employment act to enable government to use fiscal and monetary policy to create full employment, continuing farm price supports, providing for new programs of public housing and slum clearance, establishing a federal scientific research agency, expanding veterans' benefits, and building new public power and public works programs, including regional valley authorities based on the model of the Tennessee Valley Authority. He also listed a number of other needed congressional actions, including a tax cut. In special messages in the next few weeks, he added additional points: on 3 October, he asked for creation of a federal atomic energy commission; on 9 November, he asked Congress to pass a comprehensive national health program, including a compulsory national health insurance program; on 19 December, he asked for unification of the armed forces. With the addition of his civil rights program in 1947, this slate of proposals encompassed the major part of Truman's program of domestic reform, the Fair Deal.

The 6 September message symbolized for Truman his real assumption of the presidency. He later remarked that it was his way of letting "the Hearsts and McCormicks [conservative newspaper publishers] know that they were not going to take me into camp." He also claimed, with a good deal of exaggeration, that enunciation of the program opened him to a campaign of vilification unequaled in the history of the United

States, even of the world. Most of the major programs would not be passed during his presidency, although some would find full or partial acceptance later. Truman's reform slate drew a defense perimeter around the New Deal. If the line was not much advanced during the next seven years, neither was it badly breached. Thus his main contribution to domestic reform was to protect and consolidate the New Deal gains.[11]

"I'll sure be glad when this terrible Congress goes home," Truman wrote his mother and sister, as a conservative coalition of Southern Democrats and Midwestern Republicans blocked his proposals. Roosevelt had possessed a superior capacity to formulate and implement political strategy and an unsurpassed ability to dramatize issues and educate the public; Truman had none of these qualities, nor did he have many outstanding subordinates operating in domestic affairs. He had placed a dramatic program before congress but then acted as if his responsibility was over. An unwavering party man himself, he may have believed that he could count on that quality from others. When Truman was told in 1946 that three executive reorganization plans he had submitted to Congress were in trouble "he said he'd be damned if he could help it, they were good plans and it was up to Congress."

Truman gained a partial victory on 20 February 1946 when he signed the Employment Act of 1946. Conservatives, however, had modified the original proposal to remove the Keynesian thrust of making the government responsible for maintaining full employment conditions. It created the Council of Economic Advisers but eliminated any hint of government planning. In 1946 Congress also established the Atomic Energy Commission. Meanwhile, Truman's housing and health proposals, his two major attempts to expand the New Deal, were bogged down by conservative opposition and ineffective presidential leadership.[12]

If conservatives quickly realized that many of Truman's social views were unacceptable to them, liberal Democrats had a more difficult time gauging his political position. They themselves were groping for a new direction, disoriented by Roosevelt's death, by questions over future relations with the Soviet Union, and by the politics of inflation. After the first few weeks of Truman's presidency, some disenchanted liberals saw the exit of many New Dealers as a sign of a "Truman counterrevolution." They applauded Truman's Twenty-one Point message and subsequent reform proposals, only to conclude that his waffling leadership canceled his liberal stands. Indeed some believed Truman deliberately took strong reformist stands to please liberals, followed by inaction to hold conservatives in line. He ended by pleasing no one.

Truman was not an ideologically committed liberal. Although he had gone down the line for the New Deal in the Senate, many liberals suspected that he would have comfortably followed a much more conservative leader than Roosevelt. On 24 April 1945 he told an ardent New Dealer, Senator Claude Pepper of Florida, that he had supported Roosevelt "but now I am responsible for the unity and harmony of the country and I suspect most of the time you will find me about in the middle of the road." He was repelled by urban liberalism expressed in the vocabulary of New Deal "professional" liberals, like Francis Biddle and Chester Bowles, but he could accept the same ideas if they were expressed in an idiom that suited his background. He reacted strongly against eastern intellectuals with Ivy League backgrounds; they were "crackpot" liberals, of the kind he associated in his mind with the Americans for Democratic Action.

He was not interested in ideas and theories for their own sake, as were liberal intellectuals. Nor was he interested in abstract discussions of current events or even of history; he was comfortable only with concrete "facts." He did not understand modern art, music, theater, or architecture, which he associated with the "crackpot" variety of liberals; what he did not understand, he had contempt for and assumed that anyone who did express appreciation for Picasso or Frank Lloyd Wright was "nutty" or a "faker." After going to the Mellon Gallery to view works by Rembrandt and other traditional masters, he noted in his diary: "It is a pleasure to look at perfection and then think of the lazy, nutty moderns. It is like comparing Christ with Lenin. May there be another awakening. We need an Isaiah, John the Baptist, Martin Luther—may he come soon." John Snyder and Fred Vinson would not jar his sensibilities with what seemed to Truman to be bizarre tastes or ideas because their makeup was similar to his; nor would Clifford, Harriman, and Acheson, because, whatever their tastes, they were psychologically astute enough to understand and use the idiom acceptable to Truman.[13]

Later, when the anti-Communist crusade of Truman, Senator Joseph R. McCarthy, and others bludgeoned the political spectrum rightward, many liberals, who were at the same time purging their organizations of Communist contamination, saw more similarities between themselves and Truman. As they signed up for the cold war and settled for less in terms of social reform, they moved closer to the Fair Deal.

It was easier for Truman's liberal critics to crystallize differences with him in terms of personalities than in policies. By early 1946 only two of

Roosevelt's liberals remained in Truman's cabinet: Secretary of Interior Harold Ickes and Secretary of Commerce Henry Wallace. Both soon left amid circumstances that increased liberal discouragement with Truman.

Ickes resigned in a blow-up over Truman's unsuccessful attempt to make oil company executive Edwin W. Pauley, an important figure in the Democratic party, under secretary of navy. When Ickes told Truman that he was being called before Congress to testify on the appointment, Truman replied: "Tell the truth but be as kind as possible to Mr. Pauley." Ickes had the ability easily to work himself into a lather and now did so, publicly accusing Pauley of having offered the Democratic party campaign money if the government backed off its claims to federal ownership of tidelands oil land. During a press conference on 7 February, Truman was gentle with Ickes but backed Pauley. Ickes then resigned, implying that Truman had asked him to perjure himself and characterized the administration as "government by crony." The incident confirmed many people's worst fears about what was happening in Washington under Truman.[14]

After Ickes resigned, Truman asked Wallace not to leave the cabinet and told him that if any problems arose, he should talk them over with the president. Although Truman needed this last direct connection with Roosevelt, especially since Wallace had a huge and devoted following within the Democratic party, a split between the two men was probably inevitable. Wallace had long made party regulars like Truman uneasy, and by 1946 he was especially out of step with the administration's foreign policy.

Wallace believed that U.S. security depended not on building a powerful military bloc but on approaching the Soviet Union in a spirit of friendship and cooperation. He thought that belligerent Soviet behavior stemmed not from a plan for world domination but from a defensive posture resulting from the insecurity of being surrounded since 1917 by hostile Western powers. Wallace also held that past hostility between the Soviet Union and the West meant that the reality of traditional spheres of interest had to be recognized.

On 23 July 1946, he sent Truman a long letter urging reconsideration of U.S. policy. He wrote that such U.S. actions as having a defense budget of thirteen billion dollars, ten times more than in the 1930s, continuing to test atomic bombs in a world terrified of them, moving to rearm Latin American, and building strategic bombers gave the impression that Washington was paying lip-service to peace. He urged that Truman try to understand Moscow's conception of its security needs, abandon the present flawed American plan for atomic energy control, and avoid the temptation of whipping up fear of the Soviets to create unity at home.

Truman dismissed Wallace's letter as an attempt to "make a record" before he resigned, but his resignation came because of Truman's own blunders. Speaking at a huge Madison Square Garden rally on 12 September 1946, Wallace warned of the danger of another war and described how strategic bombers, atomic bombs, and guided missiles had changed the nature of war and made even the United States vulnerable to attack. After talking about relations among the great powers, Wallace then said: "In this connection, I want one thing clearly understood. I am neither anti-British nor pro-British—neither anti-Russian nor pro-Russian. And just two days ago, when President Truman read these words, he said that they represented the policy of his administration."

Wallace had indeed taken his speech draft to Truman. In his diary, Wallace wrote that Truman went over the speech page by page, frequently remarking: "That's right," "Yes, that is what I believe." Truman suggested no changes and twice thanked Wallace for his courtesy in letting him read it. Truman did not indicate that he saw any inconsistency between Wallace's speech and U.S. policy, though Secretary of State Byrnes had just delivered a hard-line speech at Stuttgart, Germany, and was then engaged in tough bargaining with the Soviets at the Paris Conference of Foreign Ministers. When Wallace returned from the White House to the Commerce Department, he told Bernard L. Gladieux, a department official, that Truman approved the speech after reading it word for word during an hour-long meeting—but that he was not sure that the president fully understood what he read.

It may be that Truman did not understand what he was reading; perhaps he just responded as he often did when confronted by a powerful personality: by indicating agreement for the sake of harmony, which had long been his pattern of behavior with Wallace. In his memoirs, Truman said Wallace came in for fifteen minutes, spoke about a number of matters, and then, just before he left, mentioned the scheduled speech: "There was, of course, no time for me to read the speech, even in part."

But in a private account written a few days after the event, Truman verified Wallace's version. He wrote that when Wallace came in, they first discussed another matter, and then Wallace pulled his speech out of his pocket and asked Truman to read it. Truman wrote: "I saw then that I was up against something." One sentence said that Wallace held no special brief for either Britain or the Soviet Union but wanted to be friends with both: "I remarked that this is the policy we are pursueing [*sic*] and he remarked he would say that was the administration's policy. There were one or two things in the paper which I thought were a little wild but didn't interpret them as contrary to the general policy." Truman said it took him thirty minutes to read the speech. He also said their relations had been friendly and that he was sure that Wallace did not intend to put anything "over on me."

Truman's first blunder was not recognizing that Wallace's speech conflicted with the administration's foreign policy. His second came at his press conference on 12 September, the day of Wallace's speech. Truman often made mistakes, some serious, in such settings because of his propensity to answer too quickly. As Dean Acheson said: "President Truman's mind is not so quick as his tongue." Reporters had a copy of Wallace's speech, including the sentence that said Truman had read these words and had said they represented the policy of the administration. A reporter read the sentence to Truman and asked if it applied to just that paragraph or to the whole speech. Truman answered: "I approved the whole speech." Later a reporter asked if Truman regarded Wallace's speech as a departure from Byrne's policy toward the Soviet Union. Truman said he did not: "They are exactly in line." These questions should have warned the president of danger ahead but did not.

Truman seemed to be about the only one who did not understand Wallace's speech. Not only did reporters recognize its implications, but that evening after Secretary of the Navy John L. Sullivan and Acting Secretary of State William L. Clayton read an advance copy of it, they telephoned press secretary Charles Ross and told him it would do a great harm to Byrnes in Paris and that the president would probably have to repudiate either Byrnes or Wallace. Ross called Truman, who did not seem alarmed, and the president did not amend his endorsement of the entire speech.

The next morning, 13 September, when the publicity explosion began, Truman finally understood what was at stake and at his staff meeting berated himself for making a "grave 'blunder.'" He and his advisers agreed to sit tight. With the storm still raging next day, they decided they had to put out a statement that Truman had approved Wallace's right to give the speech, not its contents.

Wallace graciously did not tell reporters what really had gone on at that 12 September session. Truman appreciated Wallace's loyalty and in a telephone communication on 16 September told him he did not want to hurt either him or Byrnes and thought the matter could be settled without doing so. He asked Wallace to come in to talk to him. Meanwhile, Truman seemed privately to be facing up to his responsibility for what happened. In a letter to Bess Truman on 16 September, he referred to his latest "fiasco" and said: "It was nice to talk with you even if you did give me hell for making mistakes. Looks like I'm a natural for making them."

That night Truman did not sleep much. The crisis continued; the fall elections were near. In a private note, he began to restructure his recollections. In his note on the previous day, he had written that he had taken thirty minutes to read the speech; he now said that Wallace gave him three minutes to skim it. He began to view the entire event as a trap set for him by Wallace. When Wallace and Truman met on 18 September, Truman explained that Byrnes was threatening to resign. In a long, frank conversation, both men explained their views and agreed that Wallace would not speak on foreign policy issues until the Paris conference ended.

Truman still took some responsibility for his blunder. On 18 September, he wrote his mother and sister: "Never was there such a mess and it is partly my making. But when I make a mistake it is a good one." The next day, however, the restructuring continued, and in a private note about Wallace he wrote: "I'm not so sure he's as fundamentally sound intellectually as I had thought." At their 18 September meeting, Wallace shocked Truman by suggesting that he follow Roosevelt's technique of moving leftward after elections and to the right before. That a professional politician was shocked by such tactics is itself surprising, but Truman went on to say that he was afraid that Wallace "has absorbed some of the 'Commy-Jesuit' theory that the end justifies the means." He wrote: "Henry is a pacifist 100%. He wants us to disband our armed forces, give Russia our atomic secrets and trust a bunch of adventurers in the Kremlin Politburo who have no morals, personal or public. I don't understand a 'dreamer' like that."

On 19 September, Byrnes increased his pressure on Truman, finally forcing the president to choose between him and Wallace. Firing Wallace would raise an outcry among liberal Democrats, but Byrnes's resignation would bring disorder to the international community and endanger bipartisan foreign policy at home. Truman asked for and received Wallace's resignation even as he continued restructuring the episode. He wrote Bess on 20 September: "I believe he's a real Commy and a dangerous man." He put the best face on the incident he could: "So now I'm sure I've run the Crack Pots out of the Democratic Party and I feel better over it."[15]

The Wallace affair gave added force to the potent Republican campaign slogan that fall: "Had enough?" The Gallup polls showed that Truman's popularity rating had plunged from 87 to 32 percent. Political disaster for his party followed. In November, the Democrats lost control of Congress for the first time since the Great Depression had reshaped the nation's political orientation. In the new House, there were 246 Republicans and 188 Democrats; in the Senate, 51 Republicans to 45 Democrats. Although farmers were prosperous in comparison with the past, not one Democrat survived in a midwestern rural congressional district. Labor felt betrayed by Truman because of his proposal to draft strikers, and many other voters, angered by the strikes, left the Democrats because they identified that party with labor. Among Democrats, conservatives survived while many of the liberal members lost. Of the 8 most liberal Democrats up for election in the Senate, only 1 survived; of the 69 most liberal Democratic representatives, 37 were defeated; half the 116 sponsors of the Employment Act of 1946 did not return; of the 100 strongest administration supporters, 47 lost.[16]

Truman, who seldom lost his optimism, at first thought the Democrats would win and, after that proved wrong, decided the Republican victory might be a blessing since that party would have to take responsibility for the welfare of the country. Optimist though he was, even he did not see that it was the Republican Eightieth Congress that would give him foreign policy legislation upon which he could lay claim to presidential greatness.

5

THE RUSSIANS ARE COMING

The cold war marked a new phase of a conflict between the Western powers and the Soviet Union that had begun in 1917 when the Bolsheviks came to power. After the aberrational alliance between the Americans and Soviets during World War II, the United States found itself facing a nation much less powerful than itself but one too stable to be transformed by American pressure and too strong to destroy. The Soviet Union could only be contained within the defensive bloc that it constructed as American power expanded outward.

The cold war took on a particular cast because it took place as the traditional European state system collapsed. Economic crises, the disintegration of colonial empires, and two world wars had left a bipolar world with the United States and the Soviet Union, both on the periphery of the prewar European state system, responsible for building a new international structure. The war destroyed old loyalties and traditions, fed nationalistic aspirations for liberation among colonial people, and reduced much of the world's population to even greater poverty than it had known before. The United States and the Soviet Union tried either to suppress revolutionary ferment or to direct it to their ends. In addition, Washington undertook the task of containing the Soviet Union in the hopes that it would moderate its commitment to a world Communist revolution and become more acceptable to the Americans. But the

United States itself changed, undercutting its own democratic heritage and destroying its historical role as a symbol of revolution and hope for the powerless.

In this struggle between the two great powers, the United States was by far the stronger, both militarily and economically. Its leaders sensed this power and felt called by destiny to use it to remake the world in the American image. As Dean Acheson looked back at the chaos of the immediate postwar era, biblical images came to his mind, and he entitled his memoirs *Present at the Creation*. Less grandly, journalist Walter Lippmann said Truman's task in late 1945 was to "hold up the British Empire, hold back the Russian Empire, and create a new China." Before he left office, Truman would add to the list such other tasks as rebuilding Western Germany and Japan and holding back what he viewed as the Communist hordes in Korea and Vietnam.[1]

There was much misunderstanding between the two great powers, with their different histories, economic and political systems, and ideologies. The cold war did not, however, result simply from misunderstanding or from accidents. Some degree of conflict was inevitable in a world divided between these two nations, but accord might well have been possible if the United States had been more restrained in its use of power. It is true that Truman wanted peace, but such truths do not explain much. He did not want peace badly enough to take the moderate risks and make the sacrifices necessary to achieve it. Rather, he wanted peace on his own terms; the United States could get 85 percent of what it wanted, Truman told his advisers before he met Soviet Foreign Minister Molotov in April 1945.

Most historians now agree that Soviet aims were relatively modest in 1945. Stalin made what seemed to him to be important concessions to maintain the alliance, and he carried out his agreements with Washington. Stalin, however, was in negotiation with a people who for 300 of their 350 years of habitation in North America had enslaved, pillaged, and slaughtered their way across the continent and for the past 50 years had been constructing a Caribbean and Pacific empire based on control of subject nations' economies and on suppression of resistance groups. If the Soviets were expansionistic and aggressive, they now confronted one of the most expansionistic and aggressive nations the world had ever seen and one whose appetite for empire grew in lockstep with the growth of its military and economic power.

Truman offered the Soviets little short of surrender. If he had gotten the 85 percent he expected, the other 15 percent would surely have followed from a Moscow reduced to dependency on Washington. The Soviet Union articulated an expansive Marxist-Leninist ideology that some American leaders read as a blueprint for world conquest. The Soviets, in fact, had acted in a restrained fashion, moved by traditional concerns for state security. The United States, on the other hand, without a clearly articulated blueprint, had acted in an expansive manner and came to define its security in global terms. Truman and his inner circle acted on assumptions buried so deeply in American thinking that they could not see that they were guided by an ideology and, at that, one accepted by only a small part of the world. To Truman and most of his fellow citizens, the validity of American beliefs was self-evident and required no critical evaluation. Americans bound their conception of freedom, liberty, democracy, and capitalism into one interrelated, inseparable package. They believed their version of these ideas and practices were the only valid ones and were right for all people in all places.

Truman inherited those conceptions through his commitment to Wilsonianism. Woodrow Wilson had presented a vision of a world characterized by self-determination, representative government, an open-door world economy, and international cooperation through a league of nations. Such principles, he believed, would bring peace and prosperity and would benefit all people, not just Americans. There would be no room within this benevolent world order for revolution, spheres of influence, or state-controlled economies. In his view, a stable world order required a worldwide open door or multilateral trading system, with all nations having equal access to the markets and raw materials. Truman believed that American prosperity—and the economic health of the rest of the world—depended on this open-door system. American leaders also believed that economic nationalism, resulting in a closing of doors, had created the turmoil and conflict that had led to the two world wars. Peace and prosperity rested on a foundation of free world trade, which Americans assumed required a capitalistic private property system. In his first speech to the nation as president, on 16 April 1945, Truman affirmed that the United States had achieved world leadership from moral authority, not just military power. Maintaining that leadership required Americans to revive and expand world trade. On 27 October 1945, he laid out a foreign policy based on the open door.[2]

The Soviet Union challenged the American vision. It had abolished private property, established a state-controlled economy, created instability, Americans believed, by exporting revolution, and, now in the postwar world, clearly intended to establish a closed sphere of influence in East Europe. Anti-Soviet feeling received coherent and persuasive expression in what historian Daniel H. Yergin called the Riga axioms formulated by State Department Soviet experts. These experts, based in Riga, Latvia, before Washington recognized the Moscow government in 1933, said the Soviet Union was an aggressive, expansionistic, ideologically driven state bent on world revolution and domination.

Roosevelt had not accepted the Riga interpretation of Soviet behavior and aims. He had proceeded, Yergin argued, on the Yalta axioms, envisioning the Soviet Union as a traditional great power that could be brought into the world community and bargained with in customary ways. Cooperation and world peace could be attained through negotiation, compromise, and recognition of spheres of interest. After Roosevelt died, there was no equally powerful figure left to promote his conception, and Truman found himself surrounded by those thinking in terms of the Riga axioms, toward which he also inclined.

Truman and his military and diplomatic advisers found in the Riga axioms a plan of action to counter the Soviet challenge to the American vision of a liberal, capitalistic world. They soon made an analogy between their plight and the lessons the democratic nations had learned in dealing with Hitler. Truman believed that American isolationism and failure to join with other nations in standing against Germany's aggression had led to World War II. Thus appeasement led to war; peace required democracies to maintain their national power and to be willing to use force against totalitarian aggressors.

Washington found much in 1945 and 1946 to validate these views. When the United States stood firm, as in 1946 when the Soviet Union delayed in removing its troops from Iran, and Moscow backed down, Truman interpreted the result as a sign that the lessons of history were valid rather than that the Hitler analogy was wrong and that Stalin was willing to work out an accommodation with the West. Truman also ignored the Soviet decision to allow Finland, Hungary, and Czechoslovakia a good deal of control over their internal affairs in the early postwar years, focusing instead on the harsher Kremlin treatment of Poland. The analogy, then, was validated by selective evaluation of evidence. It received further validation in 1947 and after when the Soviets cracked down on Hungary and Czechoslovakia. Washington regarded those actions as the fulfillment of Moscow's secret intentions rather than as a defensive reaction to the Truman Doctrine and other American actions that seemed provocative to the Soviets.[3]

What the American people believed about the breakdown of the alliance is open to debate. The average American's negative attitude toward the Soviet Union probably stemmed not so much from concern for the open door or the threat to private property as from its being seen as a "godless" state, where immorality was sanctioned and the family slated to be abolished. Public opinion had favored the Soviets during the war, probably because the people believed that they were becoming more like Americans.

In fact, it made little difference what the American people thought. Although Washington and Moscow always took their various cold war actions in the name of the people, average citizens played little role in formulating policy. Washington officials regarded the public as an object to be manipulated and stampeded into support for their positions. The people, conditioned by a society that consulted them little in shaping policy that affected their lives in basic ways, supported policy formulated by the administration. Under Truman, the executive branch increasingly monopolized information and worked in secrecy, giving incomplete and selective information to Americans. Although Truman eventually lost public support, especially on Asian policy, the tendency of the people was to back him on foreign policy issues. Speaker of the House Sam Rayburn expressed the view that Americans would hear repeatedly in postwar America: "America has either one voice or none, and that voice is the voice of the President—whether everybody agrees with him or not."[4]

Postwar ideology, although rooted in American history, was transformed by the development of the national security state. Postwar leaders no longer described military needs in terms of defense, a concept with built-in restraints and limitations. They talked instead of security needs, an open-ended construction. Since U.S. peace and prosperity required stability and free world trade, its interests could be threatened by the actions of nations thousands of miles from its borders, even by internal upheavals in those countries. Rather than continuing the traditional practice of making decisions based on an evaluation of an opposing power's intentions, Washington began to determine military needs based on a potential enemy's capabilities. This change substituted quantitative analysis for qualitative judgment and moved the construction of foreign policy from a flexible, restrained procedure to an inflexible, open-ended response, almost certain to lead to a spiraling arms race if an opposing power responded similarly.

During the first few years after World War II, Washington reorganized and unified its military organization, created new institutions such as the Central Intelligence Agency (1947) and National Security Council (1947), geared the economy to cold war demands, began to bend several branches of science and some educational programs to serve national security needs, and established a loyalty program to root out internal threats. Truman worked assiduously to forge bipartisanship in foreign policy, weakening traditional restraints on the executive branch and eroding older conceptions of democracy. Under his leadership, the United States prepared for a permanent state of quasi-war.

Development of these new national security conceptions and institutions had peculiar consequences. The more successful that U.S. policy was, the more its security seemed threatened. In July 1948, Secretary of State George Marshall explained to Truman and Secretary of Defense Forrestal that since Washington had successfully repulsed Soviet threats in Greece, Italy, and France, the Kremlin had responded by blockading Berlin. Marshall assured them: "Russian activity was the manifestation of the success of our policy." Thus if the United States was weak, the Soviets aggressed, and if Washington stood firm, they still aggressed. National security became a "Commanding Idea," wrote Daniel Yergin, "that explains how America relates to the rest of the world, that integrates contradictory information, that suggests and rationalizes courses of action, and that, as a court of last resort for both policymakers and public, almost magically puts an end to disputes and debates."[5]

Truman did not create a think tank to translate American ideology and security thinking into a blueprint for implementation. American policy evolved through Truman's and his advisers' reactions to specific events at specific times. Yet their conception that American liberal ideas and institutions were suitable for all people at all times guided their responses. Few Americans could conceive of the possibility that the masses of East European people might benefit from Soviet presence or that Latin American peasants might be harmed by the export of American capitalism into their lands. While they had no doubt that Soviet expansion brought terror and oppression, most Americans dismissed as cranks or subversives those who similarly characterized the American empire.

Some of Truman's advisers were cautious. George Marshall, Dwight Eisenhower, and other military leaders urged him to avoid taking positions that would break the alliance. As military men, they understood Soviet security concerns and realized that the Kremlin had scrupulously kept its military agreements with the Americans. Stimson stressed the need for Washington to understand Moscow's definition of its national security needs. Harry Hopkins, who had met often with Stalin during the war, maintained that accord between the two great powers was possible. Joseph Davies, former ambassador to the Soviet Union, tried to explain to Truman how the Soviets viewed the world, how delay in opening the second front had looked to Moscow, and how Stalin saw himself as having made important concessions in allowing his Western allies to dominate policy on Italy and Greece, expecting reciprocity on Poland. Davies told Truman that it did not make any difference if the Soviet fear of the West was unfounded because in fact they were afraid and would establish a barrier of friendly governments in East Europe, whatever the cost to the alliance. Henry Wallace argued along similar lines and said that the Soviets would match toughness with toughness.[6]

Truman's presidency made a difference in the history of the postwar world. He had a deep sense of his own and American rectitude and found it incomprehensible that decent, "right thinking" people with all the "facts" did not recognize the validity of the American vision of a proper world order. The very simplicity of his outlook, matching the mass mind, allowed him to express a vision so powerful that it provided the foundation of the foreign policy that has dominated American diplomacy since his administration.

Truman was more of a confrontationist than Roosevelt, less imaginative than his predecessor, and more reliant on the State Department hard-liners for advice. Although his views were more flexible than his blunt style indicated, his confrontational manner created an environment that invited hard-liners to come forward more openly and effectively. At Carutherville, Missouri, on 7 October 1945, Truman proclaimed that God had given Americans the destiny of showing the rest of the world the road to liberty and peace. As the cold war deepened, he described the Soviets, in simple, factual-sounding speaking style, as brutal, savage aggressors. He helped remove doubts and ambiguities from American thinking about the Soviet Union.

Truman believed that an American-imposed order would benefit the whole world. He saw American goals as selfless; Washington wanted no territory or reparations, only prosperity and peace. Although Truman had often made Wall Street a target of attacks in his Senate years, he shared business values that taught him that capitalism was the only possible underpinning for world order. In a major address at Baylor University on 6 March 1947, he expressed the open-door conception that the United States had to revive world trade based on free enterprise as the foundation of peace and freedom. He firmly held that American global economic goals would not be imperialistic, since everyone would benefit from intertwining free economies. He could not see that other peoples would have to remake themselves in the American image for his system to work as he envisioned.[7]

Few, if any, other presidents are regarded as Truman's equal in making decisions quickly and easily. These rapid decisions, however, sometimes led to cognitive shortcuts, causing him to use inappropriate generalizations and analogies, make erroneous causal assumptions, and engage in "premature cognitive closure," argues Deborah W. Larson. Sometimes he thought in cartoon-like schema, which, for example, gave him a script to understand a situation in Poland or Korea based on his mental images of what had happened in the 1930s with Germany. Any complexity of thought vanished when a current crisis fit his script. Hitler aggressed in the 1930s, the Western democracies did not act, war followed; Stalin was following Hitler's path, and the Western democracies had to stand firm to avoid a new war. His most important reactions to foreign leaders and events, with profound consequences for the future, were often based on the simplistic script he carried in his mind. It was inconceivable to him that the Soviets might have their own equally plausible interpretation of treaties or that from their point of view the Americans had broken the Yalta and other agreements. When Moscow failed to give in to American power, Truman repeated his scripted slogans that the Soviets only understood force and they never kept their word. Americans, on the other hand, were trustworthy and had no ulterior motives. The only thing Americans want, he assured his daughter, Margaret, was "Peace in the World. We may have to fight for it."[8]

In contrast to Truman, Roosevelt had been much more optimistic about the possibility of cooperation with the Soviets and had carefully worked to break down Moscow's suspicion of the West. To protect the still-fragile commitment of the public to internationalism, Roosevelt emphasized the importance of the United Nations, but in dealing with Allied leaders, he acted on the assumption that peace depended not on the U.N. but on a settlement among the great powers. Roosevelt's work with Stalin had had an effect. The Soviet premier came to Yalta in February 1945 in a strong position but conceded more than the Americans and British. He followed the Western Allies' lead on Germany, agreed to participate in the United Nations, although it would clearly be an American-dominated body, accepted delay in spelling out in detail German reparations to the Soviets, reaffirmed Moscow's intention to enter the Japanese war three months after Germany surrendered, and agreed to support Chiang Kai-shek's government against the Chinese Communists. Compared to the role that Americans would assume in the Far East, what Stalin asked in return was relatively modest: regaining the lower Sakhalin and Kuril islands, access to certain Manchurian railroads, and other concessions from China.

In Eastern European matters, Roosevelt and Churchill conceded to Stalin a sphere of influence in that region. All three leaders assumed Eastern Europe would be free within the limits of Soviet security needs for friendly governments in that region. Roosevelt left Yalta pleased, believing that Stalin's deportment and his concessions indicated that the Soviets could be dealt with as a great power with normal security demands rather than as a nation ideologically bent on world revolution and conquest. Perhaps building support for such a view would have been Roosevelt's next task, but he died a few weeks after returning from Yalta.

Stalin intended to live up to the Yalta agreements as he understood them. He was shrewd and ruthless, as anyone else would have to be to build the Soviet Union into a modern nation in a world dominated by capitalist powers. His tasks were immense. He ruled a country that had lost over twenty million people—10 percent of its population—during the war and had twenty-five million homeless citizens and devastated industry and agriculture. His nation lacked a modern air force and navy and did not possess atomic weapons. Stalin moved carefully, conceding to his Western allies unhampered control of their traditional spheres while demanding that the Soviet Union be included in the councils of the great powers and that it be allowed to build a "security belt" in areas vital to itself. Stalin focused on reconstruction of his own country, with, he hoped, a loan from the Americans and reparations from Germany. He acted as a restraining influence on the Communist parties of Western Europe, did not interfere with British suppression of Communists in Greece, and did little to help Mao Tse-tung (Mao Zedong) in China. Marxist-Leninist ideology did not pilot Stalin along a path toward world domination; history urged him to be cautious.

As the war-torn nations turned to reconstruction, the Kremlin's problems seemed immense. Truman remarked: "Russia couldn't turn a wheel in the next ten years without our aid." With Hitler defeated, the balance of power shifted to the West, and Washington moved to take advantage of a relatively weaker Soviet Union. American leaders therefore became less conscious of the many instances of Soviet cooperation and began to focus on areas of conflict. As power relations shifted, Truman and his advisers believed that Roosevelt had made too many concessions to the Soviets and began to try to establish new understandings, especially by redefining the meaning of the Yalta agreement. Truman convinced himself that the Soviets were breaking their agreements and increasingly accepted the assumption that they were bent on world conquest.[9]

Washington leaders were still confused in 1945 on how best to achieve American aims. Truman wavered, generally taking a hard-line position but periodically questioning its effectiveness. After the strong stand Truman took with Molotov on 23 April followed by the blowup over the president's stopping lend-lease on 11 May, Truman sent Harry Hopkins to Moscow. Following Hopkins's mission, Washington recognized Poland, and the San Francisco Conference successfully concluded its work on the U.N. charter. At that point Stettinius became the first U.S. representative to the United Nations, and on 3 July 1945 James F. Byrnes became secretary of state.

Although Byrnes did not find an effective way to use the American atomic bomb to encourage the Soviets to become more accommodating, the weapon became a major issue in international relations after Hiroshima and Nagasaki. When Dean Acheson heard the news of the Hiroshima bombing, he concluded that if the major nations could not develop a system of international control of atomic power, the world's people would be "gone geese." Truman, however, pursued such controls at a leisurely pace, confident that it would be many years before the Soviets could produce a similar bomb and that atomic energy was but another part of the world under American control.

On 12 September 1945, Stimson discussed with Truman a letter and memorandum that he had sent the president the day before. In the memorandum he said that with atomic weapons now entered into the equation of international power, the Kremlin would likely be tempted to push ahead to get its own nuclear arsenal, setting off a desperate arms race. He believed that to prevent destruction of human civilization, nations had to establish international control of atomic energy. He warned that continuing to negotiate with "this weapon rather ostentatiously on our hip" irretrievably embittered relations: "The chief lesson I have learned in a long life is that the only way you can make a man trustworthy is to trust him; and the surest way to make him untrustworthy is to distrust him and show your distrust." He suggested a direct approach to both the Soviet Union and Great Britain to work out a system of control of the bomb, with other nations and the U.N. brought in later.[10]

Truman brought the issues Stimson raised before the cabinet at a luncheon on 18 September and then at a formal meeting on 21 September. Despite the significance of this subject, the cabinet offered little help. Several members were misled by a phrase Stimson used about sharing the bomb with the Soviets and believed that he meant giving the bomb "secret" to Moscow, when actually he wanted to initiate discussion of international control. Secretary of Agriculture Anderson argued against Stimson on the grounds that 80 percent of the American people opposed giving away the secret. He later wrote that the decision about international control, one of the most important in the cold war, was made too casually and that he had often wondered over the next twenty-five years what path history would have taken if the administration had followed Stimson's advice. He admitted that in these cabinet discussions, he spoke as a politician, worried about its effects on the Democratic party if the administration gave the bomb away. At least two other cabinet members followed his lead on the grounds that since he was from New Mexico, where Los Alamos was located, he must have some special knowledge of the subject.[11]

On 3 October Truman announced that he would enter into discussion with Great Britain and Canada, and later other nations, to work out a system of international control of atomic energy. Although he did not follow Stimson's advice to discuss the matter directly with the Soviets, he did commit the United States to discussion of international control. At a press conference on 8 October, however, Truman emphatically stated that the United States would not share know-how or engineering knowledge with allies, and on 27 October in a major speech on foreign policy, he referred to the bomb as a "sacred trust" in American hands.

With the British and Canadian prime ministers arriving in Washington in November to discuss the issue, Byrnes asked Vannevar Bush, head of the Office of Scientific Research and Development, to draw up a plan for international control. Bush's plan provided for nations to move through a series of steps designed to achieve control under U.N. supervision. These stages would take years to negotiate, Bush said, and in the meantime the United States would maintain its monopoly. Truman and the prime ministers agreed to a plan generally along the lines Bush outlined.

In January 1946, the U.N. established the Commission on Atomic Energy. To formulate a proposal to place before it, Byrnes created a committee chaired by Acheson, with an advisory body that included David

E. Lilienthal and J. Robert Oppenheimer. The Acheson-Lilienthal group proposed an international Atomic Development Authority with control over raw materials and over plants needed to produce fissionable material. Since such tight control would minimize need for inspection, they believed this plan would ease Soviet concerns. When Lilienthal brought the advisory group's report to Acheson on 6 March 1946, however, Acheson had before him George Kennan's Long Telegram, giving a frighteningly pessimistic account of Soviet-American relations; Churchill had given his iron curtain speech the day before; Moscow seemed to be threatening Iran; a Canadian atomic spy ring was recently uncovered. With the grand alliance disintegrating, Acheson tried to balance the reality of domestic politics with that of international needs. His report to Truman included a stage system that allowed Americans to maintain their monopoly until the final step.[12]

Byrnes decided that Bernard M. Baruch, famed Wall Street operator and political adviser, had the reputation for soundness needed to sell the plan to Congress and the people. Although Truman, Acheson, and many others considered Baruch's reputation to be undeserved—he was an egotistical, conniving, old goat, Truman said—the president appointed him as representative to the U.N. commission. After the appointment was announced on 18 March 1946, Baruch used the threat of resignation to force Truman to agree that he would not just be a messenger boy to the U.N. but would help set policy. Baruch then turned to business and military advisers to modify the Acheson-Lilienthal report. The Baruch plan included the stage system, required extensive inspections, and provided for punishments, not subject to veto, for violation of the agreement. Although Acheson and Lilienthal believed presenting this plan as a final proposal would guarantee Soviet rejection, Baruch told Lilienthal that the United States could get what it wanted because the Soviet Union did not have the bomb and would not have it for many years.

The Soviets put forward their own plan, requiring the United States first to give up its monopoly before working out a mechanism for inspection and other controls. Each side rejected the other's plan, and hopes for nuclear disarmament and international control of atomic energy faded. The United States, with little to fear from the Soviet Union in the near future, refused to take even minor risks to promote any real chance of international agreement. To the American public, however, the Baruch plan, approved by Truman and Byrnes, seemed reasonable.

Years later some analysts referred to "America's dirty little secret": its policy of paying lip-service to nuclear disarmament while in fact relying on its atomic weapons to offset the Soviet Union's conventional military power in Europe. There was little incentive to give up what seemed a great advantage.[13]

While atomic energy was a new source of American power, Washington had long been confident that the United States would have unchallenged economic supremacy, which it could use to achieve a multilateral or open-door world economy. In 1944 the Americans initiated the Bretton Woods agreement providing for an International Monetary Fund and for a World Bank (International Bank of Reconstruction and Development). The Bretton Woods agreement passed the Congress in mid-1945, one of Truman's first major legislative victories. The United States controlled the operations of the monetary fund and the World Bank, on which the open-door trading structure was to be based. Washington policy prepared for a quick resumption of multilateralism. It used Allied needs for lend-lease and postwar loans, as well as the new international economic institutions, to push for the elimination of closed systems.

Despite this effort, the drive to win multilateralism foundered in the first year after the war, partly because of the Soviet refusal to integrate itself into a U.S.-dominated world economy but mainly because the faltering economies of Western Europe increasingly pushed those countries toward economic nationalism. Washington did not give up its goal of an open-door empire but groped for a new path in 1946 and 1947 to achieve its ultimate vision. Finally, in 1947, Washington decided to provide massive foreign aid to revive the economies of its Western allies, while helping them stabilize their colonial empires, and to rebuild the economies of Germany and Japan. The open door would be put off until American economic partners revived.[14]

In the meantime, American economic power provided relief to victims of war. Millions had been killed in Asia and Europe and many more injured; millions of returning soldiers and displaced persons had to be reincorporated into society. With cities in rubble, factories destroyed, agriculture production neglected and wrecked, and trade patterns disrupted, many people faced starvation. At the end of June 1945, one hundred million people in Europe were on a diet of fifteen hundred calories a day, and in some regions people had below a thousand calories, a slow-starvation level. Millions in Asia faced even more desperate conditions. Through its policies, the United States helped multitudes of people survive. It had stopped lend-lease when the war ended, but in return for economic concessions, it soon granted $3.75 billion to Great Britain, with additional loans and aid to other close allies. The Soviet Union also had requested a large loan from the Americans, but Washington chose to use this need to exact major concessions. Washington delayed too long and expected too much in return; the Soviets went their own way and rebuilt without U.S. help.[15]

Washington followed a peculiar kind of internationalism after World War II. What agencies it could not dominate, it destroyed or crippled. It converted the World Bank and International Monetary Fund into instruments to carry out American cold war policy, but it abandoned the United Nations Relief and Rehabilitation Administration, which gave aid to Communist nations in Eastern Europe, and forced it to shut down most of its activities by the end of 1946. Washington leaders also viewed the U.N. as an international instrument to further American views. Truman said that the Western Hemisphere bloc, supported by the British Commonwealth, could do anything it wanted to build a workable U.N. organization. This power lineup convinced the Soviet Union that the U.N. was just another instrument through which the United States intended to dominate the world. Adlai E. Stevenson, an adviser to the U.S. delegation at San Francisco, agreed, noting that the heavy-handed American action meant that "the Russians necessarily would tend to play their own game, not trusting the world organization." When the Soviets subsequently relied on the veto to protect themselves, their actions convinced the American public that Moscow was wrecking the U.N.[16]

Meanwhile the great powers had begun the first meetings of the Council of Foreign Ministers, established at Potsdam. In October 1945, Byrnes, in London at the first meeting, optimistically believed that the mere existence of the atomic bomb would soften the Soviet position, especially regarding Eastern Europe. He came away shaken, finding that the only thing in life that seemed to strike the dour Molotov as humorous was the American atomic bomb. When Byrnes pressed the American position in Eastern Europe, Molotov asked for a trusteeship over Libya, within the traditional Western sphere; when Americans protested being frozen out of Rumania and Bulgaria, the Soviets pointed out that they were shut out of Italy and Japan. When Byrnes complained that the Rumanian government was not representative of all the people there, Molotov asked if the U.S. government was representative of all Americans; Byrnes, from South Carolina, wisely admitted that it was not. Neither American economic nor atomic power cowed the Soviets, and the meeting soon broke up.

The next conference was held at Moscow in December 1945. Although Byrnes and Truman regarded the Soviet Union as evil and dangerous, they still recognized it as an entity that had to be dealt with. When Byrnes found that his tough stance at London accomplished little, he, one of the twentieth-century masters of political horsetrading, turned to a more open negotiating stance. Stalin agreed to broaden the Rumanian and Bulgarian governments, allowing the United States to recognize them without losing face, and the United States agreed to an Allied Council for Japan, which allowed the Soviets a nominal role. Although these and other agreements were not of great importance, they indicated that the Allies, recovering from the London impasse, could work in surface harmony.

Although Byrnes's agreements at Moscow were in line with Truman's policy, he returned from Moscow to find his enemies accusing him of having been too soft in dealing with the Soviets. Although Truman later harped on Byrnes's record of appeasement, Dean Acheson, critical of Byrnes on other grounds, concluded that "anyone who looks at what was done [by Byrnes] can't find much appeasing the Russians in it." Still, Byrnes was on slippery ground. He had worked as a loner and had kept neither the State Department nor Truman well informed of his activities. Some observers thought that Byrnes, one of the nation's most powerful figures while Truman was still an obscure senator, felt superior to the president and treated him in an offhand manner, and Byrnes's enemies played on Truman's reverence for the office of the president.

When he returned from Moscow, Truman asked the secretary to join his party aboard the presidential yacht. Although the president, in a heated session, supposedly laid down the law to Byrnes, this is just one of the many such incidents that took place only in Truman's imagination. A letter to Byrnes that Truman drafted and dated 5 January 1946 but did not deliver provides insight into the president's thinking:

> There isn't a doubt in my mind that Russia intends an invasion of Turkey and the seizure of the Black Sea Straits to the Mediterrianean [sic]. Unless Russia is faced with an iron fist and strong language another war is in the making. Only one language do they understand—"How many divisions have you?"
>
> I do not think we should play compromise any longer. We should refuse to recognize Rumania and Bulgaria until they comply with our requirements; we should let our position on Iran be known in no

85

uncertain terms and we should continue to insist on the internation-
alization of the Kiel Canal, the Rhine-Danube waterway and the
Black Sea Straits and we should maintain complete control of Japan
and the Pacific. We should rehabilitate China and create a strong
central government there. We should do the same for Korea.

Then we should insist on the return of our ships from Russia and
force a settlement of the Lend-lease debt of Russia.

I'm tired [of] babying the Soviets.[17]

This did not mark a new era in postwar relations. As soon as Truman
took office, he had started complaining about alleged babying of the
Soviets in the past. His tendency from the beginning had been to agree
with the hard-liners, but in 1945 he still held doubts about the efficacy
of that policy. His letter to Byrnes indicated that now, in 1946, Truman
would be even less open to those who urged caution in taking actions
that would cause a break with the Soviets.

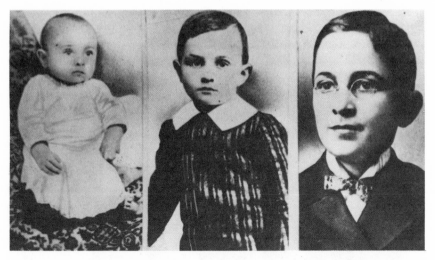

Harry Truman as a baby, at age four, and at fifteen. *Courtesy of Associated Press Photos*

The Grandview farm house, with Harry, just out of the fields, his mother, and grandmother. *Courtesy of the Harry S. Truman Library*

Captain Truman in France, 1918. *Courtesy of the Harry S. Truman Library*

Bess Truman. *Hessler Studio of Washington, D.C.; courtesy of the Harry S. Truman Library*

Senator Truman with (to his left) Thomas J. Pendergast and others at the Democratic National Convention, 1936.

President Roosevelt, Vice President elect Truman, and Vice President Henry A. Wallace, Washington, 1944. *Courtesy of the U.S. Department of the Interior*

Truman sworn in as president a few hours after Roosevelt's death. *Courtesy of Abbie Rowe, National Park Service*

Smiling allies at Potsdam Conference, 1945. Truman flanked by Winston Churchill *(left)* and Joseph Stalin *(right)*. *U.S. Army; courtesy of the Harry S. Truman Library*

Bess, Margaret, and Harry on a train platform, Independence, Missouri, 1946.
Courtesy of Bert Landfried, John Knox Village, Lee's Summit, Missouri

Truman and Republican presidential nominee Thomas Dewey, 1948.
From the General Scrapbook Volume 2, 1948–50

Truman and his cabinet, Blair House, 1949. *Courtesy of Abbie Rowe*

Truman and General Douglas MacArthur, Wake Island, 1950.
From the album, The President's Trip to Wake Island

Senator Joseph McCarthy.

Truman and advisors Averell Harriman, General George C. Marshall, Dean Acheson, John Snyder, Frank Pace, and General Bradley, 1950. *Courtesy of Abbie Rowe*

Changing of the guard: Truman and Senator John F. Kennedy, 1959. *Courtesy of the Harry S. Truman Library*

6

CONTAINING THE SOVIETS

After they left office in 1953, Dean Acheson wrote Truman: "You remember that we used to say that in a tight pinch we could generally rely on some fool play of the Russians to pull us through." In 1946 and 1947, "fool plays," real or fabricated, allowed Truman to clarify his foreign policy.

Secretary of State Byrnes reflected the tougher line. In 1946 he, Molotov, and others successfully negotiated five treaties with former enemy nations, each reflecting the power balance between the Soviets and Americans, with both sides making concessions. Rather than emphasizing the ability of the West to negotiate cooperatively with the Soviets, however, Byrnes fell in with the hard-line mood and contributed to the growing cold war atmosphere by publicly stressing Kremlin intransigence.[1]

Conflict in Iran reinforced the new hard-line policy. Before World War II, the United States had oil interests in the Middle East but deferred to the leadership position of Great Britain in that region. With Britain unable to maintain its traditional role in the eastern Mediterranean, Washington and Moscow moved to fill the vacuum. The lure of the region, in addition to its strategic geographic position, was oil. Truman was determined to keep Iranian oil out of Soviet hands, and he backed American corporations in their drive for Middle Eastern petroleum concessions. In 1946, the United States controlled 31 percent of Middle Eastern oil; this grew to 60 percent by the time Truman left office in 1953. Despite the fact that Greece and northern tier nations like Iran and Turkey lay on or close to Soviet borders, the United States haltingly moved during the Truman years to become the dominant power in the Middle East.

Great Britain, the United States, and the Soviet Union sent troops to Iran during the war to protect a vital Allied supply route. But even while cooperating to destroy Hitler, the great powers eyed each other suspiciously, and the Iranians felt endangered by all three. As the State Department assumed a more important institutional role under Truman, the Office of Near Eastern and African Affairs, staffed by strong anti-Communists, educated the president to the strategic importance of Iran. After the war, when the Soviets attempted to draw Iran into their sphere, Americans pressured them to withdraw their troops and encouraged the Iranians to resist Soviet demands. The Soviet Union removed its troops and watched calmly as Iran began to slip into the American orbit. Truman viewed the Soviet Union's withdrawal as proof that the Soviets, although aggressive and expansionistic, would withdraw when confronted with force.[2]

With the Iranian crisis as a dramatic backdrop, Churchill warned the American public on 5 March 1946 that an "iron curtain" was falling across Europe. Washington insiders had their own thinking clarified and placed in a broad conceptual framework by George F. Kennan in his now famous Long Telegram sent from the Moscow embassy on 22 February 1946. Dean Acheson later wrote: "The year 1946 was for the most part a year of learning that minds in the Kremlin worked very much as George F. Kennan had predicted they would."

Truman's comment on Kennan—"I always liked him, even though I couldn't figure out what he was talking about half the time"—illustrated the problem Kennan had in making himself understood by leaders with a simplistic view of the world. To be heard, he needed to provide Washington officials with formulas they could use to predict and guide responses to Soviet behavior. His analysis, as understood by his superiors, further narrowed their already restricted and rigid conception of global reality.

Kennan, an intellectual in a society that placed little value on ideas, identified personally with the eighteenth century and felt like an outsider in the twentieth. He empathized with the intelligentsia of czarist Russia, as did other Soviet experts he met at Riga in 1929. He detested communism, outraged at what he perceived as its degrading effect on the Russians. After World War II, from the Moscow embassy, Kennan urged Washington to accept the inevitable division of the world between the two great powers and not to give any appearance of approving Soviet actions in East Europe by continuing the alliance. He felt in 1945 as though he were plucking at the sleeves of indifferent superiors, trying to get their attention with a message they did not want to hear. Finally, Stalin on 9 February 1946 gave a speech designed to bolster the morale of the Soviet people, preparing them to endure more years of sacrifice while they reconstructed their economy. Although the speech was generally friendly to the West, Stalin portrayed the Soviet Union as a nation surrounded by hostile capitalistic powers. When the speech caused an uproar in Washington, the State Department asked Kennan for an analysis of Soviet behavior. He seized his opportunity: "They had asked for it. Now, by God, they would have it."

They got on 22 February the 8,500-word Long Telegram. Kennan found the key to explaining Soviet behavior in Russian history rather than Marxist ideology. Russian leaders traditionally felt great insecurity in relation to the outside world, and after 1917, the Soviet sense of being encircled by hostile capitalist powers created a "neurotic" view of the international scene. The Soviet Union would work to increase its strength and prestige and would push its power to the limit in places like Iran, Kennan wrote, and would work for a foothold in places like Germany and the Middle East. Kennan's passion, as well as his understanding of the kind of minds he was writing to in Washington, resulted in sentences like the following: "And they [the Soviet leaders] have learned to seek security only in patient but deadly struggle for total destruction of rival power, never in compacts and compromises with it." American policy should be based on the fact that, unlike the Nazis, Soviet leaders were not adventurists; they did not follow a fixed blueprint for domination; they did not take risks; they withdrew when they encountered danger: "Thus, if the adversary [of the Kremlin] has sufficient force and makes clear his readiness to use it, he rarely has to do so." The Soviet Union was still much weaker than the West, he argued, and its success as a system had not yet been proved. Americans should be educated to the nature of this struggle with the Soviets and end their counterproductive, hysterical anticommunism.

Sometimes Kennan's rhetoric, and Washington's reduction of his analysis to slogans and formulas, obscured or distorted his arguments. He believed that the real Soviet threat was political and psychological, rather than military, and should mainly be met by such nonmilitary containment responses as rebuilding the economy of Western Europe and improving American society. Kennan believed that U.S. power was too limited to engage in global containment, nor was that necessary; rather, there were key regions that the United States could not safely allow to fall into hostile hands: the Atlantic community nations, the Mediterranean and Middle East, and other nations running eastward through Iran, Japan, and the Philippines.

The views of Washington officials were further clarified, and hardened, in mid-1946 when Truman had his trusted staff member Clark Clifford write a report on Soviet-U.S. relations. Clifford and his assistant, George M. Elsey, interviewed top military, diplomatic, and intelligence officers and in September 1946 delivered to Truman a long report that the president found so "hot" he had all ten copies turned over to him and placed under lock and key. Clifford and Elsey's analysis was more militaristic and simplistic than Kennan's.[3]

Events in nations other than Iran continued to influence American thinking in 1946. Centuries of exploitation of the masses of people in Eastern Europe, followed by the devastation of war, led to turmoil as the people refused to allow their old masters to resume their prewar roles. Americans viewed this revolutionary ferment as the result of Kremlin-directed subversion rather than as the Soviet presence keeping mass movements from being suppressed by the old elite. American "active, noisy" foreign policy, with its continuous propaganda barrage aimed at the Soviet Union, increased Moscow's fears, and it tightened its grip over East Europe. The Soviets understood the language of force, though not as Truman assumed. Moscow felt endangered, confronted by an economically strong and aggressive power holding a monopoly on atomic weapons, and it took actions to protect itself.

In 1946, Germany replaced Poland as the main divisive element in the alliance. Negotiations concerning postwar Germany, divided into four zones of occupation by the United States, Great Britain, the Soviet Union, and France, took place within the context of the disintegrating alliance between the Soviets and the Americans, with neither side willing to risk a unified Germany falling into the orbit of the other. Although the four nations had agreed to administer their zones on a unified basis, they made little progress in 1945 and 1946 toward cooperation. France proved most recalcitrant, but as the cold war developed, Washington blamed Moscow for the discord. By 1946, Washington regarded

Germany as a necessary barrier against the Soviet Union and considered merging the western zones into one.[4]

In contrast to Washington's concern with Europe, neither Truman nor his top advisers knew much about Asia. Yet it was the political fault line under Truman's administration. Arrogance fed by U.S. power, as well as the racism and anti-Communist obsession of American leaders, kept Truman and his associates blinded to change in Asia. By the end of the 1930s, the old international structure in the Pacific and Asia had fragmented, leaving Japan and the United States warring to establish a new order. In 1945, the United States retained bases in Guam and Wake and gained trusteeships over the Marshalls, Marianas, and Carolines. It held the independent Philippines within its defensive system and occupied Japan. Yalta and other wartime agreements allowed the Soviet Union to regain the Kuril Islands and South Sakhalin and to obtain concessions in parts of China. Under the Yalta accord, both the United States and the Soviet Union would have influence in China but were to leave it as an independent nation. There had been no detailed agreement at Yalta on the future role of such colonial areas as Korea and Southeast Asia.

In 1949, Indian Prime Minister Jawaharlal Nehru tried to explain to Truman that Asians were no longer willing to endure poverty and Western exploitation and would fight to change their condition, first by destroying colonialism. In terms of its traditional anticolonial policy, the United States might have encouraged Asian nationalism; however, Washington was so intent on strengthening Europe to resist communism that it cooperated with the Europeans as they tried to reestablish their colonial empires in Asia. Americans also often found themselves supporting unpopular Asian elites who gained American support by portraying themselves as opponents of communism. Many of the nationalist leaders, like Ho Chi Minh in Vietnam, wanted both their own Asian brand of socialism and American friendship, but as the cold war mentality settled on Washington, Truman and his advisers saw such figures not as nationalists trying to combat colonialism and poverty but as stooges of Moscow. Truman ended one Asian war with atomic bombs in 1945, intervened in the Korean civil war in 1950, and moved deep into the Vietnamese struggle after 1950.[5]

In 1946 and for the next few years, China seemed to pose the major Asian problem. Americans entered that tangle with an arrogance that convinced them that China did not really exist as a nation and, as Truman and Acheson believed, had to be created by the Americans. With a peculiar mix of racism and sentimental imperialism, they assumed that the Americans had to protect the Chinese and set them on the proper road to self-fulfillment.

Truman's later view was that the whole problem stemmed from backing a "bad horse," the government of Chiang Kai-shek, the "most terrible government in the history of the world." China had been torn for years by a civil war between Chiang's Kuomintang (Guomindang) government, recognized by the Americans, and Mao Tse-tung's Communist forces. During the war, Roosevelt worked to keep Chiang afloat and encouraged him to carry through reforms to build popular support for his government. When civil war revived after World War II, however, Truman concluded that the American people would not support outright military intervention; Chiang would have to find a popular basis to survive on his own.

For his part, Stalin kept his pledge to Chiang, limiting his support of Mao Tse-tung. Mao's entry into Manchuria, under Soviet control, reflected simple power balances in northern China where Mao was strong and Chiang weak. Soviet preponderance in Manchuria was in line with the Yalta accords yet still had a great impact on American thinking. The reality of Mao's and Stalin's forces joining in Manchuria frightened American leaders and made them fear expansion of Soviet power over all of China.[6]

In late November 1945, the flamboyant Ambassador Patrick J. Hurley resigned his Chinese post with a barrage of criticism directed toward the president's policy. Truman quickly replaced Hurley with George Marshall, the most highly respected American military leader during World War II, and instructed him to arrange a truce and to mediate a settlement to unify China peacefully. Truman recognized the probability of failure of Marshall's mission; he secretly told Marshall to continue to support Chiang even if he refused to make reasonable concessions to bring about unification and to engage in constructive reform to regain popular support.

Marshall arranged a truce but failed in his efforts toward unification. Chiang, confident that Americans had no alternative to him, attempted to destroy Mao's forces. With American policy clearly tilted against him, Mao became increasingly critical of the United States, and at the end of 1946, Marshall asked Truman to terminate his mission. Truman and Marshall were in a difficult position: they believed it was impossible for Chiang to reverse the Communist tide, but they had already rejected gestures of friendship from Mao, and it seemed likely that he would soon control China.[7]

By the fall of 1946, Washington and Moscow had gone far toward forming and leading opposing blocs. In September, Henry Wallace had attempted in his Madison Square Garden speech to find a reasonable alternative, a middle ground, to head off the impending cold war and had been fired for his efforts. Secretary of State Byrnes said the United States must now draw lines and aid its friends and confront its opponents. Hopes for a global open door faded. The first necessity was to revive the economy of those within the American bloc. On 6 September 1946 at Stuttgart, Byrnes announced that failing unification of Germany—and he made clear a unified Germany could never be under Soviet power—the United States would support an economic merger of the western zones. Washington withdrew support for UNRRA, made no concessions to achieve international control of atomic energy, and prepared to act on the Riga axioms. Marshall, on 21 January 1947, replaced Byrnes, who had long before indicated his desire to resign.[8]

The gulf between Washington and Moscow widened in August 1946 when the Soviet Union formally requested a revision of the Montreux Convention, giving Turkey control over passage of warships through the Dardanelles, to allow the Soviets to have a role in control of the strait. Although the United States and Great Britain had agreed at both Yalta and Potsdam that this was an appropriate recognition of Soviet needs, the Kremlin request now appeared as a dangerous expansion of Communist power. According to Under Secretary of State Dean Acheson, in an early formulation of the domino theory, this move threatened Turkey, Greece, and the rest of the Near and Middle East and put pressure on India and China. In response, Truman sent a naval task force to the eastern Mediterranean. British and American control over the Suez and Panama canals, far from their borders, seemed entirely natural to Americans, while Soviet desire for a role in managing an adjacent waterway seemed a threat to the entire non-Soviet world.[9]

By the end of 1946, Truman was prepared to formulate postwar foreign policy more clearly. When the Republicans took control of Congress after the 1946 elections, Truman's presidency seemed to be effectively over. Reconversion made him appear indecisive and confused; the best the country could hope for, many assumed, was for him to summon some reserve of grace and dignity to get through the next two years until he could be replaced after the 1948 election. But by January 1947, the reconversion confusion was mostly over, and the country was stable and prosperous. Truman improved his staff and used it more effectively. In foreign affairs, he placed immense trust in two capable men, Secretary of State George Marshall and Under Secretary Dean Acheson. The administration ended its wavering over the nature of the Soviet threat and the proper response to it. With a revived sense of confidence, Truman, beginning in 1947, undertook a number of diplomatic initiatives on which his claim to greatness rests.

First came the Truman Doctrine. Great Britain, never recovered fully from the war, faltered during the harsh winter of 1946–47. With their economy near collapse, officials in London recognized that Britain could no longer carry out its traditional international role. Washington, pursuing its global conception of American interests, had already started shouldering the British aside in the Middle East and other places. Truman now dramatically moved to expand and make public his conception of world responsibilities. This came in the Truman Doctrine speech of 12 March 1947, in response to conditions in Greece and Turkey.

Greece had been torn during World War II by a civil war that resulted in enormous death and destruction. Great Britain had propped up an unpopular and incompetent right-wing government there, which at the end of the war had set out to destroy the Left. The popular left-wing movement defended itself, without much external aid, though it was Communist dominated and received some support from surrounding Communist nations in the Balkans. Such aid was small compared to the support that the conservative forces received from the British and the Americans. External aid for the Left, however, did not come from Stalin, who, honoring his understanding with the West, consistently worked to undermine the Greek insurgent movement.

Turkey was also under pressure although not in immediate crisis. The Joint Chiefs of Staff warned that if Moscow dominated Turkey, the Eastern Mediterranean and Middle East would probably be militarily untenable in case of war with the Soviet Union. Any faltering in Turkey would weaken the faith of other nations in U.S. steadfastness in opposing the Soviet drive to control the world. Although the immediate crisis in Turkish-Soviet relations had eased, the ambassador to the Soviet Union, Walter Bedell Smith, warned that Washington should not interpret that as a change of Kremlin attitude: "Any manifestations of Soviet reasonable consideration for Turkish rights will be tactical maneuvers for immediate partial gains. Any inaction or apparent indifference will be a matter of timing, waiting for most favorable moment to move." His statement illustrated an increasingly common American attitude: if the Soviet Union actively pursued its interests, it practiced aggression; if it took no action, it engaged in deception.[10]

On 21 February 1947, a British official delivered to the State Department notes stating that Greece was near collapse, that Turkey was under great pressure from the Kremlin, and that British resources were so limited that it would be forced to withdraw its support from the two nations by 31 March 1947. Events now presented Truman with an opportunity for dramatic action. On 24 February, Marshall characterized this as the most important decision since the end of the war and presented Truman with recommendations that called for American intervention with economic and military aid. The United States should act in dramatic fashion to educate Congress and the public to new American roles in the world.

Truman was willing to proceed on Marshall's recommendations, but he had a political problem: Republicans, controlling the Eightieth Congress, had loudly promised budget cuts, particularly in foreign aid. Yet Truman had taken care to work closely with Republican leaders, and on 27 February 1947, he invited them and major congressional Democrats to the White House for a briefing from Marshall and Acheson. Marshall, whose reputation provided him with tremendous personal influence, spoke first. Helping Greece and Turkey was not entirely a humanitarian response, he said, but was of strategic importance to American interests. If those nations fell, Soviet power might spread from France to India. Despite this dramatic forecast and his own great reputation, Marshall did not seem to move his audience. Acheson then seized his opportunity, endorsing Marshall's strategic message but bringing a passionate edge to his plea. "This was my crisis," Acheson wrote: "For a week I had nurtured it. These congressmen had no conception of what challenged them; it was my task to bring it home." He did not restrain himself to a "measured appraisal." He told the group that since the end of World War II, "Soviet pressure on the Straits, on Iran, and on northern Greece had brought the Balkans to the point where a highly possible Soviet breakthrough might open three continents to Soviet penetration." Using the image of fruit instead of dominoes, he said: "Like apples in a barrel infected by one rotten one, the corruption of Greece would infect Iran and all to the east. It would also carry infection to Africa through Asia Minor and Egypt, and to Europe through Italy and France." Only the United States could stop this. Silence followed Acheson's presentation until Vandenberg told Truman that if he would repeat that message to the American people, the senator would support him, and he thought Congress would also.[11]

Acheson and Clark Clifford carefully guided the speech-drafting process to make sure that the message was sweeping and dramatic in its presentation of the American role in the world and vivid and strong in language. Administration officials regarded it as their "All-out speech," which had to shock the people into action. It would reflect Truman's personal belief about the nature of the United States and the "free world" and of the Soviet Union and the threat it posed. It fit his conception of history as moral drama with black-and-white divisions of good and evil. His periods of wavering about correct policy were now gone, his interpretation of Soviet intent was clear, and his blueprint for action was fixed.

Some advisers urged caution. Kennan believed the speech was too sweeping in its commitment to aid any country facing subjugation. Marshall and Bohlen thought the language too flamboyant and too anti-Communist. George Elsey did not think any event warranted an "all-out" speech at that time. Acheson and Clifford designed the speech, however, to give the same clarity to congressional and public thinking that the president and his advisers experienced.

Truman delivered his message on 12 March to a joint session of Congress. He sketched the problems Greece and Turkey faced and then divided the world into two ways of life, one composed of free societies based on representative government and guarantees of individual liberty and the other subjected to totalitarian rule with a minority forcing its will upon a majority by using terror to eliminate freedom and liberty. In probably the most important sentence he delivered as president, Truman said: "I believe that it must be the policy of the United States to support free peoples who are resisting attempted subjugation by armed minorities or by outside pressures." If Greece or Turkey fell to these pressures, their collapse might spread disorder through the Middle East and have a "profound effect" on Europe: "Should we fail to aid Greece and Turkey in this fateful hour, the effect will be far reaching to the West as well to the East." He asked Congress for $400 million in aid and for authority to detail civilian and military personnel to those countries.[12]

Although Truman's sketch of the nature of Greek and Turkish society had little connection with the reality of recent events there, it gave Americans a view of the world that served them for decades. It mobilized public opinion to resist the spread of communism, and prepared the way for more extensive foreign aid programs necessary to keep world trade flowing. Truman noted that only Henry Wallace and his "crackpots" seemed to oppose the doctrine. "The attempt of Lenin, Trotsky, Stalin, et al., to fool the world and the American Crackpots Association, represented by Jos. Davies, Henry Wallace, Claude Pepper and the actors and artists in immoral Greenwich Village, is just like Hitler's and Mussolini's so-called socialist states." Increasingly, critics such as Wallace would be isolated and expelled from the mainstream of politics, which was diverted by the Truman Doctrine and the thinking behind it from placing primary concern on domestic matters.

The Truman Doctrine trapped Republican leaders by forcing them to choose between two of their highest priorities, cutting the federal budget and fighting communism. It also trapped Congress in a way that has become a familiar political ploy. The administration secretly formulated a program, wrapped it in a cloak of national security, and presented it to Congress as a fait accompli. If Congress turned the president down, it not only would pull the rug from under him but might also, according to the administration, be the final blow to Greece, weaken Turkey and Iran, and start other dominoes falling.

In closed hearings by the Committee on Foreign Relations, senators revealed that the program disturbed them. Respected Senator Walter F. George (D–Georgia) believed it was the most important step the United States had ever taken in international relations, and he had a most unusual request: he wanted time to think before the United States rushed into action. But the Truman Doctrine had already taken on a life of its own. The administration sent to the hearings an impressive array of spokesmen who seemed to have the "facts" that most congressmen did not. Acheson worked to soothe some fears by toning down the implications of the message, asserting that the United States would not intervene to help free people in areas where it could not be effective. Truman's work with Republicans also paid off. Vandenberg portrayed the problem in Greece as symbolic of a global ideological clash between communism and "Democracy." He said that perhaps this crisis was akin to Munich, when the failure to stand up to Hitler was fatal. He answered George's call for time to think by saying that the senators were not quite free agents, that this was almost like a declaration of war that they had to accept, although they could help shape it.[13]

Congress responded favorably to the Truman Doctrine and voted the aid he requested. It took its place with the Monroe Doctrine as one of the two major definitions of the American role in the world and has remained the foundation of American foreign policy since 1947. If it isolated Wallace and other critics on the Left and the Right and trapped the Republican party and Congress, it also ensnared the administration. Its language and imagery were so vivid, it explained the world so simply, and appealed so strongly to the American proclivity to divide the world into good and evil that Truman and later presidents had to follow it. Demagogues like Joseph McCarthy drew on its frightening images to harden it as the mainstream from which politicians, even Truman, could not safely deviate. A few days after the speech, Truman issued an executive order initiating his domestic loyalty program; anticommunism abroad required a similar campaign at home. By dividing the world into free and unfree blocs and including in the free world notorious dictatorships, the doctrine also debased American political language, which would increasingly become a form of doublespeak. Truman's public promise of help for all freedom-loving people, followed by Acheson's private assurance in closed hearings that he did not really mean it, was also to become a familiar ritual as the White House increasingly came to regard the American people as objects to be lied to and manipulated.

The Truman Doctrine eroded traditional diplomacy. Acheson told congressmen: "I think it is a mistake to believe that you can, at any time, sit down with the Russians and solve questions." The Soviet Union would be contained, not dealt with as a traditional power. Containment as put in place by Truman meant encirclement of the Soviet Union. It was a new form of traditional American expansionism, with the American empire pushing outward against the defensive barrier thrown up by the Communist bloc. As the doctrine took on a life of its own, it created a mind-set that supported U.S. intervention in Korea, Vietnam, and other places.[14]

American intervention did stabilize the northern tier but at the cost of taking over the Greek government. The insurgency movement finally collapsed, though mainly because of internal divisions and because in 1949 Yugoslavia premier Marshal Tito withdrew his support. The Greek economy never recovered enough to benefit its masses, but with American support, a conservative elite established a military dictatorship. Historian Lawrence S. Wittner wrote, "In short, the U.S. government treated Greece much as the Soviet Union treated its Eastern European satellites—as a piece of Cold War real estate." As the northern tier stabilized, it confirmed to Truman another "lesson": when Washington firmly opposed Soviet attempts at subversion, the forces of freedom would win. In reality, the people of those states did not gain freedom, and the Truman Doctrine probably pushed Stalin into tightening control over Eastern Europe.[15]

American officials moved rapidly in 1947 to put together the system of economic and military interdependence and political cooperation that continued to characterize the non-Communist world for decades after Truman left office. Washington, which had already provided fifteen billion dollars in postwar loans and grants to feed people in other countries and keep world trade flowing, realized that the Western economy required an even larger injection of aid, designed specifically to generate economic revival. The Truman Doctrine provided a powerful boost to a massive foreign aid program that a few months before, wrote a State Department official, seemed "fantastic" even to suggest. The Marshall Plan became the "Truman Doctrine in Action."

Many American and European leaders believed that Europe was under great pressure, internally from domestic Communist parties and externally from the Soviet Union. Britain was about to go bankrupt, Truman wrote his sister in the summer of 1947, "and if they do that it will end our prosperity and probably all the world's too. Then Uncle Joe Stalin can have his way." American and world prosperity and resistance to the Soviet Union were intertwined in Truman's mind.

By 1947, it was apparent that the capitalistic world was faltering, and American leaders had to abandon their goal of creating a global economy. Piecemeal aid programs and organizations like the International Monetary Fund and the World Bank could not hope to cope with the massive problem. The leaders also saw that if they did not head off the Western economic crisis, their own allies would embrace economic nationalism, closing their doors to protect their economies.

A major part of the problem was the sheer power of the American economy. Although the United States had productive capacity unmatched in the history of the world and global demand, fed by war devastation, seemed limitless, the world was running out of dollars to purchase American goods. U.S. loans and grants kept trade flowing temporarily, but the dollar gap steadily grew, as did political resistance to foreign aid programs. The United States had to revive its economic competitors to maintain its own economic health and to contain the Soviet Union.

Many policymakers believed that European recovery depended on German revival. The four powers occupying that defeated country had made little progress toward implementing plans for economic cooperation among the zones or on other policy matters. French recalcitrance remained the biggest obstacle, but the State Department habitually blamed such problems on the Soviets as part of its anti-Communist propaganda campaign. Washington now decided that Germany had to be partitioned and the western zones economically revived. By early 1947, Truman had made three major decisions: to cut Eastern Europe and the Soviet Union off from American trade and aid, to revive Germany economically, and restore Western European economic health. The Marshall Plan was a major instrument to achieve these goals and the Truman Doctrine a way of explaining and promoting it.

After Marshall opened discussion of the plan on 5 June 1947, Washington made it clear that the Europeans should take the initiative in drawing up the specifics of the program, that the Soviet Union and its allies were invited to participate, and that German recovery was necessary for the program to work. In the meantime, in December 1947, Congress passed an Interim Aid program, with $522 million for Europe and $18 million for China.

Fortunately for the Marshall Plan's chances of passage, the Soviet Union and other Communist nations refused to participate, for Truman got it through the budget-conscious Eightieth Congress by presenting it in a crisis atmosphere. Fear of war swept Washington during the spring of 1948 as Congress prepared to vote. On 17 March 1948, Truman delivered a hard-line speech to a joint session of Congress describing Moscow's ruthless destruction of the independence of various Eastern European nations and its intent to sabotage the Marshall Plan to prevent Western European recovery. He asked that Congress complete action on the Marshall Plan, provide for a universal military training program, and enact a selective service law. Americans had to take action to maintain peace, Truman pleaded, and unity was vital. Congress responded. On 3 April 1948, Truman signed the Foreign Assistance Act, under which the United States provided $12.4 billion to Europe over the next four years.

The Marshall Plan spurred industrial and agricultural production in Europe and promoted growth of trade within the Atlantic community. It had a great psychological effect, encouraging Europeans to invest in their own economic growth. Within the European bloc, recovery undermined the Left, broke Western Europe economic ties with Eastern Europe, and gave Western European countries strength to fight colonial wars in such places as Indochina.[16]

From Stalin's point of view, the Truman Doctrine and Marshall Plan must have seemed a dangerous turn in the old pattern of Western hostility the Kremlin had faced since 1917. Stalin had acted moderately up to this point, allowing diversity in the political and economic systems of Eastern Europe. Now he began the process of Sovietization and Stalinization of the nations of that region.

Kennan predicted in November 1947 that success of containment, especially with the Marshall Plan, would lead Stalin to clamp down on Czechoslovakia. In the winter of 1947–48, the coalition government in Czechoslovakia began to break down, and Communists moved toward greater power. The coup of February 1948 gave them control. The Americans had written off Czechoslovakia long before, giving democratic forces there little help in their attempt to maintain an opening to the West from within Eastern Europe. Now they became a symbol of embattled democrats being gobbled up by the totalitarian Stalin on his march westward. This image became part of Truman's propaganda campaign to get his program, especially the Marshall Plan, through Congress, for the Spring Crisis developed while that body was completing work on the program.[17]

Truman believed that the West faced exactly the same situation as with Hitler in 1938 and 1939. He wrote his daughter on 3 March 1948: "I just wanted you to know your dad as President asked for no territory, no reparations, no slave laborers—only Peace in the World. We may have to fight for it." On 5 March, General Lucius D. Clay, military governor of the American zone in Germany, who had been asked by the Pentagon to supply information that might be used to bolster its case for military budgets, telegrammed that war might come with "dramatic suddenness." On 10 March, Jan G. Masaryk, secretary for foreign affairs in Czechoslovakia and admired in the West, committed suicide, with Western leaders and journalists speculating that he was murdered. Truman heightened the war scare with two militant speeches on 17 March 1948. He told his staff one of the speeches was so strong that Marshall was afraid he would "pull the trigger." *New York Times* military expert Hanson W. Baldwin soon realized, he told David Lilienthal, that the Spring Crisis was totally a "Washington Crisis." It served its purpose, however. The military got a supplementary appropriation of $3.4 billion, the Marshall Plan passed, and Henry Wallace, who saw through the "crisis," was pretty well destroyed in his contest with Truman for the 1948 Democratic nomination. Truman characterized his speech on 17 March as "reading Henry Wallace out the Democratic Party." He told his audience that he would not accept support from "Henry Wallace and his Communists."[18]

The Berlin blockade increased the feeling that the world had reached the point of no return in the cold war. The Truman administration believed a revitalized German economy was central to the success of containment. It also feared that a unified Germany might fall into the Soviet orbit. Therefore Truman moved to integrate the western zones into the West European economy, inevitably partitioning Germany. He ignored all opportunities to work out compromises with the Soviets, who remained restrained on the issue. By 1 June 1948 the Americans had taken the first steps toward economic integration of the western zones with the European economy and announced that work would begin on a German constitution in the fall. Washington promised France, fearful of a revived Germany, that American troops would stay in Europe.

Moscow responded to what it regarded as high-handed American violations of the Yalta and Potsdam agreements by harassing traffic moving into the western zones of the city of Berlin, located in the Soviet, or eastern, zone of Germany. During late June 1948, the Soviets instituted a full-scale land blockade of West Berlin. General Clay, the military governor of the American zone, ordered West Berlin supplied by air.

A full-scale crisis now existed, and war seemed a real possibility. Truman, in one of his most famous and effective decisions, avoided rasher acts, such as trying to break the blockade by armed convoys, and backed the attempt at an airlift. Ambassador Robert D. Murphy, political adviser to Clay, immediately warned that if the Americans did not stand fast, their relationship with their allies would weaken, and, in a variation of the falling dominoes and rotten apples image, U.S. power in Europe would then be "like a cat on a sloping tin roof." Here then was another test of American resolve, one of many to follow. The growing American conception of its global security interests turned Berlin into a symbol of East-West cold war confrontation, though it had no strategic or economic importance. Truman told his advisers there would be no discussion; the Americans "were going to stay period."

Over the next few months, Truman remained firm as planes shuttled into West Berlin on an around-the-clock basis. The 1948 campaign for president took place during this time, and Truman benefited because the successful airlift showed his decisiveness, resolution, and apparent moderation. It also meant that his Republican opponent, Thomas E. Dewey, had to be careful not to sow disunity. Berliners, many recently returned from slaughtering Americans in World War II or from running the camps at Dachau and Bergen-Belson, now became valiant allies in an American propaganda campaign. They stood besieged in one of the outposts of freedom by the barbaric and dangerous Soviets, who until recently had been portrayed as valiant American allies.

After a year-long drubbing in the propaganda war, the Soviets, in May 1949, lifted the blockade. West Berlin remained under Western control, and war had been avoided. The blockade and successful U.S. response showed its allies that the Americans would remain engaged in Europe and reaffirmed the "lesson" that firmness resulted in success.[19]

With the Truman Doctrine in place, with the Marshall Plan economic program getting underway, with lines more clearly drawn between two opposing forces and crises occurring with great frequency (in Iran, Turkey, Greece, Czechoslovakia, and Berlin), the next phase of the cold war came with the militarization of containment through the North Atlantic Treaty Organization (NATO) and Western rearmament. Already a national security community was forming within the United States with certain industries, the military services, a few think tanks, and segments of major universities intertwined in research and development programs that had military applications. In 1947 Truman broke the long deadlock over military unification; Congress created the National Military Establishment (renamed the Department of Defense in 1949) and established the Central Intelligence Agency (CIA) and the National Security Council (NSC). The military services, especially the air force, cleverly fed the anti-Communist feeling and then asked for larger budgets. Truman found it harder to limit military spending while he steadily expanded the American definition of its security interests and magnified the Soviet threat. On 24 November 1948 he approved NSC-20/4, which said that Moscow's objective clearly was world domination.

Creation of NATO was the most important move toward militarized containment. With its organization, the United States, under Truman's leadership, broke with one of its oldest traditions, that of avoiding entangling alliances. NATO helped bolster European resolve and morale and provided a means through military spending to close the dollar gap after the Marshall Plan ended. It further intertwined Western economies, as well as their defenses.

In December 1947, Ernest Bevin proposed a Western alliance against Moscow. When Marshall responded positively, discussions quickened. The exact nature of the alliance, and the American relationship to it, emerged slowly, but on 17 March 1948, England, France, and the Benelux countries signed the Brussels Pact, which provided for collective security.

As discussions continued, Truman worked closely with Vandenberg, whose cooperation was especially important in this election year, and on 11 June 1948 the Vandenberg Resolution easily passed the Senate. The resolution endorsed a U.S. alliance with other Western nations. Diplomatic and military leaders on both sides of the Atlantic agreed to language that said an attack on one nation would be regarded as an attack on all. They also agreed that in the future, West Germany should be brought into the alliance. Twelve nations signed the North Atlantic Treaty on 4 April 1949; the Senate ratified it, and Truman signed it in July 1949.

Ratification of the treaty and creation of NATO did not immediately create a great Western military buildup. Its first effect was to act as a trigger to guarantee an American attack on the Soviets if they invaded a NATO member. To begin to put teeth into the organization, Truman asked for and Congress passed in October 1949 the Mutual Defense Assistance Act of 1949, which started a flow of American military aid to NATO members and other countries. Not until the Korean War was the administration able to begin a massive rearmament program for itself and its allies.

Since Stalin had no intention of attacking Western Europe and assumed Washington knew that, these activities added to his distrust. He responded by tightening his control within the Soviet Union and the East European satellites, just like the United States was funding allied efforts to hold their colonies and as the Americans themselves tightened their grip on Latin America. Between 1950 and 1952, Stalin doubled the size of the Soviet army, raised military expenditures by 50 percent, and formed the Warsaw Pact as a counter to NATO. The Soviets understood the language of force very well and replied in kind.[20]

Truman later wrote that there would have never been a NATO without Dean Acheson, and when Marshall retired in January 1949, the president asked Acheson to become secretary of state. With his eastern, upper-middle-class background, and Ivy League education, Acheson seemed to many to be the kind of person Truman detested, but they worked easily together and liked each other personally. Truman wanted and needed to delegate authority to a strong secretary, and his needs exactly matched Acheson's desires. Acheson was an expert manager of Truman; he knew to respect the presidency and to deal frankly with the president. He knew that Truman wanted to be kept informed and to see himself as the ultimate decision maker, even if usually he was a ratifier. They also got along because Acheson was an expert in reading Truman and expressing himself in language that moved the president. If Acheson had a deeper, subtler, and more flexible view of the Soviet Union and the rest of the world, his discourse with other men of action in those crowded years was in the black and white, simplistic terms of the Riga axioms.[21]

Containment meant drawing lines across the globe. In Europe, it was not just the Soviets who were pulling down the iron curtain; the Americans were tugging at it as well. In Asia, although the two powers generally abided by Yalta, they confronted dangerous conditions because many Asian peoples, like those in Korea and Indochina, intended to define their own future. In China, Marshall had decided in late 1946 that the United States could do nothing more to reconcile the nationalist and Communist forces and that Chiang's government was so corrupt and incompetent that it had lost the support of the Chinese people. In May 1949 Truman told Lilienthal that the Americans had poured $2.5 billion into China, and $1 billion of it was in New York banks, stolen by crooks in Chiang's government. Some advisers wanted to disassociate the United States entirely from the conflict; others wanted to open lines of communication with Mao Tse-tung; a few wanted to intervene massively to back Chiang; some wanted to divide China between Chiang and Mao. The administration did not effectively pursue any of these lines, though it did try to avoid further entanglement with Chiang. But given the rhetoric of the Truman Doctrine and the growing containment mentality in Congress, the administration could not block aid to China in 1948. Although Truman had years to prepare for the political impact that followed Chiang's fall in late 1949, he failed to do so and paid a terrible political price for this lapse.[22]

With conditions deteriorating in China, Truman tried to revive Japan as a foundation stone for his Asian containment wall. Japanese leaders and the American military government, headed by General Douglas MacArthur, faced an enormous task in 1945. Japanese agriculture, industry, and trade were destroyed or disrupted; two million people were dead; seven million soldiers had to be brought back home and reincorporated into society. In 1946, ten million Japanese were unemployed, inflation was out of control, and loss of the war challenged their fundamental values and beliefs.

The United States allowed as little interference by its allies in its occupation of Japan as Stalin allowed in Eastern Europe. MacArthur's authority was immense. He took great care to avoid affronts to the dignity of the Japanese people and calculated his every move to strengthen his position with them. More than most other Americans, MacArthur understood Japan's potential to rebuild rapidly. Despite his love of the spotlight, he also understood the need to govern through Japanese leaders, with as little open interference as possible.

The occupation reform program became MacArthur's most widely noted achievement as military governor. Legend has him writing out the fifteen basic reforms he wanted to achieve while flying to occupy Japan. Actually all of these came from Washington, were modified by the Japanese during implementation, and succeeded only if they fit prewar Japanese ideas and reform movements. Japanese and American leaders wanted just enough reform to relieve pressure for radical, leftist change without destroying the power of the elite to maintain order. With American encouragement, the Japanese adopted a new constitution that provided for a liberal parliamentary system based on government responsibility to the people. Reforms provided for the right of labor to organize and bargain collectively, free and equal education, Western principles of legal justice, one of the most extensive and successful land reform programs in modern times, legal rights for women equal to those of men, and compulsory education based on teaching of democratic values.

The Japanese found many of these reforms to be of lasting benefit, but other programs had a checkered history. To rid Japan of militarism, two hundred thousand Japanese classed as militarists were purged from positions of authority. Also, the Americans intended to break up the *zaibatsu*, the great family-based monopolies through which ten families controlled almost 75 percent of Japan's industrial, commercial, and financial structure. By attacking the *zaibatsu*, Americans began the process of democratizing the Japanese economic structure.

In 1947, with the Chinese war raging, Washington began to recognize Japan's importance as a containment barrier. Now the reverse course began; reforms that threatened economic disorder could no longer be tolerated. The *zaibatsu* were left alone; almost all the militarists were resurrected; the leftist groups began to be discredited and labor unions brought under control. Washington brought MacArthur, who still seemed intent on imposing Roosevelt's New Deal on Japan, into line and forced him to abandon his push for reforms.

Just as Washington viewed German recovery as necessary to European military health, so it saw Japanese revival as the engine of economic vitality of Southeast and East Asia. Americans had to find new trade sources for the Japanese economy to keep it from being pulled into the

Chinese Communist orbit through resumption of traditional trade patterns. Washington officials began to regard Southeast Asia as a source of raw materials and markets vital to Japanese and non-Communist Asia's economic health. This made it more important than ever before to keep Indochina and other Asian areas out of Communist hands. Washington was soon on the way to incorporating a strong Japan into its economic and military system.[23]

Containment at home also proceeded. The administration and Congress turned more attention to internal security. Truman set the tone for what followed. The attorney general compiled lists of subversive organizations in 1947; Pentagon control over the congressional testimony of its members tightened; the State Department denied passports to reporters critical of American cold war policy; the Justice Department stepped up deportation of aliens involved in Communist activities; and the Office of Education developed the Zest for American Democracy program, encouraging schools to promote patriotism. Administration officials hammered home the propaganda line set by Truman, interpreting Soviet-American relations in terms of the Truman Doctrine and blaming problems everywhere on Moscow. The Truman administration began the practices and used the language in 1947 that would three years later be labeled McCarthyism. The lineage from Truman to McCarthy was direct and clear.[24]

In 1947 the Truman administration developed its anti-Communist doctrine and made major strides toward implementing its containment programs in both Europe and Asia. It was the Korean War, however, that fully matured Truman's foreign policy and allowed its application. In the meantime, while Truman was achieving increasing coherence in the formulation and implementation of American foreign policy, he endured continuing turmoil in domestic politics and issues.

7

POLITICAL PRESSURES, POLITICAL VICTORIES

In November 1946, the Democrats lost control of Congress for the first time since the Great Depression. Truman had dissipated power, prestige, and popularity to such an extent that during the fall campaigns, Democratic party leaders kept him home in Washington, hoping, in vain, that out of sight he would be out of mind. Meat and housing shortages, inflation, confusion in the White House, and spectacular labor-management conflicts caused voters to answer affirmatively the Republican campaign slogan: "Had Enough?"

Yet pressures on Truman soon eased. The worst of reconversion was over, and the anticipated depression had not occurred. Labor-management conflicts cooled, and the government brought United Mine Workers president John L. Lewis to heel. Lewis was one of Truman's pet hates: "He is a Hitler at heart, a demagogue in action and a traitor in fact. In 1942 he should have been hanged for treason." When a coal strike began in November 1946, Truman ordered the Justice Department to seek a contempt citation, and the judge levied a massive fine on the union. When on 7 December 1946 Lewis gave in, Truman's standing with antilabor critics improved, as did his own morale.[1]

Some of his liberal supporters moved to help Truman regain his footing. Meeting secretly each Monday night at the home of Oscar Ewing, an important Democratic party official who in 1947 became director of the Federal Security Agency, they concluded that Truman was a strong, progressive leader held back by such conservative insiders as John Snyder and John Steelman. The Ewing group included, among others, Clark Clifford, Assistant Secretary of Agriculture Charles F. Brannan, Leon Keyserling of the Council of Economic Advisers, and Assistant Secretary of Interior C. Girard Davidson. These men worked out positions on major issues, always with the 1948 election in mind, and funneled their advice through Clifford, who masterfully shaped the political environment surrounding Truman.

Truman worked easily with these liberals. Their reform priorities matched his, and they framed their concerns in a practical idiom. His relationship with those whom he called "professional" or "crackpot" liberals remained tense but improved somewhat in 1947 and 1948. The Ewing group gave more direction to Truman's actions, and his battles with the Eightieth Congress to protect New Deal reforms improved his reputation. Tension also eased because liberalism itself changed. With the nation moving toward a full-blown Red scare, fostered by the administration's anti-Communist rhetoric and actions, the liberal community divided. Cold war liberals, creating the Americans for Democratic Action (ADA) in the fall of 1946, began to dominate the mainstream of the reform movement. They purged their organizations of Communists and other leftists, many of whom followed Wallace into obscurity as the center moved to the right. Although neither Truman nor the ADA wanted to admit it, their foreign and domestic programs so coincided that their fortunes were "unavoidably intertwined."[2]

As liberalism moved with Truman toward the center of the political spectrum, it lost its creative force. It had little to offer to overcome chronic barriers to social democracy: economic concentration in the industrial and financial world, stultifying work for most Americans, poverty for many, the seeming irrelevance of national politics to the everyday life of the people, sexism that held back millions of women from achieving or even recognizing their potential, and growth of de facto racial segregation within deteriorating cities. During the Truman administration years, the welfare state, military Keynesianism, and the cold war combined to produce a society characterized by an increasing degree of benevolent suppression, giving the illusion of freedom and social progress while reducing meaningful choice and maintaining the existing class and power structure. The United States, while projecting its image as a humane protector of freedom loving people, actually used its powers to extend its empire and to destroy those who stood in its way.

The national security state was Truman's true gift to future generations. It helped to stabilize the capitalist, liberal society. Within it, questioning of the fundamentals of American society was seldom seriously
entertained by men of power. The United States was so wealthy and
powerful that challenges to the basic structures of the American system
seemed out of touch with reality. Since most people benefited from an
enlarging economic pie, few had the temerity to ask that it be sliced
differently. An errant corporation might come under attack and tactics
against the Communist empire debated, but oligopolistic capitalism or
American expansionism was seldom subject to national debate.

In economic policy, the conflict between segments of big business
and many New Dealers eased. They had worked well together during the
war and slowly arrived at a consensus on important aspects of future
economic policy. Most big business leaders quit demanding the repeal of
New Deal reforms, and liberals gave up calling for economic and social
planning; they agreed that Keynesian economic techniques could promote economic growth and predictability. Keynesianism and the welfare
state carried the potential for radical change. Keynesianism could have
been tied to social planning and economic nationalism, as Lord Keynes
advocated, and the welfare state could have been used to redistribute
wealth and move toward socialism. But as combined in Truman's America, they tamed each other. Economic growth produced taxes to pay for
the welfare state rather than taxing the rich to pay for social services,
and new social and economic programs pumped money back into the
economy, producing growth and more taxes. Economic growth and welfare programs gave enough people enough security to keep them satisfied
with existing class arrangements.

The Democratic loss of the 1946 election did not represent a brief
breakdown of the Roosevelt coalition. It was, rather, the beginning of a
new postwar consensus. In 1946, Truman's troubles with the Wallacites
on the left and southern racists on the right seemed disastrous for his
political future, but cold war America converted both into extremist or
fringe groups. And as American politicians moved toward the center,
they abandoned many discordant issues, groups, and political leaders. As
a consensus politician, in both personality and political background, Truman benefited. If the programs he advocated sometimes put him ahead
of public opinion, the actions he took brought him back to the center.
He portrayed himself as the protector and leader of the common people,
but he also believed that American society was fundamentally sound and

that domestic reforms had to take a backseat to foreign policy and military needs.[3]

In 1947, the immediate problem Truman faced was the Eightieth Congress. Early in the year, Truman had tried to conciliate the Republican majority, but that party's leadership interpreted the 1946 election as a mandate to destroy much of the New Deal legacy. Southern Democrats, watching with dismay the increasing power of blacks and labor leaders in the party, joined with conservative Republicans to block Truman reform initiatives in housing and health care. Yet they and their Republican friends misread the election. Voters, although angry with reconversion and Truman's leadership, continued to support the New Deal. Public support for the New Deal programs, divisions among conservatives, vigorous action by moderates and liberals of both parties, and judicious use of Truman's veto prevented major damage to Roosevelt's programs.

The most explosive fight in the Eightieth Congress came over the Taft-Hartley Act. When the Eightieth Congress opened, 66 percent of the public wanted legislation to restrain unions, and the Taft-Hartley bill passed both houses in early June 1947. Among many restrictions, it outlawed the closed shop, gave the government authority to impose an eighty-day cooling-off period to end strikes, placed limitations on union political activities, and required union officers to submit affidavits that they did not belong to the Communist party. On 20 June, in a scathing attack on the Republicans, Truman vetoed Taft-Hartley. The House overrode his veto on the same day and the Senate a few days later, but Truman pleased union leaders by standing against the "slave labor bill."

In line with his strategy to project himself as a battler for the common people, Truman reiterated his full reform program in his 1948 State of the Union message and soon began flaying Congress for its inaction. Attacking the Republican-dominated body for not passing his domestic program allowed him to project his action-oriented image without having to assume responsibility, and pay the political costs, for real social change.[4]

Truman's cabinet and staff stabilized by the end of his first term. Marshall had replaced Byrnes at State, and Forrestal took over the newly created National Military Establishment. In December 1947, Jesse M. Donaldson, a career civil servant, replaced Robert Hannegan as postmaster general and served to the end of Truman's administration. After he fired Wallace, Truman turned to Averell Harriman, who served as secretary of commerce from October 1946 to April 1948, when he went to Europe to help implement the Marshall Plan. Harriman, a liberal in the context of the Truman administration, was replaced by Charles W. Sawyer, who served until the end of Truman's presidency and allied with fellow outspoken conservative John Snyder. Clinton Anderson left the cabinet in April 1948, returning to New Mexico to run successfully for the Senate. Charles F. Brannan, a strong voice for liberal reform, replaced him and served until Truman went home to Independence. After Secretary of Labor Schwellenbach died, Maurice J. Tobin took his place in August 1948 and remained until 20 January 1953. Although not considered a forceful leader, he did improve relations with organized labor.

After the initial confusion while Truman's largely untested staff jockeyed for position, more order came to White House operations. Charles Ross and Matthew Connelly remained close advisers, and John Steelman and Clark Clifford became increasingly important. Steelman was the "administrator of the normal, ongoing, every day work of the White House," and special counsel Clark Clifford acted as political troubleshooter, speechwriter, drafter of bills, and crisis manager. Truman had no chief of staff but allowed Steelman and Clifford to lead the rest of the staff as first among equals. Steelman was a low-keyed man who deliberately stayed in the background. By contrast, Clifford was a handsome, exciting, ambitious man who read Truman skillfully and created a political environment within the White House to promote his goals. Other aides, like Charles S. Murphy, were more studious and organized in their presentation of information to Truman, and David E. Bell and David D. Lloyd were better idea men, but "Clifford was, without equal, the synthesizer and operator," recalled Leon Keyserling.[5]

The loyalty and political capability of Truman's staff and cabinet were fully tested in the tense months before the 1948 elections as he took up two of the most complex and controversial issues in modern times: civil rights for American blacks and a homeland for the world's Jews.

Truman inherited southern racial attitudes. His four grandparents came from Kentucky and were slaveowning southern sympathizers during the Civil War. The people in his home region of Missouri shared southern values and passed them along to Truman. He later said that there had been no "color line" in Independence, but like many other southerners, he believed blacks' staying in their place, not challenging Jim Crow institutions, meant that good race relations existed in his community and that segregation was a voluntary matter. Truman attended segregated schools and as county judge administered racially separate institutions. Independence largely solved its racial problem by using slum clearance and community redevelopment projects to drive most blacks to Kansas City.

After he left the presidency, Truman wrote: "All my life I have fought against prejudice and intolerance." His memory, however, was selective. In 1911, at age twenty-seven, he wrote Bess:

> I think one man is just as good as another so long as he's honest and decent and not a nigger or a Chinaman. Uncle Will says that the Lord made a white man from dust[,] a nigger from mud, then He threw up what was left and it came down a China man. He does hate Chinese and Japs. So do I. It is race prejudice I guess. But I am strongly of the opinion that negros ought to be in Africa, yellow men in Asia[,] and white men in Europe and America.

He continued using the words *nigger* and *coon* throughout his life. He also spoke of "kikes" and carried a Jewish stereotype in his mind. In 1935, after winning money from a man in a poker game, he wrote, "He screamed like a Jewish merchant. He is a Jew I think. At least he looks and talks like one." A fellow reserve officer was a grand person, he wrote in 1941, "Name's Rosenbloom but doesn't act it at all."

Despite his racist views as a young man and his racist language, Truman was the first president to make civil rights a major part of his program. As he advanced politically, he loosened the bonds of racism that held most of those around him. Truman benefited from black support in county politics and voted favorably on civil rights in the Senate. The contrast between his early exposure to southern values and his later education in an urban machine made him understand the diversity of the Democratic party coalition and the need to serve all elements within it. As president, he found it difficult personally to challenge segregation and accept social equality, but he believed that blacks had a right to equality under the law and deserved equal opportunity. When his brother protested his Fair Employment Practices Commission (FEPC) proposal, Truman replied that Vivian was wrong; the legislation was part of the Democratic party platform, "and I expect to put the whole program over before I leave this office because it is right."[6]

After more than a hundred years of being exploited and terrorized by white Americans, blacks were organizing to take control of their own destiny with a force that could no longer be entirely suppressed. The development of the cold war also boosted the black position and enabled Truman to see more clearly the need for change. With Washington wanting to mobilize the free world to hold the containment line, the United States had to improve its image with African and Asian leaders. Truman said: "The top dog in a world which is 90 percent colored ought to clean his own house."

In 1945 and 1946, blacks examined very closely Truman's actions regarding the FEPC, which Roosevelt had established during the war to deal with minority employment problems. Although Truman proposed retaining the commission as a permanent agency, a southern filibuster in early 1946 persuaded him and Democratic party leaders to abandon the agency, and it died. Many observers believed Truman had merely given the FEPC lip-service to maintain black support and still not anger southern congressmen.[7]

Like his successors in the White House, Truman found that the middle ground on civil rights rapidly eroded. Blacks were pushing for an end to discrimination and demanding a role in Democratic party matters. Black veterans returning to the South challenged traditional racial mores. The relative disinterest with which most southerners received Truman's first actions on minority matters faded, and horrible acts of violence occurred in 1946. In February, a South Carolina policeman blinded a black veteran still in uniform. In July, two black veterans, with their female companions, were killed in Monroe, Georgia. Other killings and acts of violence followed, and the Ku Klux Klan increased its activities.

White House aide David K. Niles and his assistant, Philleo Nash, dealt with minority matters in a low-key, almost secretive manner, quietly handling problems blacks faced within the executive branch and maintaining liaison with minority organizations. In 1946, Niles and Nash discussed the possibility of responding to racial tensions by creating a blue-ribbon commission. The opportunity came on 19 September 1946, when Walter White, executive secretary of the National Association for Advancement of Colored People (NAACP), led a delegation of black leaders to urge Truman to take action against mob violence. As they described to Truman details of some of the attacks on blacks, Truman became pale, and his voice trembled as he promised action. He soon issued an executive order to create the President's Committee on Civil Rights. Niles and Nash carefully filled the fifteen-person committee with prominent Americans who would be sympathetic to civil rights.

In 1947, while the committee deliberated, Truman did little to promote civil rights. Although federal establishments harbored segregated facilities and federal housing and hospital and other agencies engaged in discriminatory practices, he took no executive action to ensure equal treatment. But on 29 June 1947, at an NAACP rally at the Lincoln Memorial, he told his audience that he believed the United States had reached a turning point in racial relations: "Every man should have the right to a decent home, the right to an education, the right to adequate medical care, the right to a worthwhile job, the right to an equal share in making the public decisions through the ballot, and the right to a fair trial in a fair court." The night before he spoke, he had written to his sister: "Mrs. Roosevelt has spent her public life stirring up trouble between whites and black[s]—and I'm in the middle. Mamma won't like what I say because I wind up by quoting old Abe. But I believe what I say and I'm hopeful we may implement it."[8]

The civil rights committee worked hard and well and reported to the president on 29 October 1947 in a document entitled *To Secure These Rights.* From this point on, civil rights moved to the forefront of the liberal reform agenda. The committee recommended establishment of a civil rights division in the Department of Justice, a permanent commission on civil rights, and a permanent fair employment practices commission. It urged Congress to strengthen existing civil rights statutes, pass an antilynching law, and provide new protection for voting rights. To move toward desegregation, the government must discontinue federal funding to private and public bodies that practiced discrimination, prohibit discrimination in private employment and in health services, and seek court action to end restrictive covenants in housing.

Truman faced a dilemma. The report was stronger than he had expected, yet he had portrayed the committee as sound and had promised action. He now had to respond to this aggressive agenda while trying to hold Southern Democrats behind him. On 9 December 1947 he told Clifford to formulate a civil rights program based on the report. By this time, Clifford and former Roosevelt aide James H. Rowe had written a long memorandum to Truman outlining an election strategy based on the assumption that he would run against Dewey and Wallace. To win, Truman should assume that the South would remain safely Democratic, and he should seek the votes of farmers, labor, blacks, and Jews.

As Truman prepared to make public his civil rights program on 2 February 1948, he noted in his diary that Congress would probably re ceive the message "coldly": "But it needs to be said." He placed the program in the context of the Truman Doctrine and pointed to the need to bring about change at home to justify American leadership of the free world and to reaffirm the American tradition of freedom and equality.) He called on Congress to establish a fair employment practices commission, a joint congressional committee on civil rights, and a commission on civil rights and to provide an additional assistant attorney general to head a new civil rights division within the Department of Justice. He endorsed strengthening and expanding existing civil rights statutes, passing antilynching legislation, and eliminating poll taxes. He did not take up the committee recommendations to move against segregation except in interstate transportation. He also promised an executive order to forbid discrimination in or by the federal government.

Truman misjudged southern reaction. The South had been fairly quiet on racial matters in 1945, but during 1946 many politicians had been warning that southern institutions were endangered by change within the Democratic party and by unionization drives in the South. Politicians nervously noted black political activity stirring even in the Deep South and cases challenging virtually every aspect of segregation moving through the court system. Although southern leaders had long concluded that Truman was not one of them, his 2 February 1948 message directly repudiated their values. A revolt began, led by South Carolina Governor J. Strom Thurmond, who four months earlier had called for Truman's nomination for president. Except for Claude Pepper of Florida, one of Truman's least favorite politicians, all southern congressmen, even those closest to the president, reacted negatively to the message.

Truman had intended to send an omnibus civil rights bill to Congress and to issue an executive order to end discrimination in the federal government. Now he backed away. Philleo Nash told historian Barton J. Bernstein that the strategy was deliberate: "To start with a bold measure and then temporize to pick up the right-wing forces. Simply stated, backtrack after the bang." At a press conference on 11 March, Truman said it was not a good idea for the executive branch to write bills for Congress. Actually he had already sent an omnibus bill to Senate Minority Leader Alben W. Barkley but now held it back; nor did he issue his promised executive order. In a June 1948 campaign warmup tour, he mentioned civil rights in only one of seventy-three speeches.

Truman had come to recognize the exploitation and humiliation blacks suffered, but other minority groups were not powerful enough to force him to confront seriously their conditions. His views toward women also remained those of the Victorian age. John Truman had instructed his sons that decent women were to be placed on a pedestal and were to be respected and defended by men. Vivian and Harry were to protect their sister, respect their mother, and exalt women generally. Harry wrote Bess that "the best man in the world is hardly good enough for any woman." He came to view women as the crucial force in shaping the American character and maintained that position until the end of his life: "Because the women in the set up under our program are those who maintain the morals of the community, and when you take them down off the pedestal and they become the common everyday street women—then we are gone, and I am not in favor of it. I want my women to be ideal, and they are."

This Victorian conception limited and imprisoned women. Truman's sister, Mary Jane, trapped by her family's expectations, watched her brothers marry and pursue careers while she stayed home to run the family farm and take care of their mother. She died embittered, as did many other women of her generation, by the thought that the boys had pursued their dreams while life passed her by. Early in Truman's presidency, Mary Jane wanted to go to a political meeting in Oklahoma. Truman's letter to her reveals much about his attitude toward women:

> It won't help me a bit for you to go to Oklahoma to a political meeting and it will give these columnists like Drew Pearson and the rest of the gossips a chance to say that my family, particularly the women of my family, are courting the limelight. So please don't go. . . .
>
> I want you and Mama to have everything I can possibly give you and I want to see you enjoy as many things as you desire but political appearances are not in the category of the enjoyments I anticipate for you.
>
> I have kept Bess and Margaret out of the political picture as much as I can and I am still trying to keep them from being talked about.

He reminded her: "You remember what awful places the Roosevelt relatives were in the habit of getting him tied up with." "Thank heaven," he wrote after receiving a letter from Eleanor Roosevelt, "there are no pants wearing women in my family."

Truman was not comfortable with women in politics. He refused to follow Roosevelt's example and appoint a woman to the cabinet; he believed their presence made discussion among males awkward. Truman was always courteous when Eleanor Roosevelt and others pressured him to appoint women to executive branch positions, but he never acted. Although India Edwards, the highest-placed woman in the Democratic National Committee, claimed that Truman had appointed more women to key posts than any other president, she could identify only about nineteen such appointments, and they were not in important policymaking positions. In a list of over one thousand of Truman's major appointments, only about thirty were female. He gave fewer than five of over two hundred high diplomatic positions to women.[10]

Although Truman overcame his racial prejudices enough to move the nation forward on civil rights, his sexism was so deeply ingrained that he could not seriously confront women's issues. The major feminist goal in the immediate postwar era was the equal rights amendment (ERA). Although as a senator he had endorsed ERA in a public letter to Democratic National Committee member Emma Guffey Miller, he did so in a way that reflected his chauvinistic conception of women's roles: "I have no fear of its effect on the home life of the American people. Nearly every man has his woman on a pedestal anyway and this will only make the legal aspects of the situation more satisfactory from the standpoint of the legal rights of the women of the country."

By 1946 the issue had became political dynamite, David Niles warned him, because many women's and labor organizations believed ERA would endanger legal gains already won. Truman did not publicly withdraw his endorsement of the proposed amendment—it was part of the Democratic platform—but he refused to support it actively. When Miller wrote him in 1950 seeking renewal of his support, he replied to her gracious and well-reasoned letter: "It has been my experience that there is no equality—men are just slaves and I suppose they will always continue to be." Miller regarded his reply as a "slap in the face," but she let the matter drop. Truman's admirers often dismissed lack of successful action on Fair Deal proposals by explaining that the president at least set the reform agenda for the future; however, Truman never found room on the agenda for equal rights for women.[11]

In the case of highly organized Zionist pressures to build a home for Jews in the Arab land of Palestine, Truman did take action, but with disastrous consequences for millions of people. He regarded the Palestinian problem as the most complex he faced and one of his major failures. Truman never entirely understood the human dimension of this issue. Westerners like Truman, blinded by "orientalism," developed the myth of arrested Arab development—of Arabs being the opposite of the Westerners in all respects, of Arab backwardness resulting from that people's own weaknesses. This orientalism prevented him from seeing the Arabs as fully human. In endorsing the British Balfour Declaration of 1917, which called for creation of a Jewish homeland, Truman said: "This promise, I felt, should be kept, just as all promises made by responsible, civilized governments should be kept." He ignored the promises that Great Britain and the United States had made to the Arabs. He wrote: "The Balfour Declaration, promising the Jews the opportunity to reestablish a homeland in Palestine, had always seemed to me to go hand in hand with the noble policies of Woodrow Wilson, especially the principle of self-determination." It seems not to have occurred to him that the principle of self-determination might have some implication for the Arabs, the majority population in Palestine. Using the reasoning that Americans used as they dispersed the Indians, Truman said the land of Palestine had been the scene of conflict since the age of Darius the Great, "and the pity of it is that the whole area is just waiting to be developed. And the Arabs have just never seemed to take any interest in developing. I have always thought that the Jews would, as of course, they have." The Arabs, under Jewish guidance, would have the benefit of Western-imposed ideas of Wilsonian self-determination, New Deal development projects, and Jeffersonian democracy.[12]

Truman inherited a problem that had been centuries in the making. The Romans had expelled the Jews from the land later called Palestine, leaving behind their Semite "cousins," later conquered by the Arabs. For centuries before World War I, the area was part of the Ottoman Empire, and the few remaining Jews lived peacefully with the majority Islamic population. In the late nineteenth century, as anti-Semitism erupted in Europe, Jewish leaders turned to Palestine as a haven for their people. They created the World Zionist Organization and called for Jewish immigration to Palestine.

After World War I, Great Britain took over the area as a League of Nations mandate. As Jewish migration to Palestine increased, especially with the rise of nazism, conflict between Arabs and Jews increased. When Germany began the extermination of the European Jewish population during World War II, Great Britain would not let the Jews into Palestine nor would the Roosevelt administration allow their mass migration into the United States. Many politicians, including 411 of the 535 members of Congress, began to back the Zionist demand for a Jewish commonwealth in Palestine. Arabs watched as Washington refused to lower barriers to Jewish immigration into the United States and instead expected the tiny country of Palestine to solve a problem not of its making.

With the end of the war, Truman pressed the British to admit 100,000 displaced European Jews into Palestine, but he refused to promise the British that Washington would help by supplying troops and money to deal with the disruption that would follow. He could not visualize the impact of his policy on the Arabs, and his White House advisers fed his ignorance. David Niles told him that he did not have to worry about hostile Arab reaction because the Arabs were practitioners of Mahatma Gandhi's philosophy of nonviolence.[13]

Most of Truman's diplomatic and military advisers warned him against caving in to Zionist pressures. Secretary of Defense Forrestal and others believed that the West needed Arab friendship because of Middle Eastern oil and strategic location. Truman tried to relieve domestic political strain by pushing for admission of displaced persons to Palestine while following his national security advisers' caution to protect strategic interests by not giving in to larger Zionist demands. As criticism mounted from both sides, Truman finally struck out in anger against alleged anti-semitism in the State Department and against Zionist pressures on him. He could not please the Jews, he angrily remarked in July 1946; "Jesus Christ couldn't please them when he was here on earth, so how could anyone expect that I would have any luck?"

The British, trying to buy time and force Truman to accept some responsibility for the consequences of his actions, proposed in October 1945 that the two nations create an Anglo-American Committee of Inquiry (AACI) to study the problem. Truman agreed, and in April 1946 the AACI recommended that the British allow 100,000 displaced Jews to enter Palestine at once, that the U.N. and the British prepare Palestine for independence as a binational democratic state, and that the Jewish and Arab communities determine future immigration policy. Truman endorsed the politically popular proposal for immediate admission of 100,000 people and ignored the rest of the report, which would have required some American responsibility for its implementation.

As conditions deteriorated in Palestine, the British, increasingly under attack and finding it difficult to maintain order, could not gain American help. Foreign Minister Ernest Bevin developed almost "pathological" bitterness toward Truman, one observer found, and in June 1946 asserted publicly that Americans wanted to put the Jews in Pales-

tine because they did not want them in New York. With the 1946 elections approaching, Truman, on Yom Kippur, a Jewish holy day, called for
immediate admission into Palestine of substantial numbers of immigrants
and went further by endorsing the idea of a Jewish state, an issue he had
previously tried to sidestep. Washington no longer had a coherent policy
on the Palestine problem; Truman's shifting positions confused even
insiders.[14]

In February 1947, Britain announced that it was turning the Palestine problem over to the United Nations to find a solution. That fall
a U.N. committee unanimously recommended making Palestine independent, with a majority of the committee recommending partition into
two states. Most Jewish spokesmen in the United States supported partition, and in October 1947 Washington officially endorsed that position. The White House put its client states under intense pressure, and
the United Nations voted for partition in November 1947. Washington,
despite its role in getting partition through the United Nations,
now refused to assume responsibility for its implementation. Disorder
mounted in Palestine, and by 18 January 1948, 720 people had been
killed. Britain finally refused to accept responsibility for implementing
partition, and on 16 February 1948 a U.N. commission announced it
could not establish order without substantial military force, which the
State Department and Defense Department opposed.

Another flip-flop was in order. State Department officials and Truman decided that partition was unworkable and threatened disorder that
endangered American security. In early March, Truman decided that
rather than partition, the United Nations should assume a trusteeship
over Palestine. Marshall told U.N. ambassador Warren Austin to announce the switch at the earliest appropriate time. On 18 March 1948,
Truman assured Zionist leader Chaim Weizmann that despite rumors to
the contrary, Washington firmly supported partition. The next day, Austin announced the change. The timing of Austin's speech surprised Truman and eliminated his opportunity to prepare Zionists. He subsequently
tried to blame the State Department for acting on its own and claimed
that policy really had not changed. Truman had, however, approved the
speech, and it was surely a change in the American position. As was
often the case, Truman could neither stand the heat nor get out of the
kitchen.

This reversal created turmoil in Palestine, in many world capitals,
and in the United Nations. Although it soon became apparent that trust-

eeship would take more troops to impose than partition, Washington refused to make commitments to help maintain order. With Britain withdrawing on 15 May, time was running out, and the United Nations was paralyzed.

Meanwhile, the 1948 election was approaching. Wallace challenged Truman on the left, and the Dixiecrats assailed him on the right. New York Governor Thomas E. Dewey, the leading candidate for the Republican nomination, was making a bid for the Jewish vote, which was concentrated in a few key states like New York. Party bosses in these states put pressure on Truman to placate the Zionists, who saw trusteeship as a step away from their goal of a Jewish state. Clifford, Niles, Connelly, and other White House aides pressed Truman to meet Zionist demands. In disgust, Secretary of State Marshall delegated Palestine matters to a subordinate because he said it was a domestic rather than an international problem.

With time running out and with Palestinian Jews preparing to proclaim a Jewish state when the British left on 15 May, Clifford pushed Truman to recognize the new government. After an explosive meeting with Marshall and other officials, Truman agreed to recognize the new state and did so a few minutes after Jewish leaders proclaimed the existence of Israel. This reversal of policy shook the United Nations but steadied many Democratic politicians. [15]

Truman's inability to develop a consistent policy prevented the United Nations and other bodies from devising plans to deal with the crisis. Washington's paralysis stifled everyone else. War followed the proclamation of Israeli independence; peace, such as it was, was finally established by force of arms.

Truman's political sensitivity to black and Jewish voters did not seem to be enough to bring him success as the 1948 election year opened. In January 1948, only 28 percent of the voters said they would favor Truman in an election against Dewey. Such polls obscured Truman's strengths. White House politicos believed that his natural strategy for 1948, which fit his self-conception, in any case, was to project himself as a battling protector of the common man. He should concentrate on holding black, labor, and farm votes and focus his attack on the Republican record in the Eightieth Congress, which was vulnerable on issues important to these groups. Truman's tough foreign policy fit the growing anti-Communist mood of the public, fed by the Spring Crisis and the Berlin blockade. The Democratic party was the majority party, and the

New Deal reforms remained popular. The country was prosperous and stable. Thus Truman had a solid foundation for his campaign.

Despite these underlying strengths, through most of 1948 only Truman's weaknesses seemed visible. Although most liberals, who now had signed on for the cold war, did not follow Wallace out of the Democratic party, they still deplored Truman's lack of style and often seemed more aware of his fainthearted actions than his courageous stands. Many searched for a replacement. Some favored Supreme Court Justice William O. Douglas, but he would not agree to challenge Truman, nor would Dwight Eisenhower, the popular general who enchanted many liberals in 1948. By the time of the Democratic convention, liberals had only Truman.

Still, the president faced revolt from the conservative wing of his party. Despite his caution, the civil rights issue exploded again at the Democratic convention in July. Party leaders tried to find a way to meet black demands without driving out the southerners, but the convention accepted a strong civil rights plank. Although most southerners stayed, voting for Georgia Senator Richard B. Russell for the nomination, those who bolted, the Dixiecrats, met to nominate South Carolina Governor J. Strom Thurmond for president and Mississippi Governor Fielding L. Wright for vice president.[16]

At the convention in Philadelphia, Truman had to wait until the last minute to find a vice-presidential nominee. Douglas refused to join the ticket as the vice-presidential candidate because, Truman heard, he did not want to be a "number two man to a number two man." He belonged to the "crackpot" crowd anyway, Truman wrote, and added: "No professional liberal is intellectually honest." Truman accepted Alben W. Barkley as running mate after the popular senator from Kentucky gave a rousing keynote address. Barkley was an old friend and had strong ties with Southern Democrats.

After party regulars delivered the nomination to him, Truman appeared at 2 A.M. on 15 July in a hot, stuffy convention hall, facing several thousand tired, dispirited Democrats. He brought them to their feet by proclaiming: "Senator Barkley and I will win this election and make these Republicans like it—don't you forget that!" He quickly listed the benefits farmers and workers had received from the Democrats, attacked the Republican record, and announced that he was calling the Eightieth Congress into special session to meet on July 26 in order to give the opposition a chance to make good on their platform promises without waiting until 1949. To demonstrate his own willingness to act, he waited until the convention ended and issued two executive orders on civil rights, one setting up a mechanism within the executive branch to handle complaints on discrimination and the other calling for an end to discrimination within the armed forces.[17]

The romantic image of Truman's waging a one-man battle in the 1948 campaign is misleading. It overlooked the strong support he had from an able White House staff, from the regular Democratic party machinery, and from many executive branch officials, like Secretary of Labor Maurice Tobin who made 150 campaign speeches. Dewey also had liabilities. He had been an effective governor of New York, but he seemed cold and aloof to many. He could not attack Truman's foreign policy, both because he approved of it and because major parts of it had been passed by the Republican Congress. His views on domestic policy were similar to Truman's, but he was tied to a Congress that Truman hammered at day by day for being a do-nothing body that betrayed the common man. The special session accomplished little, further underscoring the president's message.

Truman campaigned hard in the face of constant predictions from experts that he had no chance. He traveled 31,700 miles, giving 356 speeches, most of them during whistle-stops from the back of a train as it paused a few minutes in small towns. He went on week after weary week. Only 10 percent of the nation's daily newspapers supported him. Experts were soon debating the makeup of Dewey's cabinet; many bureaucrats opened communications with the Republican camp, hoping to find a place in the new administration, and all major polls predicted Dewey's victory. But unnoticed by most observers, Truman's crowds were huge and growing. In his speeches, to shouts of "Give 'em hell, Harry," he flayed the Republican Congress and stressed the Roosevelt-Truman record of working to help the common people.

Meanwhile, the Dixiecrat movement fizzled since most southerners found it difficult to break with the regular party. The Wallace campaign on the Progressive party ticket also fell apart. Wallace tried to provoke a serious discussion of the need for extension of New Deal reforms and of the merits of the containment policy, but blacks and Jews responded to Truman's initiatives on civil rights and Palestine. Labor, now purging leftists from its own ranks, also abandoned Wallace. Cold war liberals engaged in unrestrained Red-baiting. Many liberals of the sort who belonged to the Americans for Democratic Action attacked Wallace so thoroughly on the Communist issue that the Democrats had to do little of the dirty work themselves. Truman, however, did not keep his hands clean. After warning reporters to watch for an interpolation in a speech on 17 March 1948, he told his audience: "I do not want and I will not accept the political support of Henry Wallace and his Communists. If joining them or permitting them to join me is the price of victory, I recommend defeat. These are days of high prices for everything, but any price for Wallace and his Communists is too much for me to pay. I'm not buying." Such Red-baiting, along with events like the coup in Czechoslovakia and the Berlin blockade, buried Wallace and the last major postwar attempt to raise fundamental questions from the left about the direction Truman was taking in foreign and domestic policy.

On 2 November, election day, Truman went to a small resort outside Kansas City to be alone. After sleeping soundly that night, he awakened to find that he had won. The final popular vote was 24,105,695 to 21,969,170. Truman lost New York, because of the Wallace vote, and lost four usually Democratic southern states; however, he carried other key states, including Ohio and California. He held the Far West and the farm states in the Middle West. Still, neither Truman nor Dewey excited the public. Only 51.1 percent of the people voted, and Truman won with 49.5 percent of the vote.[18]

The president and many of his supporters had anticipated a new surge in reform after the 1948 election, but the election taught politicians that straying from the center was dangerous. It validated Truman's cold war foreign policy and endorsed the status quo in domestic programs, with advances in such fields as civil rights as were politically required and acceptable. Voters backed the existing New Deal agencies, but Truman had not built support for extensive additions to the reform agenda.

8

THE NATIONAL SECURITY
STATE IN ACTION

In the spring of 1948, Truman complained to his staff that the whole government had "gone warlike." The armed forces pushed the White House for more men and money as the Pentagon struggled to match with military power the global responsibilities that civilian policymakers were assuming. In 1949 and 1950, Truman joined the warriors and began to accommodate the demands of military leaders. The Korean War, coming in mid-1950, was the crucial episode that allowed the administration to implement a rearmament program.[1]

By 1949, Washington and Moscow had constructed mirror images that they used in explaining and predicting the actions of the other. American leaders saw the Soviet Union as an empire bent on fostering world revolution as an instrument of global domination. Truman and most other Americans saw themselves differently. They believed their nation was democratic and humane and that it reluctantly entered world politics not to build spheres of influence or to exploit other people but to help itself and the rest of the world achieve peace, prosperity, and freedom. Truman believed this. He also found that division of the world into a bloc of good nations confronting a sphere of evil ones had a practical benefit in mobilizing public support for the administration's foreign policy and made the American people willing to assume new burdens of international responsibility that resulted in heavy taxes, physical danger, and the erosion of many of their domestic traditions.

Kremlin leaders, on the other hand, believed that their government had been surrounded since 1917 by hostile powers bent on its destruction. Stalin watched the Red army melt away after the war, to fewer than three million soldiers in 1948, while Washington mounted a propaganda campaign against the Soviet Union in Eastern Europe, established a military role in Greece, Turkey, Iran, Saudi Arabia, and Japan, constructed NATO, established scores of bases near the Soviet border, and tried to maintain its atomic monopoly. While the Soviet economy was in shambles, the United States entered a long period of unchallenged economic supremacy. Stalin heard Washington officials proclaim their allegiance to the open door as a necessary foundation for world peace and prosperity yet make exceptions for American protected interests, watched Washington use international bodies like the United Nations to serve American global hegemony while destroying or withdrawing from international bodies that could not be so used, and saw Truman condemn spheres of influence while tightening Washington's control over the Western Hemisphere and the Pacific.

Both Americans and Soviets constructed fearful images of the other, which were partly true. Both took actions to guard against the danger they saw; these actions seemed offensive rather than defensive to the other and fleshed out the image they were forming.[2]

Many memories of Truman focus only on his feisty, blunt personality or on dramatic events such as his ordering the atomic bomb dropped on Japan or intervening in the Korean civil war. Truman also led the nation as it prepared itself less sensationally to endure the permanent quasi-war status it entered in the postwar period. Under his leadership, Congress created a modern defense structure, the administration formulated economic concepts that allowed permanent huge military budgets, American and allied leaders accepted the idea of collective security, and the armed forces developed new technologies and strategies. The nation prepared to enter the age of guided missiles carrying hydrogen bombs as Truman left office. These changes affected the United States politically, socially, and intellectually and transformed its diplomatic, military, and economic structure. These results, not pithy aphorisms and dramatic decisions, were Truman's true legacy.

Despite the historic transformation involved as he constructed the national security state, Truman accomplished his task with relative ease.

The president's policies largely coincided with the views of leaders in Congress, business and labor, the media, universities, and the military and diplomatic corps and received bipartisan support because they fit the conceptions of such Republican leaders as Thomas Dewey, John Foster Dulles, and Dwight Eisenhower.

As the nation entered the postwar era, many were concerned that American military power seemed to be disintegrating; the military forces fell from over 12 million people in 1945 to fewer than 1.6 million by mid-1947. The military budget fell from over 37 percent of gross national product to less than 5 percent in fiscal year 1948. Yet this postwar low point still left the American military four times its prewar size, with the strongest navy and air force in the world, and with a monopoly on nuclear weapons.

Not only did the publicity over the declining state of military power ignore its huge size compared to America's historic peacetime posture, but government officials and the press also magnified Soviet military power. The Soviets demobilized as rapidly as the Americans in order to concentrate their resources on economic recovery. In 1948, the Soviet military force had slightly fewer than 2.9 million personnel, only enough, given its huge landmass, to maintain minimum defense and occupation chores. Yet American military planners grossly inflated the size of the Soviet military organization—saying it had a minimum of four million men—to persuade Congress to increase the U.S. budget.[3]

Truman wanted to use the military budget more efficiently by unifying the armed forces. Beginning in 1947, as the contours of the national security state emerged, the whole nation would have to be placed on permanent quasi-war footing. Truman and most army leaders supported merging the armed forces into a tightly unified department of defense. The navy, fearing that it would be eclipsed by the air force and its long-range bombers, opposed drastic change and finally forced a compromise. Truman signed the National Security Act in late July 1947. The act created the National Military Establishment (NME) headed by a secretary of defense with little more than coordination authority over three separate Departments of Navy, Army, and Air Force, each with its own cabinet-level secretary. It must have amused Truman to appoint James Forrestal the first secretary of defense, with responsibility to administer this organizational nightmare. Forrestal, as secretary of navy, had worked for a weak central authority.

Many believed it was the hard-working, duty-driven Forrestal's attempt to bring order to the NME that broke his confidence and drove him to suicide in May 1949, a few months after he left office. During Forrestal's term, budgets remained tight while the political leaders assumed more and more global responsibilities requiring military backing. Forrestal, who had been a major figure in shaping early cold war thinking, was pulled into the morass of the defense establishment. Truman came to see him as weak and indecisive. He wrote in his diary: "Forestal [sic] can't take it."

Forrestal soon recognized that he needed more authority and recommended further unification. Truman agreed and in August 1949 signed a bill creating the Department of Defense. It left the military establishment in a holding-company form of organization with separate military services but increased the authority of the secretary of defense to direct, not just coordinate, them. This came too late to help Forrestal, but it was a major step toward Truman's original goal.

Truman replaced Forrestal with Louis Johnson, former assistant secretary of war and national commander of the American Legion. Johnson proved to be a tough leader and probably as good an administrator as one could be in the Department of Defense in that turbulent period of transition. He cracked heads and beat down a revolt of the admirals to carry out Truman's policy. But he was undiplomatic, overtly ambitious, and a ferocious battler over turf. He made war on Acheson so intensely that it sometimes paralyzed cooperative relations between the departments. His enemies multiplied.

Johnson held the budget in line, following Truman's policy. When young, poorly trained and equipped American men died by the hundreds in the early days of the Korean War and criticism mounted over American unpreparedness, Truman let the buck stop with Johnson; the secretary of defense became the scapegoat for White House policy. In September 1950, Truman forced the weeping Johnson to resign, and his tough, ambitious lieutenant loyally went quietly into oblivion. "The blow was hard," he later wrote Truman, "harder than you can realize— and the going has been rough, at times it has seemed almost too much." Truman turned once again to George Marshall, who returned to public service as secretary of defense even as the Korean War broke the budget caps and eased conflict among the services.[4]

In the minds of civilian leaders, caps on military spending seemed reasonable because behind the conventional military force lay the atomic bomb. After destroying Hiroshima and Nagasaki, Washington had put forward the Baruch plan for international control of the weapons and at the same time initiated a program for domestic development of nuclear energy. In a message to Congress on 3 October 1945, Truman asked for legislation to create an atomic energy commission to control nuclear research and development, raw materials, and plants. Despite resistance from the military, Truman on 1 August 1946 signed the Atomic Energy Act incorporating most of his recommendations and establishing the Atomic Energy Commission (AEC), a major achievement of Truman's administration. Although the AEC was under civilian control, over the next few years, those who directed it found its activities geared to military needs. The nation made little progress under Truman toward peaceful uses of atomic energy. With Truman's knowledge, the military committed such abuses as testing atomic bombs in Nevada without warning people of the danger to which they were exposed.

The great powers made no progress toward international control either. Stalin, it was said, met with Soviet atomic scientists the day after Hiroshima and told them to catch up to the American nuclear program regardless of cost. Truman issued orders that the United States must stay ahead. In February 1949, Truman told David Lilienthal, the chair of the AEC, that nuclear weapons were "the mainstay" and only they had kept the Soviets from taking all of Europe.[5]

All of Truman's strategic thinking was shattered on 21 September 1949 when he learned that the Soviets had exploded an atomic bomb. With his contempt for Soviet technological capability, he considered it a "phony" that could not knock down the White House, but the matter was potentially too serious to ignore. His military and scientific leaders concluded that the American monopoly was broken, and on 23 September Truman announced that an atomic explosion had occurred in the Soviet Union.

Military planners, some scientists, and a few congressmen had already been pressing to speed up the nuclear program, and now they pushed Truman to leap ahead of the Soviets by developing the "super" or hydrogen bomb. On 30 October 1949, the AEC's general advisory committee, chaired by Robert Oppenheimer, voted against such development. The hydrogen bomb was in a different category of danger from the atomic bomb, it said, without any inherent limits to its power. Lilienthal agreed that the H-bomb would create an even more dangerous arms race and on 9 November 1949 reported to Truman that the AEC by a three-to-two vote opposed developing the new weapons.

Truman then set up a committee composed of Acheson, Louis Johnson, and Lilienthal to make a recommendation to him. There were alternatives, such as international controls, but Truman had not seriously pursued that option since he had ordered the destruction of Hiroshima and Nagasaki. Truman's decision to develop the H-bomb probably was inevitable given his assumptions. He believed that the Soviets were bent on destroying the United States and that only superior power would prevent it. He also accepted the theory that the H-bomb would be a bargaining chip in dealing with the Soviets, an insidious theory that resulted in self-generated escalation of the arms race. By the time the Acheson committee recommended that the president initiate a program to determine the bomb's feasibility, Truman had already decided to do so and in March 1950 ordered a crash program for its development. The United States exploded its first thermonuclear device in November 1952, the Soviets in August 1953.[6]

Dean Acheson said that ten seconds after Truman heard about the Soviet A-bomb test, despite his contempt for their technology, the president realized "it changed everything." From this realization came NSC-68, a fundamental policy statement that summarized and clarified American cold war objectives, promoted American rearmament, and provided parameters for American thought and action toward the Soviet Union for years in the future. Forrestal believed that American security needs should determine military budgets; Truman had counted on the A-bomb monopoly to offset the budget limitations. What he realized in a few seconds was that his strategic assumptions had been shattered.

NSC-68 said that Washington confronted a challenge that involved not just the potential destruction of the United States but of civilization itself. The purpose of the United States was to further democracy, freedom, and dignity of the individual. The Kremlin's purpose was to build absolute power by destroying on a global scale non-Communist governments and replacing them with Kremlin-controlled satellites. The United States was the main society slated to be destroyed as the Soviet Union conspired to dominate the world. The Kremlin already had military power to overrun Western Europe, even if it were defended by American nuclear arms, to threaten oil fields in the Middle East, and to attack with atomic weapons Britain, Canada, and the United States.

Negotiations were meaningless, NSC-68 authors said, because the Soviet Union would not change. But to satisfy world opinion, Washington must enter into negotiations in such a way as to place failure to achieve disarmament and other goals on the Kremlin. The United States and the West must rebuild the free world's military and economic power.

The United States must be strong enough to deter war or, failing that, to survive an attack and have second-strike winning capability. The survival of the non-Communist bloc depended on the United States.

NSC-68 exuded cynicism and overstatement, but the Truman Doctrine had prepared the American people to accept this approach. The document itself remained classified until 1975, but Acheson and others spread its essential message. Keynesian economics showed these policymakers a way to raise American military budgets from the $13 billion range Truman had insisted on to the $50 billion or more envisioned by NSC-68. Government military spending would expand the economy, and that expansion would pay for more arms. NSC-68 also shifted fundamental assumptions about the nature of containment. Kennan had regarded containment as limited to the protection of strong points, the vital industrial centers of the world. NSC-68 shifted from strong point defense to perimeter defense; any Soviet move anywhere was a challenge and threat to American interests. This new conception of containment meant that the Soviets would now determine America's vital interests. Threats were also not just physical but psychological. Even if an area like Korea had no geopolitical relevance to Washington, a Soviet challenge would test American will. This thinking "rendered all interests vital, all means affordable, all methods justifiable."[7]

Asia was both the source of much cold war thought and its implementation zone. American leaders tried to maintain their focus on Europe, but events in the Far East kept intruding and finally became controlling. Although Washington had previously viewed most of the Far East as peripheral to its interests, it, reflecting the assumptions behind NSC-68, now began to regard nations there as vital interests requiring military commitment.

Events in China shaped Washington's thinking about the Far East. Since 1947, most American leaders believed that Chiang Kai-shek and his nationalist government was doomed. Truman, however, failed to educate the American people about the realities of the situation. They were stunned when in December 1949 Chiang and many of his supporters fled to the Chinese island of Taiwan, and Mao Tse-tung's Communist forces consolidated their hold over the mainland.

Within the United States, the Truman administration had successfully established a bipartisan foreign policy, built ideologically on the Truman Doctrine and programmatically on the Marshall Plan and NATO, but that bipartisan relationship had not extended as clearly to the Far East as to Europe. Acheson hoped that as the dust settled from the fall of China, Washington could recognize Mao's government and establish some sort of acceptable relationship with it, perhaps hastening the break, predicted by many experts, between Mao and Stalin. As it turned out, Acheson had to move too slowly. McCarthyism was growing, and Republicans found the "soft on communism" charge an enticing weapon to use against the administration. Truman, too, had to be educated. While discussing the Communist takeover of China, he told his cabinet on 19 January 1949: "We can't be in a position of making any deal with a Communist regime." The Truman Doctrine had trapped its promulgator. He was too cautious, too indecisive, and too complacent. By the end of 1950, China and the United States were at war with one another, and Truman would not consider dealing with the "thugs and murderers" in Beijing. After the blundering policy of the Truman administration, it took twenty-five years to normalize relations with China.[8]

Fast on the heels of Chiang's fall, the Korean War nearly brought about the collapse of the Truman presidency, clarified and hardened cold war thinking and policies, and reduced alternatives for dealing with the Soviets and Chinese. It allowed a massive rearmament program and encouraged opposition to a Communist takeover of Vietnam.

The Koreans, whose nation had been annexed by Japan in 1910, expected freedom with Tokyo's defeat in World War II. Instead they found themselves cold war pawns, with Washington and Moscow often speaking in the name of the Korean people but having little regard for their self-determination. Roosevelt moved to carve out an American role in Korea by proposing a four-power trusteeship, with Korea to become independent "in due course." The allies agreed on the trusteeship idea, and, in an offhand way, without settling the details, they agreed that the Soviets would accept the Japanese surrender above the thirty-eighth parallel and the Americans below.

The Korean economy had been characterized by peasant agriculture, with most land in the hands of landlords. When Japan colonized Korea, it began slowly to build a market economy, pulling about 10 percent of the peasants into industry. At the end of the war, the masses were ready to carry through extensive social reform, including land redistribution, to win some of the benefits of modernization. To keep order following the Japanese surrender, Korean nationalist leaders formed the Committee for the Preparation of Korean Independence, which on 6 September 1945 proclaimed the Korean People's Republic (KPR). The KPR coalition was composed of nationalist leaders on both the Left and Right. Many were Communists but were also Korean nationalists, with no wish to be directed by Moscow or any other foreign body. The KPR leaders promised extensive reform, including giving all citizens over eighteen the right to vote, nationalizing major industries, redistributing land, and opposing foreign interference in Korean affairs. KPR units spread through Korea, kept order, fed the people, and built mass organizations. Meanwhile, many on the Right, emboldened by news of the coming American occupation, built their own party, the Korean Democratic party (KDP). KPR existed through mass support, while KDP had to be propped up by the Americans.[9]

By the time the war started in June 1950, 100,000 Koreans had already been killed as factions warred over Korean reconstruction. The United States entered this civil conflict blindly, assuming that it could bring freedom to the Koreans. Truman's representatives in the occupation forces were military copies of himself, totally self-assured in their view of the world and in their assumption of the moral right to lead people they considered less civilized than themselves. The occupation leader was General John R. Hodge, who had the reputation for being an excellent soldier but who had no special training for occupation duty. He started with the assumption that the Koreans were the enemy, saying "Koreans are the same breed of cats as Japanese." When he landed at Inchon, the Japanese guards, still armed, fired on and killed several of the Koreans who gathered to greet their liberators. Hodge then praised the Japanese for maintaining order.

Hodge instinctively regarded reform agitation and social strife as the work of Communists, and he and his advisers increasingly turned for advice to conservative elements, who were more likely to lead a life-style familiar to Americans. He responded positively when they told him Korea needed order but he could not understand that Korean masses wanted radical change. By the end of 1945, Hodge was already basing his reports to Washington on cold war assumptions not fully acceptable yet among his superiors. He turned more and more to the conservative leader, Syngman Rhee, who had lived in the United States since 1910. He accepted Rhee's leadership reluctantly because even Hodge could see that Rhee did not fit Korea's needs, nor was he easily controlled.

Until the spring of 1950, Washington had not seen Korea as vitally important. Military planners said it had no strategic value to the United States. But within the context of the deepening cold war, Washington's view changed because control of the peninsula became a test of will with the Soviets. When the trusteeship arrangement stalemated, Washington, keeping up its propaganda barrage against Moscow, placed the matter before the United Nations, which damaged its prestige by meekly becoming part of the American campaign. The United Nations held elections in South Korea in July 1948, and Rhee was elected president. The North Koreans established the Democratic People's Republic of Korea that fall, and the Kremlin withdrew Soviet troops. The United States stayed on to strengthen South Korea and finally withdrew its troops in June 1949, although many believed Rhee's government, increasingly unpopular, could not survive.

Kim Il Sung, a young guerrilla leader in the war against Japan, took control of North Korea. He led his nation through the social revolution that all of Korea had been moving toward when the Americans intervened. The North Koreans established their own mix of communism and nationalism, and most North Koreans gained what liberation had promised. Kim had Stalin's backing, but he developed charismatic ties with his people, minimizing Moscow's need to interfere, while Rhee had to be propped up by the Americans. Both Kim and Rhee were dictators, but Kim had the support of his people; Rhee relied on the support of the United States.

In the early morning of 25 June 1950, Korean time (about 3 P.M., 24 June, Washington time), the North Koreans attacked across the thirty-eighth parallel, driving toward Seoul, the South Korean capital. Reasons for the timing of the action are still unclear. Republicans soon flayed Acheson for a speech he gave on 12 January 1950 in which he traced the American "defensive perimeter" and left out Korea. This supposedly signaled Moscow, whom Americans assumed ordered the attack, that Korea would be an easy conquest on its road to world domination. Actually Acheson had said that the United States would fight to counter aggression within the perimeter, while areas outside would rely first on their own resources and then on U.N. support. Acheson's speech aside, both Rhee and Kim intended to try to unify the peninsula, and Kim moved first. According to Nikita Khrushchev, Stalin gave Kim reluctant approval for the attack, acquiescing in the plan of a fellow Communist leader to extend communism to his countrymen. Kim evidently believed that Rhee's government would fall almost at once, before the United States could intervene. [10]

While Truman regarded his decision to intervene in Korea as the toughest and most important one he made as president, his previous activity and his view of world relations actually left him little to decide.

The "loss" of South Korea, following the Communist takeover in China, would, Truman believed, weaken American allies in Japan and Vietnam, as well as other parts of Asia, and might undermine the credibility of the newly established NATO. Although Truman often said he had to intervene in Korea to avoid undermining the United Nations, he told Acheson that the United States would have intervened unilaterally if the United Nations had not acted.

Truman's thoughts were influenced by analogies he made with events in the 1930s. He assumed that Kim acted on the orders of Stalin. The West, he believed, faced another Munich. He wrote Vandenberg: "The present Russian feeler in Korea is an exact imitation of Japan in Manchuria; Hitler in the Rhineland and Mussolini in Ethiopia." If Truman did not act, World War III would inevitably occur. In a logic that made sense to Truman, he had to go to war to maintain peace.[11]

At 9:26 P.M. on 24 June 1950, a Saturday evening, while Truman was at home in Independence, the Department of State received word of the attack from Ambassador John J. Muccio. Officials began to collect at the State Department and Pentagon, and those at State immediately decided that the United Nations must intervene. Acheson, notified at his home, agreed and then called Truman who approved, as did U.N. Secretary-General Trygve Lie. The South Korean government prepared to evacuate Seoul, while General Douglas MacArthur had already decided on his own to send ammunition and other supplies to Rhee. State and Pentagon officials worked all night and then continued on Sunday gathering information and formulating responses to present to Truman. That afternoon, with the Soviet Union representative boycotting meetings in protest over another issue, the U.N. Security Council approved a resolution that said that the attack was a breach of peace and called on North Korea to withdraw.

Truman returned to Washington on Sunday afternoon. As he left from the Kansas City airport, an aide remarked: "The boss is going to hit those fellows hard." Truman radioed ahead asking his top military and diplomatic advisers to meet with him at Blair House. Truman, assuming enormous power as commander in chief, made decisions during the next few days that resulted in the death of many people and that had long-term consequences for the entire world, including the potential for global war. He made these decisions in consultation with a small group of State and Defense Department figures, usually from five to fifteen men, during the first week. Truman did not seek advice from congressional leaders, nor did he bring into the meetings any of his own White House staff. He made decisions rapidly, delaying only to allow the situation to clarify, not to consult more widely or to consider alternatives to military intervention. Acheson took pride in the fact that no one raised the possibility of not intervening.

When Truman's plane landed in Washington, he told Acheson and others who met him: "By God, . . . I am going to let them have it." Later at Blair House Philip C. Jessup heard him muttering: "We can't let the UN down!" Thus the commander in chief set a framework for his advisers that narrowed options rather than encouraging them to challenge his assumptions. Truman silenced Under Secretary of State James Webb who told him before the meeting not to act too rapidly and later suggested that they discuss the political aspects of the situation. Truman decided, based on Acheson's suggestions, to authorize sending supplies to Korea, to send in a survey group, to move elements of the fleet to the area, and to use air and naval power to cover evacuation: "We would wait for further action until the UN order is flouted," he said. Several Pentagon officials, while approving of resistance to aggression, warned of the difficulties of sending ground troops onto the Asian mainland.[12]

On Monday 26 June, Truman received word that Rhee had fled Seoul, and Muccio said that the military situation was disintegrating so quickly he was not sure that all Americans could get out. At 9 P.M., Truman met again at Blair House with the same group. He now lifted restrictions on American air and naval strikes south of the thirty-eighth parallel. He took a step into the Vietnamese quicksand by agreeing to increase aid to Indochina and to send a military mission there. He agreed to move the Seventh Fleet to a position between Taiwan and the mainland to prevent the Chinese from taking that island, which Chiang's forces occupied. Although Truman believed that Taiwan legitimately belonged to China, this move tied the United States in a continuing relationship with Chiang and added a new point of contention that fueled Chinese-American conflict for decades. On 27 June, the Security Council, again with the Soviet delegation absent, voted to aid South Korea to repel the attack and to restore "international peace and security in the area."

Although the State Department controlled the initial responses to the North Korean attack, by mid-week, MacArthur was taking the lead. On Friday 30 June, Truman authorized MacArthur to utilize all the troops under his command. Truman, who prided himself on his knowledge of military history, had committed U.S. troops to land war in Asia, violating a basic American military doctrine.

Truman made another fateful decision when he refused Webb's suggestion that they discuss political matters at the first Blair House meeting. He rejected all suggestions to go to Congress for a resolution of support. Truman, setting the pattern of postwar executive arrogance, believed that presidential power, on which, in his view, survival of the nation depended, was at stake. Instead he followed the advice of those who said that such a request, even if approved by Congress, would create a debate and reveal division within the government. But as early as 28 June, Senator Robert Taft began to raise questions, suggesting that Washington's bungling had led to the war and doubting Truman's legal grounds for intervening without congressional approval.[13]

Decisions arrived at in the pleasant, calm atmosphere of Blair House, following dinners with fellow "movers and shakers" of history, thrust American soldiers into a bloody nightmare. The first U.S. troops landed in Korea on 1 July. Americans there and at home expected the Asian peasants to flee in terror when they realized they were fighting soldiers from the mightiest nation in the world. The American troops were told to stop the North Korean offensive as far north as possible of Pusan, at the tip of the peninsula. On 5 July, the 540-person initial force saw action and hardly slowed the North Korean sweep; scores of Americans were killed and many fled, abandoning their wounded. Week followed disastrous week as hundreds of poorly trained, poorly equipped Americans died as symbols to Asia that Washington would keep its cold war commitment.

By the end of July, the Americans and South Koreans had established a defensive perimeter around Pusan, fighting with their backs to the sea to keep from being pushed off the peninsula. Despite the initial power of its offensive, the North Korean attack slowed as its supply lines extended, becoming more vulnerable to air attack, while American men and material poured into Pusan. By the fall of 1950, MacArthur had eight American divisions and several regimental combat teams in Korea, commanded there by General Walton Walker.

During July, Truman put the nation on a war basis; he brought four national guard units into federal service and expanded the draft. The United Nations asked the United States to name a U.N. commander of the forces in Korea, and Truman appointed MacArthur, although at age seventy the general was well past retirement age and was fully occupied in Japan. Fifteen nations eventually sent troops but not enough to affect the war dramatically. It was a U.S. operation directed from Washington, behind a U.N. front.

On 15 September, MacArthur, ignoring the doubts of many military colleagues, successfully carried out an amphibious landing at Inchon, behind North Korean lines. North Korean troops, tired and battered from pounding by American air power, scrambled back up the peninsula to avoid being cut off. The North Korean army disintegrated as the American and South Korean offensive pushed out from the Inchon and the Pusan areas. Truman's confidence grew, strengthened when, a few days after Inchon, he fired Louis Johnson and brought George Marshall in as secretary of defense. Truman believed that the difficult part of the war was over.[14]

Within days of the Inchon landing, those North Korean forces not killed or captured retreated from South Korea; U.N. forces "liberated" Seoul before the end of the month. Truman now confronted probably the most fateful decision of his presidency: should U.N. troops stop at the thirty-eighth parallel, on the grounds that they had achieved their aim of restoring peace, or should they cross the parallel to unify Korea by force? Debate started before Inchon. On 21 August, George Kennan told Acheson that American goals in Korea were not clear, that the nation was engaged in an emotional and moralistic crusade, that MacArthur was not being kept under control by Washington, and that American policy tightened rather than loosened ties between China and the Soviet Union. He believed the proper solution would be to leave Korea as nominally independent, with the Soviet Union as the dominant influence, to be replaced someday by Japan. He saw American policy in Asia pushing the nation toward disaster.

The CIA and the State Department Policy Planning staff also pointed out the dangers of crossing the parallel, but MacArthur had no doubts about the proper course. He had great contempt for those "asses in Washington" and had pushed his authority to the limits and beyond. While American and South Korean forces were still retreating in early July, MacArthur was already discussing with visiting superiors his plans to destroy the North Korean army and unify Korea. Yet while Truman's defenders often made the general the scapegoat for mistakes in Korea, it was not MacArthur's decision to cross the thirty-eighth parallel, nor was it his fault that the decision brought disaster. Truman was commander in chief; he made the decisions. If MacArthur had been exceeding his authority since 24 June, Truman knew it and did not stop it. MacArthur scoffed at warnings that the Chinese might enter the war, but it was

Truman who had access to intelligence sources on a global basis, including many warnings that the Chinese would enter.

Truman said that after the North Korean attack, he never had anything else in mind but unification of Korea. He was a Wilsonian who felt a moral imperative to help the Koreans achieve unification under benevolent American guidance while upholding the authority of the United Nations. Truman viewed Inchon as another brilliant performance by an extraordinary military leader; MacArthur seemed unstoppable. Why not seize the opportunity to roll back the Soviet empire? Truman's aggressive mood was enhanced by the moderate tone of the Kremlin through these months. Moscow put out peace feelers in August, and Soviet moderation emboldened Truman, already enticed by the prospect of a brilliant coup. From the perspective of a public conditioned by the Truman Doctrine, even containment seemed weak, but a rollback would be viewed as daring and strong. In addition, many Americans had died by October 1950; if Truman had stopped at the thirty-eighth parallel, not punishing the North Koreans further, the political uproar generated by the fall of China and by McCarthyism, would have intensified manyfold. Harriman said: "It would have taken a superhuman effort to say no. Psychologically, it was almost impossible not to go ahead and complete the job."[15]

On 9 September, the administration, in NSC-81/1, said that the U.N. goal was Korean independence and unity and that this was in the national interest of the United States unless it provoked a general war. NSC-81/1 recommended allowing MacArthur to begin a rollback of Korean forces north of the thirty-eighth parallel if there was no "major" Soviet or Chinese intervention. On 27 September, Truman approved orders to MacArthur, implementing NSC-81/1. After sending South Korean units across the parallel, MacArthur began his full-scale invasion on 9 October. The North Korean army began to collapse within a few days, and U.N. forces took Pyongyang, the North Korean capital.

On 15 October Truman took some advisers and thirty-eight journalists and traveled to Wake Island in the middle of the Pacific to meet MacArthur and reap the political benefits of reflected glory. Ambassador Muccio, traveling with MacArthur, found the general "mad as hell" for being used politically, but both the president and the general judged the conference beneficial when it was over. Truman's later stories about MacArthur's trying to make the president's plane land first were figments of his imagination. During the conference, MacArthur said he hoped to withdraw the Eighth Army by Christmas. He discounted the probability of Chinese intervention but did not flatly assert that it could not happen.

Most of the conference was spent planning for the expected North Korean surrender. Despite the thousands of miles Truman and MacArthur traveled, the conference lasted only a few hours, and MacArthur left before lunch. There was ample time for press coverage, and so Truman's major purpose was achieved. MacArthur left with the feeling that Truman had given him a free hand to conduct the war as he thought best.[16]

Even while the nation's top military and civilian decision makers met at Wake Island, the Chinese were infiltrating 100,000 troops—180,000 by November—across the Yalu River into North Korea. After 25 October, U.N. forces began to come into contact with Chinese units, and by 1 November, the Chinese had attacked with such power that the U.N. offensive was blocked. MacArthur on 6 November said his forces were threatened with destruction.

Then the Chinese broke off the attack and moved back into the mountains. Washington policymakers tried to figure out what was happening. The Chinese had been warning all along, publicly and privately, that they would intervene if American forces invaded North Korea. The attack was a surprise only because Washington refused to heed clear warnings. Breaking off the offensive was a final attempt to warn Americans. The Chinese tried to show their lack of hostile intent, sometimes not even disarming American prisoners before sending them back to their units. Truman and his advisers did not take seriously Asian sources of intelligence conveying the warnings and believed that if China did intervene, it could not put together an army of peasants that could stand against the most powerful nation in the world. Truman allowed the offensive to continue.

Some analysts later concluded that Truman and his advisers engaged in groupthink. (Symptoms of groupthink include an illusion of invulnerability, group rationalizations to discount warnings, belief in their own inherent morality, and a view of the enemy as too evil to negotiate with.) They were made arrogant by their sense of American power. Instead of working to increase their ability to make good decisions in these few weeks, among the most crucial in twentieth-century American history, they narrowed it. Even the disaster that followed Truman's invasion of North Korea did not destroy his mind-set, which continued for years to prevent settlement of the war. Rather than rethink his assumptions, Truman, bolstered by his closely knit group, blamed his difficulties on the Soviets, Chinese, MacArthur, or Republican newspaper publishers—every one but himself, Acheson, Marshall, and other advisers.[17]

The Americans did not take advantage of the opportunity that the

Chinese gave them to reconsider, and MacArthur pushed on. Finally, in late November, at the beginning of the bitter Korean winter, the Chinese attacked in full force. On 28 November MacArthur reported to the Joint Chiefs of Staff that he confronted 200,000 Chinese troops—actually probably 300,000—and that "we face an entirely new war." His shattered forces began the longest military retreat in American history. Truman's dreams of a rollback had ended, and now the question was whether U.N. forces could hold a base at all in Korea. Acheson, years later, wrote to Truman: "The defeat of the U.S. forces in Korea in December was an incalculable defeat to U.S. foreign policy and destroyed the Truman Administration."

Despite Chinese intervention, decision making continued to be distorted by a view that the whole operation was Soviet directed. How China saw the war and what its leaders wanted seemed irrelevant. Truman, Acheson, and others assumed Mao Tse-tung was carrying out Stalin's orders and focused on Moscow. This interpretation benefited Washington's global plans because if Korea was only a diversion by the Kremlin, then military buildup had to continue to meet the real test that would come elsewhere. Some advisers, like MacArthur, wanted to widen the conflict and carry on a full-scale war to China; others, especially Acheson, held the line for a moderate response, staying, if possible, in Korea but not widening the war. On 16 December Truman declared a national emergency.

Many of the U.S. allies were dismayed. They had gone along with the Americans on the assumption that the war would be short, but now it seemed that the conflict might widen. Clement Attlee held meetings with the president beginning on 4 December, but Truman rejected the prime minister's suggestion that the United Nations settle the war. Attlee found that the Americans thought of themselves as so "pure and clean" that they could not understand that many Asians regarded them as imperialists. He noted that although it was supposedly a U.N. war, Truman could not find a compromise settlement in Korea because it would be "political dynamite" for him domestically.[18]

In Korea, U.N. forces began recovering from the Chinese attack, regrouped far down the peninsula in South Korea, and in January 1951 began a minor offensive under General Matthew Ridgway, who replaced General Walton Walker after Walker had died in a road accident.

This slow recovery failed to rebuild Truman's political position; instead he called down a fire storm of criticism on himself in April 1951 by firing MacArthur. Truman had never liked MacArthur, but he respected him and from the first days of the war had allowed the general to exceed his directives. During the months after Chinese intervention, MacArthur pushed constantly to remove the restrictions on his conduct of the war and became increasingly public with his criticisms. Then, in late March 1951 Truman believed that MacArthur deliberately sabotaged a U.N. peace effort by issuing a bombastic statement, a virtual ultimatum, to the Chinese.

Before Truman reacted, MacArthur answered a request from House Minority Leader Joseph W. Martin for information on the general's views on Far Eastern policy. Martin, without MacArthur's permission, made the general's letter public on 5 April. MacArthur said he approved Martin's advocacy of unleashing Chiang's army against the Chinese even at the cost of widening the war and said that it was in Asia, not Europe, that the "Communist conspirators" had chosen to challenge the free world. MacArthur told Martin: "As you point out, we must win. There is no substitute for victory."

This was standard rhetoric from MacArthur, and when an aide, Roger W. Tubby, took a United Press copy to show the president, Truman, who disliked the press even more than he did MacArthur, reacted in typical fashion by charging that the journalists probably had put the general up to it. When Tubby explained that MacArthur was challenging the presidency, Truman exploded. It became a personal test; he told his staff that people did not think he had courage to fire MacArthur.

Truman discussed the matter with the joint chiefs, Marshall, and Acheson, as well as congressional leaders. Although there was a consensus that Truman would be justified in firing MacArthur on the basis of his insubordination, several advisers warned the president of the political consequences of such action. Truman finally narrowed his options to either firing the general or leaving him in place, rather than finding a way to ease MacArthur out and letting him fade away with honor. The final mistake came when the White House panicked on hearing that word of the firing had leaked to the press. It scuttled its plan to let Secretary of Army Frank Pace notify MacArthur personally and called a press conference at 1 A.M. on 11 April to announce that one of the nation's greatest military heroes had been relieved of command.[19]

Near hysteria seemed to grip many Americans. Republican leaders discussed the possibility of impeaching Truman. Senator McCarthy charged that Truman was drunk when he made the decision to fire the general, and Republican Senator William E. Jenner said the country was in the hands of "a secret inner coterie which is directed by agents of the

Soviet Union." MacArthur was mobbed by tens of thousands of admirers when he landed in San Francisco; five hundred thousand met him in Washington, where he delivered to a joint session of Congress one of the most emotionally charged major addresses in modern American history. Congressman Dewey Short said: "We heard God speak here today, God in the flesh, the voice of God." The public not only admired MacArthur but agreed with his theory that the United States should either fight the war to win or get out of Korea. Sixty-nine percent of people polled supported MacArthur, and only 25 percent believed he should have been fired.

Truman's act of firing MacArthur may have been a courageous one, but it was unwise and unnecessary. Some defended it by saying that his action upheld civilian supremacy over the military and protected the power of the president. Yet given the damage it did to Truman's administration, the main lesson it taught future presidents was to avoid hostile confrontations with national heroes. If such powerful figures as Eisenhower and others had not stood behind Truman, he might have lost ability to govern.[20]

After the Chinese intervention and the MacArthur firing, Truman never recovered his popularity and power. As the MacArthur controversy eased, Truman had about a year and a half left as president and less than a year until his announcement that he would not run for reelection in 1952. His administration never recovered its balance. Crippled, it entered a period of holding action as it tried to cope with McCarthyism, internal scandals, inability to end the Korean War, and continued low popular support. Yet despite these problems, Truman had successfully put into place his military program, as envisioned in NSC-68, to support the containment policy, and he continued the Korean War without a congressional declaration of war.

9

FIGHTING COMMUNISM AT HOME AND ABROAD

Truman's expectation that his upset victory in the 1948 election would open the way for important legislative achievement quickly proved illusive. His Fair Deal program hopelessly bogged down in Congress, and he was increasingly occupied by powerful challenges from McCarthyism, increasing opposition to the war in Korea, and spreading evidence of corruption within his administration.

In his State of the Union speech on 5 January 1949, Truman put forward the entire slate of reform proposals he had offered in his first term. Although reaffirmation of this program cheered reformers and frightened conservatives, those who expected a repetition of the success of Franklin Roosevelt's hundred days in 1933 overlooked significant differences. Truman won the 1948 election with a little less than 50 percent of the votes cast, and over half the eligible voters did not vote at all. Most Americans were relatively prosperous; consumerism excited people more than confronting social problems as new products flooded the market and old ones flowed from the reconverted assembly lines. Only blacks and a few white allies felt deep commitment to civil rights reforms. Labor's biggest demand, hardly bold, was to repeal Taft-Hartley, and farmers, basically prosperous, wanted higher prices. McCarthyism placed dangerous obstacles in the path of some legislation like the Brannan Plan and health insurance, both attacked as socialistic. The Korean War diverted already slackening energy from domestic concerns.

The new Congress was not elected on a tide of support for the Fair Deal, and by the end of 1950, Truman decided there were "more morons than patriots in it." Nor was the Eighty-second Congress, elected in 1950, any better from his point of view. The Democrats lost five Senate seats and twenty-eight House seats, which, although good for an off-year election, diminished further Truman's chance of making gains on domestic reform. With the Korean War absorbing his attention, he offhandedly reaffirmed his support for the Fair Deal in 1951 and 1952, without high expectations.

During his second term, the administration lost on public power development, on Taft-Hartley repeal, and on the Brannan Plan, designed to gear farm programs to the needs of small farmers. The American Medical Association, spending millions to fight Truman's national compulsory health insurance program, successfully persuaded Congress that it was socialized medicine, potent words designed to scare.

Not all reform proposals were lost. On 15 July 1949 Truman signed the National Housing Act, his major reform achievement. After the initial glare of publicity about the shortage of homes at the end of the war, problems remained while stories of veterans living in abandoned automobiles faded from the front pages of newspapers. Yet millions of people still lived in city slums and millions more in substandard rural dwellings. The 1949 housing act included provisions for 810,000 units of public housing and passed mainly because Southern Democrats from urban areas split with the conservative coalition. Opponents need not have been concerned. By the time Truman left office, just 60,000 of the 810,000 units had been built. Housing continued to deteriorate, and slums spread after the act passed.[1]

Civil rights also presented a mixed record. Blacks, poised to force breakthroughs in many American institutions, guided crucial cases upward through the court system and exerted more power within the Democratic party. Truman responded to black pressure in 1948 and put forward his civil rights program, which he then reasserted in 1949. Opposition to the program remained strong, culminating in one of the major filibusters in Senate history. Instead of building a bipartisan coalition in Congress for his program, Truman pulled the rug from under Republican and Democratic moderates who were proposing a compromise to end the filibuster. He soon gave in to southern pressure in order to get higher-priority issues through, deciding that nothing should interfere with foreign policy legislation.

Blacks made greater gains in desegregating the armed forces. Although they had long seen military service as a way to win recognition from the white community, they had traditionally been forced into segregated military units and generally found themselves treated as a problem rather than as an asset. Black anger at military discrimination reached explosive levels in World War II, and civil rights leaders threatened demonstrations and other forms of direct action if it continued after the war. Truman responded to black pressure with his 1948 executive order to establish equal treatment in the military services. Although the services resisted change, the Korean War forced a breakthrough, and by October 1953, 95 percent of black soldiers served in integrated units.

Blacks made some gains in other areas. The Justice Department entered amicus curiae briefs on behalf of cases that the NAACP and others brought against housing contracts that bound owners not to sell or rent to minorities. In May 1948 the Supreme Court ruled that such restrictive covenants were not enforceable. Nevertheless, the Federal Housing Administration (FHA) continued to underwrite segregation by withholding loans from areas threatened by "Negro invasion" and by building segregated public housing units. Truman pressured the agency to lessen discrimination, but by 1952, nonwhites had access to only fifty thousand out of three million FHA-insured units.

The Justice Department expanded its ability to litigate in civil rights matters, although the attorney general had to hide money used for such activities rather than openly placing it in the budgets submitted to Congress. The department fought segregated housing and transportation and entered cases against separate-but-equal education. Blacks also made some gains in federal hiring practices, although Truman did not push hard for change in such areas or appoint many minority people to high positions.[2]

During the Truman administration, Native American policy reverted to older forms. Truman proclaimed the merits of the "patriots" who fought the European invaders and acknowledged that Americans had treated the Native Americans badly. He believed that if treated properly, they would have voluntarily assimilated into white American culture. It was inconceivable to him that people would choose to remain separate from the mainstream. Most white American reformers wanted Indians to accept Western European concepts of individualism, capitalism, and democracy, and, eventually, through education, become like the majority population. Through programs designed to achieve assimilation, whites grabbed much Native American land, severely damaging the vitality of tribal communities and threatening their personal identity.

During the New Deal, Bureau of Indian Affairs (BIA) director John Collier, aware of deep flaws in Western civilization and tolerant of cultural pluralism, tried to find ways to protect the Native American cultures and their tribal communities. Opposition to Collier's program was formidable—from within the Native American population where many individuals had already assimilated and from without by whites who feared that revival of Indian consciousness and organization would limit their access to Indian land and resources and might in some regions pose a political threat to the white power structure. These opponents found new strength as World War II and the cold war allowed them to stress the need for national unity and cohesion and to describe such practices as collective landownership as communistic.

Under Truman, the federal government moved again to a policy of assimilation and abandoned Collier's support for the traditional community. Despite his admiration of "patriotic Indian leaders," Truman had little interest in Native American problems or in their culture. When he signed the Navaho-Hopi Rehabilitation Act of 1950, designed to achieve economic growth along capitalistic lines, he said the bill was a model for "the complete merger of all Indian groups into the general body of our population." Truman's BIA director, Dillon S. Myer, prepared the way for Dwight Eisenhower's policy of tribal termination, which resulted in disaster for many Native Americans.[3]

How did Truman's Fair Deal program stand at the end of his nearly eight years in office? He got the housing and full employment acts through Congress, extended social security coverage and raised its benefits, raised minimum wages, achieved limited gains in civil rights, and consolidated various New Deal programs. Generally, however, Truman displayed a lack of skill or will to build a coalition for new reform proposals, such as national health insurance and civil rights. He frequently sacrificed the Fair Deal to get his foreign policy legislation through Congress. His most important legacy in domestic legislation was to protect the New Deal reforms from critical erosion.

The White House operation itself ran more smoothly than it had during Truman's first term. In late 1950, press secretary Charles Ross died and was replaced by Joseph H. Short, who served competently until his death in September 1952. John Steelman continued his important role in dealing with operational problems, but in January 1950 Clark Clifford, in debt and worn out, resigned to enter private law practice. Charles S. Murphy took his place as counsel. Murphy, a man of high intelligence and sound judgment, was as liberal as Clifford and closer to the president, replacing Ross as a restraining influence on Truman.

Truman's cabinet remained rather stable in his second term. Acheson, Snyder, Brannan, Sawyer, Tobin, and Donaldson served until the end of his administration. Marshall, replacing Louis Johnson as secretary of defense, served until September 1951, when he was replaced by Robert A. Lovett, a competent man already familiar to Truman from his earlier service in the administration. In December 1949, Truman replaced Secretary of the Interior Julius Krug with liberal and respected Oscar L. Chapman. Truman named Attorney General Thomas Clark to the Supreme Court and replaced him with J. Howard McGrath in August 1949. McGrath mixed liberal ideas, practical machine politics, intelligence, and poor administrative ability with a mercurial temperament. In a blowup over the attorney general's handing of the scandals that engulfed the administration, Truman fired his friend McGrath and replaced him with James P. McGranery in May 1952, who inherited a mess and had little time to get it straightened out.

In 1970, sixty-five law school deans and professors, historians, and political scientists rated all the Supreme Court justices since 1789. According to these scholars, Truman's record in choosing good justices was by far the worst of any other president in history. Truman appointed three of the eight justices ranked as failures: Chief Justice Frederick M. Vinson, Harold H. Burton, and Sherman Minton. Thomas C. Clark, who Truman himself later concluded was the worst appointment he made as president, ranked average. The nation's regulatory apparatus also declined under Truman because of his many mediocre appointments to the administrative law system.[4]

Truman did not make much effort to spread top people through the executive branch, but he did pay close attention to the structure of government. In 1945, he took control of an executive branch that had mushroomed in size as the government responded to the depression and war crises. Roosevelt and Congress had fragmented administrative organization and scattered agencies throughout the executive branch with little concern for organizational rationality. Truman believed that Roosevelt had left labor, housing, and welfare programs in an administrative mess and that the State Department and military services were organizationally unprepared to cope with the new problems of the postwar era.

Truman won two grants of reorganization authority (the Reorganization Acts of 1945 and 1949), under which he submitted forty-eight reorganization plans, thirty-three of which passed. Since 1900, many administrative reformers had struggled to bring the modern bureaucratic state under unified direction. Truman went far toward establishing the managerial presidency that reformers advocated. When the Republican Eightieth Congress created the Hoover Commission to find ways to dismantle New Deal programs following the anticipated defeat of the Democrats in 1948, Truman subverted the commission, using it to improve rather than destroy the existing structure. He then allied with Herbert Hoover, and the two men, so different in many ways, guided through Congress the most extensive reorganization program in American history. Truman, with congressional approval, unified housing, transportation, and social welfare functions as a preparatory step to creating cabinet-level departments in those fields, which later presidents achieved. Congress, under his guidance, rebuilt the Department of Labor and created the Department of Defense. By 1953, he had thoroughly overhauled the structure of government.

He also built a powerful presidency. Truman was a modest, unassuming man, kind and thoughtful, especially to the powerless with whom he came into personal contact. He retained his down-to-earth style and never lost his humility. When rain one night blew through an open window into the White House, Truman characteristically got on his hands and knees to mop it up rather than to disturb servants. Observers noted Truman's tendency to distinguish between himself as a private person and as the president. He would frequently switch from referring to himself as "I" to referring to "the president." People saw this as a sign of humility and as evidence that he did not confuse the man with the office. On the other hand, it also allowed him to formulate an unrestrained conception of presidential power: he was not fighting for power or glory for Harry Truman, the unassuming man from Missouri, but to protect and honor the office of president.

Truman helped create the imperial presidency. He used executive reorganization to create a more hierarchical form of government, moving ultimate power further from the bottom of the structure, where it was closer to the people. Many of his seemingly most innocuous reorganizations transferred authority from bureau chiefs to their bosses, the department secretaries. Congressmen often embedded statutory authority to administer specific programs in specified bureaus in order to keep the functions tied to precise constituencies, that is, to bodies of citizens organized into interest groups. Truman attempted to change that by centralizing the programs in the secretaries, responsible to the president.[5]

More subtle changes occurred too. Truman formulated policies and programs and presented them to Congress as national security issues that required quick action and unity. He often surrounded his actions and policies with secrecy that limited congressional and public ability to evaluate them. It was ironic that Truman's folk hero status developed in the 1970s partly because the public viewed him as a striking contrast to Richard Nixon. Historian Athan G. Theoharis found the reverse to be true. He noted "striking parallels" between the Truman and Nixon administrations, including political and illegal uses of intelligence and investigative agencies, unilateral and secret global foreign policy actions based on claims of inherent powers and executive privilege, and opposition to the principle of congressional oversight of executive branch activities. Executive power had always expanded during wars, and in Truman's America, the nation was in permanent quasi-war status. National security thinking regarded executive powers as almost unlimited in an increasingly dangerous world that required constant vigilance and ability to respond immediately to threats.

Two important new agencies adding to the president's ability to engage in unilateral action, while limiting congressional ability to review, were the Central Intelligence Agency (CIA) and the National Security Council (NSC), both created by the National Security Act of 1947. Truman believed that American intelligence operations during World War II had been defective. When he became president, uncoordinated intelligence information from twenty-five agencies overwhelmed him. Since he wanted a central body to coordinate and weigh intelligence operations and information, he had Congress establish the CIA. He had been warned by a number of individuals that such an agency would be difficult to control, and by the time he left office, it was already engaging in covert operations and clandestine collection of information and even domestic surveillance, supposedly forbidden by the 1947 act. The cold war atmosphere made such activities, traditionally deemed a violation of American ideals, seem acceptable, even necessary. In NSC-10/2 in June 1948, Truman agreed to supplement U.S. foreign policy by covert activities. The CIA would carry out these operations: "Specifically, such operations shall include any covert activities related to: propaganda, economic warfare; preventive direct action, including sabotage, anti-sabotage, demolition and evacuation measures; subversion against hostile states, including assistance to underground resistance movements, guerrillas and refugee liberations groups, and support of indigenous anti-communist elements in threatened countries of the free world." The CIA unit that carried out this broad mandate grew from 302 employees in 1949 to 2,812 in 1952, with 3,142 additional overseas contract personnel. By 1952, tight control and supervision of such activities from above had already loosened.

The second of the two new agencies was the National Security Council, which helped supervise the CIA and provided a secretariat to gather and weigh national security policy. It brought together in one body diplomatic, military, and resource information to help plan long-term policy, identify problems, and even, as in the Berlin blockade, meet in a decision-making capacity.[6]

While Truman was establishing a government structure and programs to deal with the Communist threat abroad, others were more concerned about the home front. On 9 February 1950 Senator Joseph R. McCarthy (R.–Wisconsin), speaking at Wheeling, West Virginia, claimed that he had a list of names of Communists working for the federal government. Such charges were old; the names from the list he read to his Senate colleagues on 20 February 1950 were from 1947 files accumulated by the House Un-American Activities Committee (HUAAC). Most people listed no longer worked for the government or had been investigated and cleared by the Federal Bureau of Investigation (FBI). McCarthy himself had been making such charges for years, as had many other Democrats and Republicans. His speech, however, came a few months after Mao Tse-tung had taken control of China, less than three weeks after former State Department official Alger Hiss had been found guilty of perjury in trials involving his denial that he was part of a Washington-based spy ring, and a few days after news that Canadian citizen Klaus Fuchs had turned atomic bomb secrets over to the Soviet Union. McCarthy explained that the United States "lost" China because men like Alger Hiss infested the Washington bureaucracy and led the government into betraying Chiang Kai-shek and his anti-Communist forces. McCarthy and his followers tapped politically a feeling of unease among Americans, who had experienced in a very short time many disturbing technological, social, and economic changes in their lives, had recently assumed frightening global responsibilities, and had still to come to terms with permanent peacetime big government and welfare state.

McCarthy spoke at the right time to capture headlines, and media attention heightened as the administration responded to his attacks. He proved to be a demagogue with a flair for drama and no inner restraints.

McCarthy lied and when caught lied more, while attacking those expos-
ing his dishonesty as Communist dupes or agents. As his attacks caught
on, Republican leaders used him to hammer at the Democrats on the
Communists-in-government issue. Senate Democrats quickly asked respected Senator Millard E. Tydings (Maryland) to investigate his
charges. The Tydings subcommittee exposed the fraudulent nature of
McCarthy's claims but did not even dent the anti-Communist movement, now set to run its course over the next few years.

McCarthy became the symbolic head of an anti-Communist crusade
that he did not start and could not control. *McCarthyism*, a term used
to describe a movement much broader than the senator's activities, had
its roots in periodic campaigns against left-wing radicalism that went far
back into American history. After 1945, this deep-rooted fear of radicalism had focused on the Soviet Union and communism, and the cold war
was almost certain at some point to trigger a Red scare.

As the cold war tensions heightened in 1947, fear mounted of Communist conspiracy in the United States. The abstract danger of subversion took on faces and names in July and August 1948 when Elizabeth
T. Bentley and Whittaker Chambers testified publicly that they had been
undercover Soviet agents working with many Washington officials. They
named several important people in the Roosevelt and Truman administrations: Lauchlin Currie, administrative assistant to Roosevelt; Harry
Dexter White, assistant secretary of treasury; and Alger Hiss, an important State Department official under Roosevelt, who became president
of the Carnegie Endowment for International Peace. Attention focused
on Chambers, a *Time* magazine editor, who charged that Hiss had been
a member of Chambers' spy ring. Hiss denied these charges, and in August 1948 Truman sneeringly dismissed such spy hunts. On 21 January
1950, however, after two spectacular trials, a jury convicted Hiss of perjury relating to the spy charges, and he went to prison.

Hiss was a friend of Secretary of State Dean Acheson, who helped
him plan his testimony before HUAAC. Acheson, showing more moral
courage than political caution, publicly announced that he would not
turn his back on Hiss, and McCarthyites used that as evidence that
Acheson also was implicated, either as a dupe or an agent. When Acheson apologized to Truman for the uproar his statement caused, with the
unspoken offer to resign, Truman, remembering a similar outburst when
as vice president he attended the funeral of Tom Pendergast, said: "God
damn it, Dean, if you think a man who followed an old criminal to his
grave because he was his friend would have you do anything different

than you did you don't know me." Truman, however, did not think Hiss was innocent. He told a friend that he thought "the s.o.b. is guilty, and I hope they hang him."

Many other government officials, especially State Department figures, faced charges of subversive activity and had their careers destroyed. Others outside the government were caught up in the anti-Communist hysteria and were ostracized, harassed, and blacklisted from their occupations. Some suffered worse fates. Julius Rosenberg evidently passed atomic secrets to the Soviet Union, and his wife, Ethel, probably knew about it. They were sentenced to death during the Truman administration and executed just after he left office. Flawed trial procedures and harsh sentences imposed on them were the product of the anti-Communist hysteria of the time.

By 1950, the anti-Communist persuasion had taken new intensity as prominent people and dramatic activities captured newspaper front pages month after month. Republicans used the Communist issue against the Democrats, politicians from both parties used it against each other, liberal labor leaders used it to purge radicals from union leadership, businessmen found it useful to fight unions and New Deal reforms, and reformers attacked communism to show that they were good Americans. Liberals played their role in feeding McCarthyism. Many of them had engaged in Red-baiting and Wallace bashing in the 1948 campaign; most did not defend the rights of Communists to hold jobs, speak freely, and engage in political activity but contented themselves with showing that they or their friends were not Communists.[7]

Truman did nothing to help American Communists as they came under attack. He, too, saw them as security threats; he differed with the McCarthyites only in that he believed that he had already fired all of the Communists from the government. He defended himself not by defending the rights of Communist citizens but by stressing his own anti-Communist record. Truman disliked McCarthy and deplored McCarthyism, but his own rhetoric and programs had helped shift the American political culture to the right, and he found little secure ground on which to stand to fight the movement.

Long before McCarthyism peaked, Truman had set up his own loyalty program. The 1946 election revealed increasing fear of domestic subversion, and on 21 March 1947 Truman issued Executive Order 9835. Although he intended to use the order to remove the issue from public concern, his action seemed to verify that Communist infiltration of the government was a real danger. Since the loyalty program came just a few days after the Truman Doctrine speech, it signaled that Truman was moving against the threat of communism at home as well as abroad. The executive order required a loyalty investigation of employees as they were hired and made agency heads responsible for firing disloyal personnel. Accused employees could appeal adverse findings through a series of bodies up to the Loyalty Review Board. Such employees had right to counsel but were allowed to read only a summary of charges against them and did not have the right to confront their accusers.

Truman said he wanted no witch-hunts in his administration, but his program was flawed in conception and practice. It placed government concerns ahead of historic protections for the individual and shifted traditional concepts of Anglo-American law from punishing acts that had been committed to taking preventive action against people, such as those individuals Truman labeled "potential subversives." The order also authorized the Attorney General's List of subversive organizations. The very existence of such a list chilled freedom of thought and association. The order made it easier to accuse dissenters from government policy with disloyalty and to view the disloyal as security risks.

In practice, the loyalty program led to injustices, as well as affronts to decency and common sense. The boards often harassed blacks involved in civil rights activities; board members sometimes quizzed people on their attitude toward the Truman Doctrine and Marshall Plan; some asked if employees voted for Henry Wallace, provided religious training for their children, read suspect books, or listened to records by the left-wing entertainer Paul B. Robeson. Truman tried to tighten supervision of the program to prevent government witch-hunting and fought against the Internal Security Act of 1950 (the McCarran Act), which passed over his veto, but even he had to admit that some of his boards were engaged in "un-American activities."[8]

McCarthyite activities by the Truman administration were widespread: groups could be placed on the Attorney General's List without any public review procedure, and even expired membership in such organizations could cost individuals their jobs; associations placed on the list were often damaged or destroyed. By 1953 the administration had arrested three hundred radical aliens for deportation and lifted the passports of such radical citizens as Paul Robeson. Truman continued a wartime operation under which RCA, ITT, and Western Union allowed government officials to read telegrams of foreign citizens and of certain designated Americans.

J. Edgar Hoover's abuse of power, more widespread and damaging than McCarthy's, has been well documented. The FBI fed McCarthyism, by conducting its own anti-Communist propaganda campaign. It secretly gave information to HUAAC and to favored journalists and congressmen, intimidated witnesses who challenged HUAAC, conducted surveillance of Congressman Vito Marcantonio (American Labor–New York), a dissenter from Truman's cold war policy, compiled massive lists of people to be detained in times of emergency, the compiling of which invaded the privacy of thousands, conducted a wide surveillance of domestic political activities, including wiretaps, and placed informers in unions and other organizations.

The FBI became stronger under Truman, and although Truman might growl and snap at Hoover behind the director's back, the president, like most other politicians, smiled to his face. Hoover often used Truman's friend Harry Vaughan as a conduit into the White House, sending him reports on people inside and outside government. The crudity of these documents and their heavy-handed attempt to influence Truman is still shocking. Hoover also fed Vaughan massive stacks of transcripts of wiretaps on the telephone of former Roosevelt aide Thomas Cochran, who placed calls to people all over Washington. By this means, the White House received transcripts of conversations of journalists, executive branch officials, congressmen, and even Supreme Court justices. Truman, rather than being repelled by this activity, wrote Bess in June 1945: "I went to bed at 10:30 and read a gossip phone conversation between a Justice of the Supreme Court and one of Drew Pearson's stooges in Vinson's office. It was funny but also bad business. The so-called Palace Guard [Roosevelt loyalists] hate to give up. I'm causing them much worry I'm afraid." Such documents and Hoover's reports may well have influenced Truman's appointments to office, as well as other of his actions.[9]

While under attack for being soft on communism at home, Truman continued the war on the Korean peninsula, killing alike Communists and non-Communists, civilians and noncivilians. Half of the South Korean people were homeless refugees by early 1951, trudging along roads among bombed-out villages, fleeing opposing armies, and hiding from strafing aircraft.

After Truman failed in his attempt to roll back communism, the U.N. forces slowly fought their way up the peninsula to the thirty-eighth parallel but this time did not cross. The war settled into one fitting the containment pattern. Truman led the nation during its first "limited" war, although it was not limited for Koreans and Chinese and others who died by the hundreds of thousands. Expanding the war into China would have endangered the unity of the Western alliance and diverted Washington from what it thought was still the major threat: Soviet power in Europe. Limited war also served Washington leaders by allowing them to use an expanded military budget to continue to rearm the United States and Europe.

Problems mounted at home. Republican attacks on Truman's handling of the war increased as his popularity fell. As early as January 1951, two out of three Americans favored getting out of Korea. By November 1951, only 23 percent of Americans approved of Truman's handling of the war. Americans did not take to the streets against Truman policy as they did to protest the Vietnam War in the 1960s, probably because patriotic attitudes aroused during World War II were strong enough to support completing a national goal even if it came to be regarded as a mistake. In addition, the civil rights movement had not given Americans a lesson in the efficacy of democracy in the streets, nor had a revolution yet occurred in the values of the young that caused them to question many things that their elders regarded as truisms. Finally, strong Republican criticism of Truman's inability either to win or to end the Korean War provided a release for the outrage many felt.

Despite his unpopularity, Truman carried out an effective wartime economic policy. After the Chinese intervention, Truman, in December 1950, declared a national emergency and established wage-price controls. There was a brief initial inflationary spurt, but then prices stabilized, probably because of the economy's extraordinary capacity to expand rather than because of the controls.

Despite his success in controlling inflation, Truman lost another economic battle when the Supreme Court slapped down his seizure of the nation's steel mills. After the United Steel Workers voted to strike for higher wages on 9 April 1952, Secretary of Defense Lovett convinced Truman that a strike would threaten national security by hurting the war effort. Rather than use the Taft-Hartley provision allowing the president to call an eighty-day cooling-off period, Truman, on 8 April 1952, exhausted and shaking, issued Executive Order 10340, seizing the steel mills to prevent the strike. He based his action on the president's power as commander in chief. With Truman now as unpopular as any other president had been in the twentieth century, this action struck many as a high-handed outrage by a discredited president. Congressmen introduced fourteen separate resolutions of impeachment. The steel companies went to court to block Truman's action, and federal judge David A. Pine found the seizure illegal. Truman was dumbfounded.

Truman remained confident as the case went to the Supreme Court. Attorney General Clark, before he went to the Supreme Court, had assured him he had legal authority to prevent an economic breakdown. Truman also had consulted Chief Justice Vinson, who had told him to go ahead. Truman had appointed four of the nine justices and with his conception of loyalty no doubt believed they would come to his aid. But on 2 June 1952, the Supreme Court ruled six to three that Truman had exceeded his constitutional authority. *Youngstown Sheet & Tube Co. v. Sawyer* remained a historically important case, and judges, legal scholars, and others turned to it in controversies over presidential power during the Vietnam War era and the Watergate scandals. The decision affirmed that the president is not above the law and that the executive branch does not determine its own constitutional powers. Although in his memoirs Truman said he could not understand how the Court ignored the threat posed to national security, the strike continued for fifty-three days without serious effect on the war effort.[10]

While checked by the Supreme Court in his attempt to seize the steel mills, Truman displayed the power of the modern presidency by continuing military action in Korea. After the U.N. forces held back the initial Chinese offensive and regained ground to the vicinity of the thirty-eighth parallel, Washington signaled its willingness to negotiate. Talks started in July 1951, but Truman dragged his feet, unwilling to be seen as needing peace. His confusion over who was directing the war, which he regarded as Moscow's operation, and his moralistic bombast about the "cut throat organization" in China run by a bunch of "murderers and crooks," prevented him from fully understanding what the war was about. He fantasized giving the Kremlin an ultimatum to comply with his directives or face atomic destruction: "It must stop and stop now. We of the free world have suffered long enough." The Soviets must stop kidnapping and murdering children and engaging in other evil deeds, Truman wrote. It must accept Washington's "fair and just proposal" or be destroyed. He would instruct Soviet leaders in morality and read the Declaration of Independence to them, as well as the fifth through seventh chapters of Saint Matthew.

While Truman composed imaginary ultimatums for Stalin, the war continued. By January 1952, peace talks had gone far enough to settle most issues, but then the question arose over whether prisoners of war held by the U.N. forces would be forcefully repatriated to the north. Truman, working himself into moral outrage and not wanting to give up a propaganda opportunity to show how the Chinese and Koreans hated their Communist governments, took positions that caused the war to continue. The morality of killing Koreans and Chinese because of their symbolic value in cold war gamesmanship apparently never bothered him. The Americans even escalated air attacks on the already devastated North Korea. Eisenhower finally ended the war, by surrendering, Truman believed.

The Korean War left the peninsula divided after having killed hundreds of thousands of people—perhaps 12 to 15 percent of the North Koreans. The war further undercut the chance to achieve such domestic social goals as a health program or even to implement the housing program already authorized, although since 1945 the Truman administration had in any case relegated domestic concerns to secondary priority. By the time national leaders turned back to domestic reform in the 1960s, another Asian war awaited to drain more resources into military adventure while U.S. cities decayed, education declined, and millions of blacks and other poor Americans lived in misery.

The war hardened cold war attitudes. It confirmed to Washington that Moscow would use military means in its drive to achieve world domination. It built a stronger coalition behind containment, with many liberals and moderates viewing limited war as a regrettable but rational way to carry out that policy, even if they criticized Truman's execution of it. Dissent from the Left almost disappeared from the mainstream of American politics. Instead the debate was between critics who wished to go all out to win and those who supported Truman's policy of limited warfare. Truman learned that by spotlighting the supposed threat of the Soviet Union, he could at least hold the center behind his military and diplomatic programs. Others learned lessons as well. Right-wing dictators everywhere, watching the "free world" defend Rhee, realized that they could also appeal to the fear of the Kremlin to gain American support for themselves.

The war also allowed Truman to implement NSC-68. American defense spending tripled during the war, demonstrating that the economy could easily absorb such expenditures. These levels soon seemed normal. Only a portion of these funds went to Korea; much went to the general military buildup. U.S. military forces rose from 1.46 million men and women to 3.64 million. Americans poured resources into building NATO, and Washington began carefully preparing its European allies to accept German rearmament. The Mutual Security Act of 1951, with appropriations of $7.3 billion, went almost entirely to military assistance.[11]

When Truman left office, his conceptual and administrative components of the national security state were in place, as was a clearly formulated foreign policy toward most areas of the world. Future presidents modified parts of it, but Truman's policy has continued to serve as the fundamental guideline to American diplomacy.

The conflict over Eastern Europe stabilized after the United States acquiesced to Soviet power there. Washington did not seriously contemplate a rollback of the Soviet presence but seized opportunities to promote "heretical communism," as in Marshal Tito's Yugoslavia. Through the Marshall Plan and NATO, the Truman administration worked to build the economic and military power of Western Europe, binding it, including Italy and West Germany, together in a strong anti-Soviet bloc. It build a network of bases in Europe and the Mediterranean from which it could launch atomic bomb attacks on the Soviet Union.

In the Third World, the United States intervened in hot spots, but generally the poorer countries were of only secondary interest to Washington. To a considerable extent, the Truman administration relied on the open-door policy and private corporations to secure U.S. interests in such areas. Global corporations looked to Washington for help in gaining favorable agreements and in maintaining stability in countries where they had investments; they gained profits for themselves, grew in size and influence, and kept Third World resources out of Soviet hands. For its part, the Truman administration paid lip-service to requests from Third World nations for help in furthering their economic development, but most of Washington's interest and money went to Europe. Truman promised through the Point Four program to export American technological resources to help these nations. His proposal reaped great propaganda rewards, but the much-lauded plan never amounted to much except as a publicity device.

In Latin America, an area of traditional concern to Washington, U.S. foreign policy took a new turn as the cold war encouraged Americans to find ways to control the region without resorting to the crude methods of the era before the Good Neighbor policy. Since the late nineteenth century, as American economic interests in Latin America increased, Washington took more responsibility for maintaining political stability in the region. The United States always proclaimed that it acted in the interests of the people of Latin America, but those who benefited most were the United States and Latin American elites. Roosevelt's Good Neighbor policy changed the rhetoric of government officials and eliminated overt control through military intervention, but the United States continued to follow a policy of maintaining a "closed hemisphere in an Open World." In the Truman years, Washington saw no contradiction in building a solid anti-Soviet bloc in Latin America while resisting similar but cruder Soviet control of Eastern Europe. Thousands died over the decades resisting or maintaining the American-imposed order in Latin America.

By the end of the Truman administration, American control seemed so secure that Washington officials did not give the region much thought. In 1950, George Kennan told U.S. ambassadors to Latin America that communism must not be allowed to establish a foothold in the region: "The final answer might be an unpleasant one, but . . . we should not hesitate before police repression by the local government. This is not shameful since the Communists are essentially traitors. . . . It is better to have a strong regime in power than a liberal government if it is indulgent and relaxed and penetrated by Communists." Latin American oligarchies looked with increasing favor on U.S. power entering the region since that power served their interests.

Truman's policy toward Africa was similar, although the continent was hardly even of tertiary interest to Washington. U.S. wartime rhetoric underscored traditional American hostility to colonialism, commitment to self-determination, and recognition of the evils of racism. After the war, African and Asian nationalists slowly came to realize that while this was the American rhetorical position, its policy was to place European interests first.

One part of the Third World was of great concern to Washington. It was in the Middle East that Washington officials had so often since 1945 used the image of falling dominoes or spoiling apples. The presence of oil and the region's strategic location made the Truman administration determined to prevent any Soviet influence from extending into the Middle East. American government and corporate interests intertwined as the big oil companies profited by acting as instruments for Washington's cold war policies. While largely relying on private corporations to protect its national interests, the U.S. government also propped up "strong regimes," like that in Turkey, while building its own military power in a network of bases and shoring the position of pro-American elite groups. Americans were soon involved in trying to maintain the established order, while the Middle Eastern masses lived in misery. The area remained explosive. Not only did Washington have to deal with Arab nationalism, but its support for Israel placed it on the tightrope that it would walk for decades.[12]

In Asia, Americans helped suppress the hukbalahap rebellion in the Philippines and generally supported the colonial regimes in the Far East. It did withdraw support from the Dutch in Indonesia but only because it came to view the ineffective Dutch government as a greater source of instability than a new nationalist government would bring. The Communist revolution in China and the Korean War had led the United States to hold South Korea for the free world, to protect Chiang on Taiwan, and to establish Japan as the American forward power base in Asia.

Washington looked to Southeast Asia as the key to allowing Japan to rebuild its economy. The kind of thinking found in NSC-68 blurred distinctions between vital and peripheral interests and made Southeast Asia loom bigger in American eyes. In late March 1950, well before the Korean attack, Truman told a State Department official that developing proper policy toward Indochina was one of the most important problems the government faced.

France, trying to hold Indochina, faced revolt by left-wing nationalists led by Ho Chi Minh, Vo Nguyen Giap, and others, who fought first against the French and then against the Japanese occupation during World War II. Roosevelt had little sympathy for the French desire to retake the area when the war was over: "France has milked it for one hundred years," he said. He did not, however, envision immediately freeing Indochina but proposed a U.N. trusteeship period of tutelage by Western powers. China accepted the Japanese surrender north of the sixteenth parallel and the British to the south.

The British and French were intent on regaining their colonial possessions and faced weakening opposition from Washington when Roosevelt died. Truman used traditional American anticolonial rhetoric, but colonial people remained abstractions to him. When he came to perceive Ho Chi Minh as a Communist puppet directed from Moscow, he lost any ability to see him as man representing the national aspirations of the Vietnamese people. Ho wrote several letters to the United States asking for help in achieving Vietnamese independence. Truman did not respond. As Truman focused his attention on the Kremlin, Indochina faded from his attention except as a pawn in the cold war. In August 1945 Truman met French Premier Charles de Gaulle and assured him that the United States would do nothing to prevent a French return to Indochina.

A few days later, Ho proclaimed the Democratic Republic of Vietnam. Conflict developed rapidly as the French expelled the Viet Minh from Saigon and other cities in the south, while Ho strengthened his position in Hanoi and the north. He swore to aid the southerners in throwing their colonial masters out and sent supplies and men to help the resistance fighters. Ho and the other Communist leaders soon absorbed the Vietnamese nationalist spirit and movement.

Washington wanted stability in Southeast Asia and realized that Asian nationalism would create instability as long as France stayed. Yet Truman saw Ho as a puppet of Moscow and by 1946 believed that the United States had to oppose him. In November, Acheson told the French government that the United States was ready to be "helpful." As Truman and his national security advisers watched conditions deteriorate in China, Ho seemed more dangerous since his takeover of Vietnam would represent another area falling to communism.

By 1949, the Truman administration had become even more concerned with Southeast Asia. The region was important economically, especially for Japan; militarily, in terms of communications and certain crucial raw materials; and symbolically as a place to hold the line against further Communist expansion. It was also important in domestic politics because the administration already faced mounting attacks for being weak in its support of Chiang Kai-shek. Mao's victory in China made it essential that Ho fail in Southeast Asia.

Americans also recognized that French victory would be difficult if that nation did nothing to satisfy Indochinese nationalism. Attention focused on the Bao Dai solution as the way to defeat communism while bowing to nationalism. The French established former Vietnamese emperor Bao Dai as head of a new government, putting him forward as a Vietnamese alternative to the Communist Ho. Although Washington recognized that Bao Dai had little support among the Vietnamese people, by 11 December 1948, the American ambassador to France was warning that if the United States did not take strong action and recognize Bao Dai, other areas, including Burma, Siam, and Malaya, would fall to communism "like overripe apples." By May 1949, Acheson had decided that Bao Dai was the only alternative to a Communist government. The United States would consider recognition and aid at a proper time but in the meantime would pressure France to give the Bao Dai government enough independence to shed its image of being a puppet to Paris. On 1 February 1950, a State Department working group summarized the problem: "Unavoidably, the United States is, together with France, committed in Indochina. That is, failure of the French Bao Dai 'experiment' would mean the communization of Indochina. It is Bao Dai . . . or Ho Chi Minh . . . ; there is no other alternative. The choice confronting the United States is to support the French in Indochina or face the extension of Communism over the remainder of the continental area of Southeast Asia and, possibly, further westward." Acheson recommended recognition to Truman, and on 7 February 1950 the United States recognized Laos, Vietnam, and Cambodia.

On the same day, Ambassador David Bruce said that France expected the Soviets to increase aid to Ho and believed that Washington should regard the French effort as part of the general struggle against communism in Asia. On 8 May 1950 Acheson recommended economic and military aid to the French in Vietnam. U.S. involvement was open-ended since any support increased American symbolic commitment to preventing the expansion of communism.

By mid-1950 the United States was paying 40 percent of the French cost of the war and providing other support for the French operations. One effect was to increase Washington's role in setting policy in the war, including the determination that there would be no negotiations with Ho.

Kennan warned Acheson on 21 August 1950 that "we are getting ourselves into the position of guaranteeing the French in an undertaking which neither they nor we, nor both of us together, can win." Acheson recognized the danger of being trapped there, but in the typical Acheson, and Truman, fashion of valuing action over thought wrote: "I decided . . . that having put our hand to the plow, we would not look back." Not until the late 1960s did most Americans pause to look back, a look that revealed a horrifying picture of death, destruction, waste of resources, and erosion of American democratic values.[13]

10

THE MERRY-GO-ROUND
SLOWS

The presidency ground on Truman incessantly. In 1951 he turned sixty-six and at times seemed dangerously exhausted. Much frustration and few achievements awaited him in his last two years in office. The war continued, McCarthyism raged, the Fair Deal remained stalled, and attacks on the Truman administration multiplied as scandals surfaced. After he announced on 29 March 1952 that he would not run for reelection, Truman had to endure the humiliation of being a lame duck.

This disheartening status added to the anger and hurt that had accumulated over his lifetime and that often bubbled to the surface in his last two years in office. Every election from the 1920s on had been an ordeal for him. He had been scarred by personal attacks from which he could not shield his family. In his second term, the barbs came continually. The 1948 election, with its cheers of "Give 'em hell, Harry," had enhanced his self-image of being a battling, feisty, blunt man. After his upset victory, many people lauded him as a political genius. He became more certain of his positions and less tolerant of journalistic and congressional critics.

Frequently the attacks were not criticisms of policy but cutting assaults that portrayed him as a laughable bumbler. He often wrote letters to Bess or notes to himself listing past humiliations—a litany including bankruptcy, portrayal as Pendergast's water boy, taunts like "Had enough?" and "To err is Truman" in 1946, and attempts to dump him from the ticket in 1948. He tried to make her happy, he wrote Bess in June 1949: "Did I? I don't know. All I can say [is] I've tried. There is no one in the world anyway who can look down on you or your daughter. That means much to me, but I've never cared for social position or rank for myself except to see that those dear to me were not made to suffer from my shortcomings."[1]

Truman's rage often focused on the press. Although he was accessible to journalists, averaging 3.4 press conferences a month, a recent study of the press and the presidency concluded that "deep down, he hated the press with a corrosive passion exceeding any of those who preceded him." Margaret Truman believed his attitude stemmed from the "reactionary" attacks on him beginning in 1949. Truman said his dislike was directed toward editors and columnists rather than reporters, but his hatred, which had started long before he became president, often flared at reporters as well as their bosses.

Truman's view of the press stemmed partly from a view of loyalty that regarded as betrayal criticism from those he befriended or aided, as he had many newsmen, or from newspapers he considered Democratic: "There was never a newspaper man who can understand what the word loyalty means." He was always quick to attack the "sabotage" press as traitorous and to blame it for all of his problems, from the Chinese intervention in Korea to McCarthyism.[2]

In his last years in office especially, Truman felt sure newspapermen were engaged in a conspiracy to destroy him by hanging a corruption label on his administration. The issue had been building for some time. There were minor problems in the first administration but nothing serious until 1949, when a number of scandals began to emerge. In February 1951, a Chicago newspaper called for Truman's impeachment on the grounds that he was "crooked as well as incompetent." In 1952, 52 percent of the people believed there was a great deal of corruption in Washington; most people believed Truman knew what was going on.

Early questions revolved around such close Truman associates as Harry Vaughan, Jake Vardaman, and Edwin Pauley. The blowup over Pauley had been serious enough to lead Secretary of Interior Ickes to resign in early 1946. Several of Truman's men used their positions to do minor favors for friends or to engage in commodity speculation after Truman had forbidden it. Truman sent some of his cronies home and unloaded others on agencies outside the White House. A few, like his old friend Harry Vaughan, he kept with him until the end of his presidency.

The venality involved in these early scandals by the "Missouri gang" was small in scale and often involved stupidity as much corruption in the usual sense.

More serious scandals surfaced in 1949 and after. Congressional investigations revealed questionable business judgment and possible favoritism on the part of officials of the Reconstruction Finance Corporation (RFC). Investigators charged that Truman aide Donald S. Dawson, among others, used his position to influence RFC directors to grant favored individuals loans. When an investigating subcommittee outlined such charges, Truman referred to the report as "asinine," which caused subcommittee chairman Senator J. William Fulbright (D–Arkansas) to go after the RFC with such fury that the agency never recovered and would later be abolished. Charges of corruption spread to the Bureau of Internal Revenue (BIR), where investigation revealed favoritism, payoffs, and other acts of corruption by government employees. The BIR scandals were damaging politically because taxpayers were sensitive to favoritism in an agency that affected their interests so directly.

Pushed by his White House staff to take action, Truman reorganized the Bureau of Internal Revenue but then undermined his cleanup campaign by directing Attorney General J. Howard McGrath, a political operator who inspired little confidence, to investigate these and other charges. McGrath did not take the scandals seriously, and on 3 April 1952, after he bungled the investigation and had an angry public confrontation with Truman, the president fired him.

It may be that the Truman scandals were relatively minor episodes that occur in every administration but were blown out of proportion because of deep frustrations over the war in Korea and other issues. But Truman himself was mainly responsible for the public perception of a mess in Washington. Rather than facing the fact that some of his friends and associates had betrayed his trust by engaging in unwise, if not illegal, actions, Truman often blamed newspapers, sometimes the corrupters (while usually saying there was no corruption), and almost always the investigators. His narrow conception of loyalty, learned under Pendergast, blinded Truman and made him back friends who came under fire, even when they had betrayed the public trust through venality or poor judgment. The "mess in Washington" soured the closing months of his administration and gave Republicans plenty of ammunition to use in the 1952 elections.[3]

Truman for some time had been thinking about his future. He later said that reading newspapers from across the country during his first term convinced him that after twenty years, the people were fed up with the Democrats. After winning vindication in 1948, he felt it would be proper for him to step aside at the end of his term. On 16 April 1950, he privately noted that he would not accept renomination in 1952: "There is a lure in power. It can get into a man's blood just as gambling and lust for money have been known to do." Roosevelt set a bad precedent for a republic by running for more than two terms, Truman believed, and he wanted to reestablish the traditional pattern. On 19 November 1951, he told his closest staff of his decision but decided to wait for an opportune time to announce it publicly, both to retain as much influence with Congress as he could and to choose the best moment to establish the Fair Deal as the agenda for the Democratic party in 1952.

Truman's choice as a successor was his friend, Chief Justice Fred Vinson. Although Vinson did not strike most observers as a man of great vision, many Washington insiders admired him. Truman regarded him as competent, noting that his service in all three branches of government would be especially useful to the country. He discussed the matter with the chief justice several times, but, to his surprise, Vinson refused to leave the Court.

As Truman discussed other candidates with his advisers, the name of Illinois Governor Adlai E. Stevenson came up. As early as May 1950, Truman had noted him as a possible successor. He met with Stevenson in January 1952 and again in March, but Stevenson refused to enter the race, perhaps because he believed 1952 would not be a good year for a Democratic candidate. By 1956, he would have fulfilled his commitment to the people of Illinois and then could run for the presidency.

After Stevenson's first refusal, Truman met at least twice to discuss the election with his most trusted advisers, including Charles Murphy, Clark Clifford, and Vinson. He evidently was reconsidering his decision not to run. Murphy recalled that the group did not respond positively, although Truman's notes on one of the meetings indicated he heard encouragement from some of those present. Truman was tired, Murphy believed; the administration was running down and having difficulty getting good people. Bess and Margaret also encouraged Truman to stand by his decision not to run, and Bess finally told him she could not survive four more years of the presidency and did not think he could.[4]

As the convention neared in late July 1952, Truman, finally and reluctantly, agreed to support Vice President Barkley, aged seventy-four, whom Truman considered too old to run. But Barkley could not gain labor support and withdrew. Stevenson on the afternoon of 24 July 1952 called Truman and asked if it would embarrass Truman for the governor to enter the race: "I told him it not only would not embarrass me but that it would please me in every way, that I have no commitments and if he is nominated I would put forth every effort possible to see that he is elected and he will never hear from me after the election is over unless he sends for me." After Stevenson won on the third ballot, Truman, Stevenson, and other party leaders caucused to choose Senator John J. Sparkman as the vice-presidential nominee.[5]

Stevenson faced a formidable opponent. On 7 January 1952, NATO Supreme Commander General Dwight Eisenhower announced that he was willing to accept the Republican nomination. Eisenhower later told journalist Robert Donovan that he would not have run if he had known that the Democrats would nominate Stevenson; Eisenhower entered because he wanted to keep Truman from governing the country for another four years. While Truman often had expressed admiration for the general, Eisenhower had been polite and noncommittal in return. Eisenhower, with ties to the liberal Eastern Establishment within the Republican party, was part of the "vital center." He accepted New Deal reforms but intended to administer them with more fiscal responsibility and efficiency than the Democrats, and he was an internationalist in foreign policy. He believed that the country had to be saved from the irresponsibility and incompetency of Truman, whom Eisenhower regarded as a "congenital liar," from the isolationists, like Robert Taft, and from such "disciples of hate" as Joseph McCarthy.

Truman had admired Eisenhower, believing him to be an outstanding general who seemed to have retained the democratic values and manners of the Midwest. Truman had known since 1945 that Eisenhower was a hot political property; in fact he had tried to recruit him for the Democratic party. But Eisenhower had refused to get involved in the 1948 campaign, and on 6 November 1951 Truman still believed the general would stay out in 1952: "He is at the pinnacle of his fame right now because he has done a wonderful job on this European defense program. There is nothing he can gain by sitting at this desk, except to lose his character, just like Grant did."

Stevenson was not eager to run against Eisenhower because he thought he could not defeat him and because he fundamentally agreed with Eisenhower on domestic and foreign issues. On domestic policy, Stevenson's positions were usually less liberal than those of Truman. Stevenson was a man with a clear vision of what the United States should be and was able to express his ideas with more eloquence and clarity than

Eisenhower or Truman or probably any other major political leader of the time. Congressman Ken Hechler (D–West Virginia), who worked for both Stevenson and Truman, contrasted the two men: "Truman had an instinctive, visceral feeling about issues that concern the common man, and his reactions were basic, immediate and forceful. Stevenson had an intellectual, many-faceted knowledge of world problems and sought intelligent solutions to every issue."

The 1952 campaign was difficult for both men. Stevenson wanted to distance himself from Truman. He replaced Truman's chairman of the Democratic National Committee, moved his campaign headquarters from Washington to Springfield, Illinois, and, repeating a reporter's phrase, publicly referred to the "mess in Washington." Truman was deeply hurt and wrote letters, never mailed, to Stevenson and Sparkman, deploring "snub after snub" to which he felt they had subjected him. He believed that amateurs were in charge of their campaign and resented the fact that they neither asked him to help nor defended his record: "I'm telling you to take your crackpots, your high societies with their noses in the air, run your campaign and win if you can." Stevenson later gingerly negotiated a limited number of appearances by Truman, which the president stretched into a hard-hitting campaign reminiscent of 1948.

Although Truman remained confident that he could have guided Stevenson to victory, the president's involvement probably hurt Stevenson. With or without Truman's support, however, Stevenson had little chance. Eisenhower's victory was a personal triumph. Americans in the 1952 election did not vote to reject the New Deal–Fair Deal domestic program or the containment policy. The election represented a repudiation of Truman personally rather than of his program.

Truman congratulated Eisenhower on his victory and offered to cooperate to achieve an orderly transition. In the next few days, the two men agreed that Eisenhower's representatives would work with counterparts in the Truman administration. Truman and Eisenhower held their own fence-mending meeting on 18 November. Not much was accomplished; campaign invective created insurmountable distrust and anger between the two men. Yet Truman so successfully carried out this first formal transition planning operation that he established it as a routine procedure that allowed future presidents to take over the government smoothly.

Eisenhower and Truman met again on inauguration day and tensely rode together to the inauguration platform. Attention of the press and people turned to the Eisenhowers, and after the ceremony, Harry and Bess took the train to Independence, following a farewell party at the house of Dean Acheson.[6]

By the time he left office, Truman evoked anger and contempt from a good part of the public. One study of presidential popularity found that presidents since 1945 have averaged 53 percent approval rating; Truman's average was 45 percent, lower than any of his successors. No one rose as high or fell so far, from 87 percent approval in his first weeks to 23 at the end, although Richard M. Nixon dropped to near that level. In the 1950s the general public usually ignored him, and his periodic forays into political life on behalf of friends seldom succeeded.

In the 1960s and 1970s, his reputation revived. The disunity and confusion of the 1960s caused Americans to look back on Truman's years with nostalgia. The loss of the Vietnam War, the Watergate scandals, the bland mediocrity of the Gerald R. Ford and Jimmy Carter presidencies, and the trickle-down economic approach of Ronald W. Reagan caused a revival of interest in the Missourian. Many people forgot the issues that caused so much anger at the time. A mixture of fact and legend came together, wrote historian Franklin D. Mitchell, to turn Truman into a folk hero who stood up to Soviet leaders without flinching, who battled for the common man, and who fought with integrity, morality, and directness for his beliefs. Merle Miller, in his best-selling book, *Plain Speaking,* summarized this Truman: "You never had to try to figure out what Harry was up to; he told you what he was up to. . . . There was not a duplicitous bone in his body." Miller had forgotten much: "Once Harry found out that a couple of his appointees had been 'influence peddling' . . . and, without hesitation, he threw them downstairs, right out in front of God, the electorate, and everybody."

Historians' rating of Truman never quite fit that of the general public, ranking him higher than the general community early and a little lower later. Liberal historians, whose writings dominated in the 1950s and 1960s, rated Truman high as a president, in the mold of Woodrow Wilson and Franklin Roosevelt. Beginning in 1962, polls among scholars consistently ranked Truman among the top ten presidents, with the broadest poll placing him in the near-great category. A recent biographer, Robert H. Ferrell, predicted that eventually Truman would rank as the nation's second greatest president, just behind Lincoln. Yet based on their 1981 poll, Robert K. Murray and Tim H. Blessing suggested that

Truman's popularity among scholars may have peaked; they found that the oldest historians ranked Truman highest, with middle-aged scholars finding him less meritorious, and young historians harshest in their evaluation. Historian William E. Leuchtenburg found that Truman specialists tended to rank Truman lower than did the rest of the profession.

Leuchtenburg's comment pointed to a change in historians' interpretations of Truman. Many liberal historians admired Truman as a battling proponent of internationalism and domestic reform. Beginning in the 1960s, revisionists reexamined the cold war, the origins of McCarthyism, the achievements of New Deal–Fair Deal reform programs, and the efficacy of Truman's leadership. "In sum," wrote Franklin D. Mitchell, "revisionist historians have cast Truman as a cold warrior, an anti–civil libertarian, ingrained conservative with a liberal gloss, and an ineffectual leader."[7]

Truman's achievement's seemed obvious to many. Winston Churchill told him: "You, more than any other man, have saved Western civilization." Churchill no doubt had in mind the containment policy, enunciated in the Truman Doctrine and put in place through the Marshall Plan, NATO, and the intervention in behalf of Berlin and South Korea. Truman helped to revive and draw together Western Europe into a free world bloc and to establish liberal, democratic governments in West Germany and Japan. Truman's primary domestic achievement was to consolidate and protect the New Deal legacy. He achieved the most extensive reorganization of the government in the twentieth century, institutionalized the presidency, and put forward a number of proposals achieved in some form by later administrations: the Saint Lawrence Seaway, Hawaiian and Alaskan statehood, national health insurance in the form of medicare, and civil rights legislation. Truman often listed avoiding a third world war and maintaining prosperity as his major achievements.

In evaluating Truman, one must keep in mind that he inherited from Roosevelt a reform agenda, a broad outline of foreign policy objectives, and, especially in foreign and military affairs, many of Roosevelt's officials. He worked within a framework partly shaped by Congress, his own bureaucracy, stable and powerful interest groups, needs and demands of allies and adversaries, as well as by forces outside American control entirely, like Asian nationalism. He inherited direction of the most powerful military and economic power on earth, which in itself helped set his agenda. American economic power, for example, meant that Washington assumed certain responsibilities in the world economy. Another president might have lost or gained more in a domestic program or made the cold war harsher or milder, but the welfare-regulatory capitalist state would have continued without much modification and with some degree of conflict with the Soviets.

Truman brought his own personal qualities to his presidency. He was an energetic, hard-working man, generally in good health. He was not driven and obsessed with managing every detail of government operations, as were Lyndon B. Johnson and Jimmy Carter, nor was he as withdrawn from operational particulars as were Eisenhower or Ronald Reagan. He was an optimistic, happy individual, confident that he would do the best he was capable of and sure his best was better than average. Truman possessed optimism, flexibility, an interest in achieving productive results through government action, and an ability to shed resentment and frustration, which he felt but did not become obsessed with, as did Richard M. Nixon.

Truman thought of his presidency, and his life, in terms of decisions he made. Great men made history through making decisions, and Truman saw this as his major role as president. He also thought of himself as a good decision maker. Actually he often acted too rapidly, without thinking deeply about the implications of his actions and the assumptions behind them. His decisions were usually made in the company of a rather narrow range of males who shared similar views of the world and who disagreed mainly on how to carry out a policy rather than on the policy itself.

Ultimately Truman's place in history rests on the cold war—its origins, strategies, and effects. Truman and Stalin drew lines across the globe that endured with remarkable stability for decades. Truman reinforced the American people's belief in the moral rectitude of the United States and its goals in the world. He implemented as the foundation of American policy the Riga axioms, and the rhetoric and action of his administration burned those views so deeply in the minds of the American people and Washington leaders that no other view of the world is taken seriously. Serious foreign policy debate is almost always over what actions or tactics to take within the framework of those axioms. Working from those conceptions, Truman set the pattern for future American leaders to suppress the attempts of other peoples of the world, as in Korea or Vietnam, to gain control of their resources and set their own destinies.[8]

Domestic society has been affected in a variety of ways. Although Eisenhower was on his way out of office before he spoke about the military-industrial complex, in December 1948, Lilienthal noted the "tie-up" between the military and business and believed it would perhaps be the biggest issue in the future. Truman admired military men and appointed an unprecedented number of them to such high civilian positions as secretary of state and of defense, CIA director, occupation governors in Germany and Japan, and ambassadorships. Admirals William D. Leahy, Robert L. Dennison, and Sidney W. Souers were important White House advisers.

Truman demonstrated the efficiency of "military Keynesianism" as a spur to the economy. Under his administration, the services learned to stop feuding over shares of limited budgets and to build support for a large budget with plenty for all. Congressmen learned that even if the legislative branch was losing power in setting national security policy, they still benefited by being able to provide constituents with military jobs and contracts. Early in the postwar years, university administrators and scientists discovered that colleges and laboratories stood to gain from the military-technological revolution. During the Truman administration, government entered the universities in a major way, recruiting graduates into government programs and guiding the direction of research through the allocation of government funding.

Truman could maintain control of national policy despite his loss of public support because he had the military and diplomatic elite behind him within the executive branch, as well as support from powerful congressmen. The nation's most influential press, like the *New York Times*, backed his policy, as did such Republicans as Dewey, Eisenhower, Stimson, Vandenberg, and Dulles. A number of businessmen held powerful positions within his administration: W. Averell Harriman, Robert P. Patterson, Paul G. Hoffman, Robert A. Lovett, David K. Bruce, and James V. Forrestal.[9]

There was little countervailing power arrayed against this powerful government-business-educational complex. Labor had its teeth pulled. Radical leaders were purged from its mainstream, and the movement ceased to grow in numbers and political power, focusing instead on gaining as much of a share of the product of military Keynesianism as corporate leaders chose to award it in return for accepting a quiet, subordinate position in cold war America.

Most liberals crowded their way into the vital center, where they contented themselves with fighting with conservatives over foreign policy tactics and over how much of the budget would be left for butter after the guns were paid for. Even Henry Wallace abandoned the few remaining Wallacites and signed on with Truman in support of the Korean War. With McCarthyism freed by the cold war atmosphere, popular front activities became picturesque relics of the past. A few old progressives remained after World War II to rail against the liberal, corporate state and to warn of the consequences of cold war internationalism, but they were isolated, with little more impact on political discourse than socialists, Communists, or conservative isolationists.

The architects of the cold war created such a clear and compelling image of a Moscow-directed Communist conspiracy to control the world that they were able to reorder the American economy, politics, and governmental structure, as well as other American institutions, including universities and labor unions. The danger they saw was so convincing to others and so immediate that it imposed conformity of thought on society. Much criticism was directed toward cold war tactics or centered on whether more attention should be paid to this or that domestic program, but little examination took place of fundamental cold war assumptions or of the kind of society that liberal capitalism was producing. Truman had so frightened America, Carl Solberg wrote, "that he silenced a whole generation of its young." This was the main impact of the cold war, believed Isaac Deutscher: "While still holding the threat of the physical holocaust [of nuclear war] over our heads, it delivers us immediately to the moral holocaust; it aims immediately at the destruction and mutilation not of our bodies but of our minds; its weapons are the myths and the legends of propaganda."

Despite all of Truman's rhetoric about the common man, the movement begun in 1929 toward a slightly more egalitarian income distribution stopped; income distribution largely stabilized, with the rich beginning to regain a little of their lost ground. Middle-class Americans flocked to the suburbs to live in one-family homes, while older communities and inner cities declined. These suburbanites were often young veterans, building their homes and new-style communities under government programs. The baby boom of these years would have a continuing impact as the boomers moved through the educational system. Americans became more mobile than ever before and especially affected in many subtle ways the nature of American life as they continued to move from rural areas. Within the big cities, minority populations, especially the black community, grew rapidly.[10]

The meaning of many of these characteristics of postwar America

175

were just beginning to emerge as Truman's enemies and friends bade him farewell as he left Washington in 1953. Even at the lowest point of his popularity, Truman had staunch admirers, though many of them believed it was time for him to retire. One group, including much of the nation's elite, admired him for taking what they considered to be brave and wise actions to mobilize the free world against the Communist threat. Many others admired him because he represented to them the democratic ideal, the average man who rose to the highest office in the nation and never forgot his origins. Many of the first group bade him farewell at Dean Acheson's house after Eisenhower's inauguration, and thousands of the latter lined the streets there and other places as he and Bess made the train trip back to Independence. He noted in his diary: "Mrs. T & I were overcome. It was the pay off for thirty years of hell and hard work."

Harry and Bess settled back into the life of Independence, interspersed with travels to Europe and other places they had dreamed of visiting. Both Independence and Kansas City were growing, with Independence largely losing its identity as it was relegated to suburban status. A large part of the old family farm at Grandview became the site of Kansas City's first mall. Yet many of the Trumans' relatives and old friends still lived in the area. Bess settled back into her social network, and Harry found the area alive with friends and associates and memories of the past. His devotion to Bess and Margaret never wavered, and he found new family interest when Margaret married and in 1957 presented him with his first grandchild.

Enjoying old friends and savoring memories did not consume all of Truman's energies. He would have liked to return to the Senate or the House, but even if it had proved politically feasible, Bess would not have allowed it. Nor would he yield to those who wanted him to run for president in 1956: "That's not saying I couldn't," he wrote Margaret, "Wish I could be 50 instead of 70. I'd take 'em around the bend[,] you bet." Although Truman felt he had knowledge and understanding that would benefit the nation, Eisenhower kept him at arm's length, not even extending pro forma honors to him. Truman normally restrained himself publicly in relation to Eisenhower and Vice President Richard Nixon, "Alibi Ike" and "Tricky Dicky" to him in private.

Acheson remained Truman's close friend and adviser and tried to restrain, or at least channel, Truman's impetuous involvement in politics after he left the presidency. He often failed. In 1956 Truman supported Harriman rather than Stevenson for the Democratic nomination, and one observer said his endorsement of Harriman did not bring a single vote to his former associate. By the 1960 election, Truman was even more out of touch.

Acheson tried to keep Truman out of trouble. He encouraged Truman to keep quiet on civil rights issues. With Martin Luther King, Jr., leading a campaign of civil disobedience to end segregation, Truman's remarks often seemed racist. Truman opposed John Kennedy's nomination. He thought he was too young and inexperienced and that a Catholic could not win. Truman detested John's father, Joseph P. Kennedy: "It's not the Pope who worries me, it's the pop." During the next year, Truman seemed to accept the reality that his time had passed. "There couldn't be any doubt how your commencement speech would turn out," he wrote Acheson on 7 July 1961: "wish I could be as certain how my statements would come out. I have been calling off meeting after meeting on that account."

Other work was more productive. He left an important legacy for scholars and others. Before he left the presidency, he urged his friends and associates to help Jonathan W. Daniels gather material for an excellent biography, *The Man of Independence,* which appeared in 1950, and he cooperated with William Hillman to produce in 1952 an interesting and useful book, *Mr. President.* With the help of a number of associates, he wrote his two-volume memoirs, published in 1955 and 1956, which, although often inaccurate, provide the basic record of his administration. He wrote newspaper columns and delivered thousands of talks on the presidency and on his views of life and moral issues. In 1961, he taped 141 interviews with Merle Miller, who used parts of those in *Plain Speaking,* published in 1974. The Truman who appeared there was the man many came to admire in the 1970s. Although few statements of fact in the book can be trusted, it was an interesting expression of Truman's self-image. Much of Truman's time and energy after 1953 went to the Truman Library, his greatest legacy to scholarship.

In these years, Truman achieved more financial security than ever before. Although he received $600,000 from *Life* magazine for his memoirs, only $37,000 of it was left after he paid his staff's salary. In the mid-1950s, however, he sold most of the Grandview farm to a developer, gaining financial security for himself, Vivian, and Mary Jane. In 1958, the government also began to provide pensions for ex-presidents.

Still, retirement was difficult in many ways. Since 1922, Truman had been at the center of political activity at some level of government. Now he could advise power brokers, but he was no longer the decision maker. Also, although Truman loved to instruct and had a deep desire

177

to pass on his understanding of history, politics, and morality to others, he was not a good teacher or writer.

His health broke. He became seriously ill in 1954 and had difficulty recovering from an operation. The real decline started in the 1960s. In 1963 he had a hernia operation followed by a difficult recuperation. In October 1964 he fell, fracturing his ribs and injuring his head. He told an audience that year: "I hope you will remember what I have been and not what I am today." His trips fell off after that, though he still continued to go to his office at the Truman Library until late 1971. Health problems multiplied, and on 26 December 1972, he died. Bess lived for nearly another decade and died on 18 October 1982. Both were buried in the courtyard of the Truman library, a few blocks from where they had first met in 1890.[11]

CHRONOLOGY

8 May 1884	Harry S. Truman born, Lamar, Missouri.
December 1890	Truman family moves to Independence, Missouri.
September 1892	Enters first grade at Noland School in Independence.
May 1901	Graduates from Independence High School.
1901–1906	Enters working world, employed most of this period at a large Kansas City bank.
1906–1917	Works the family farm at Grandview, Missouri.
1917–1919	Serves in World War I as captain in the 129th Field Artillery of the 35th Division.
6 May 1919	Receives discharge from army.
28 June 1919	Marries Bess (Elizabeth Virginia) Wallace.
1919–1922	Owns and operates a men's clothing store in Kansas City, Missouri, with partner Edward Jacobson.
7 November 1922	Elected Eastern District judge of the Jackson County Court.
17 February 1924	Daughter Mary Margaret Truman born.
4 November 1924	Defeated for reelection as Eastern District judge.
1925–1926	Works with Kansas City Automobile Club.
2 November 1926	Elected presiding judge, Jackson County Court.
4 November 1930	Reelected presiding judge, Jackson County Court.
7 August 1934	Wins Democratic primary for U.S. Senate.
6 November 1934	Elected to U.S. Senate.

6 August 1940   Wins Democratic primary for reelection to U.S. Senate.

5 November 1940   Reelected to U.S. Senate.

1941–1945   Wins national recognition as chairman of the Special Committee to Investigate the National Defense Program (Truman Committee).

21 July 1944   Receives nomination as vice president to run with Franklin D. Roosevelt.

7 November 1944   Roosevelt and Truman win election.

20 January 1945   Takes oath as vice president.

12 April 1945   Takes oath as president, following Roosevelt's death.

8 May 1945   Announces German surrender.

16 July 1945   Successful test of atomic bomb in New Mexico.

17 July–2 August 1945   Presides at Potsdam conference meeting of the Big Three Allies.

28 July 1945   Senate ratifies the U.N. charter.

6 August 1945   United States drops atomic bomb on Hiroshima, Japan.

9 August 1945   United States drops atomic bomb on Nagasaki, Japan.

14 August 1945   Announces Japanese surrender.

6 September 1945   Sends Twenty-one Point Address to Congress, containing most of his domestic program later called the Fair Deal.

20 February 1946   Signs the Employment Act of 1946.

25 May 1946   Asks for legislation to draft into the army striking workers under certain conditions.

1 August 1946   Signs the Atomic Energy Act of 1946.

20 September 1946   Requests Henry Wallace's resignation as secretary of commerce.

5 November 1946   Republicans win control of House and Senate in the Eightieth Congress.

12 March 1947   Delivers the Truman Doctrine speech.

21 March 1947   Establishes federal government loyalty program.

5 June 1947	Secretary of State George C. Marshall outlines what becomes the Marshall Plan.
20 June 1947	Vetoes Taft-Hartley Act.
26 July 1947	Signs National Security Act of 1947, unifying the armed forces.
29 October 1947	Receives report of President's Commission on Civil Rights, *To Secure These Rights.*
2 February 1948	Submits his civil rights program to Congress.
3 April 1948	Signs Foreign Assistance Act, implementing the Marshall Plan.
14 May 1948	Recognizes state of Israel.
June 1948	Berlin blockade and airlift begins, lasting almost a year.
15 July 1948	Accepts nomination as Democratic candidate for president.
26 July 1948	Issues executive orders directing end of discrimination in armed services and federal government.
2 November 1948	Wins 1948 election.
20 January 1949	Inaugurated as president.
4 April 1949	Signs North Atlantic Treaty.
15 July 1949	Signs Housing Act of 1949.
23 September 1949	Announces that an atomic explosion has been detected in the Soviet Union.
6 October 1949	Signs Mutual Defense Assistance Act, providing aid to North Atlantic Treaty members.
December 1949	Nationalist government officials flee from the mainland of China to Taiwan.
31 January 1950	Announces order to construct a hydrogen bomb.
9 February 1950	Senator Joseph R. McCarthy's reveals that he has a list of names of Communists in the Department of State.
24 June 1950	Learns of North Korean attack on South Korea.
30 June 1950	Commits ground troops to Korea.

15 September 1950	General Douglas MacArthur successfully lands troops at Inchon.
15 October 1950	Meets with MacArthur on Wake Island.
November 1950	Chinese intervention in Korean War shatters U.N. offensive.
11 April 1951	Relieves General MacArthur of his command.
10 July 1951	Negotiations begin for a truce in Korea.
29 March 1952	Announces he will not run for reelection.
8 April 1952	Issues order seizing steel mills.
2 June 1952	Supreme Court strikes down Truman's seizure of steel mills.
4 November 1952	Dwight D. Eisenhower elected president.
20 January 1953	Attends Eisenhower inaugural and returns with Bess to Independence.
1955–1956	Publishes his two-volume memoirs.
July 1957	Attends dedication of Truman Library.
26 December 1972	Dies at age eighty-eight in Kansas City.

NOTES AND REFERENCES

1. ROOTS

1. Harry S. Truman to Martha and Mary Truman, 16 April 1945, Post Pres.:*Memoirs*, Truman diary note, 12 April 1945, PSF:Appointments, Harry S. Truman Papers, Truman Library; [Mary Martha Truman] to [Nancy Bentley], 2 May 1884, Nancy Bentley Papers, Truman Library.

2. Richard S. Kirkendall, "Harry S. Truman: A Missouri Farmer in the Golden Age," *Agricultural History* 48 (October 1974): 470–73; first quotation in Harry to Bess Truman, 4 August 1941, Papers Pertaining to Family, Business and Personal Affairs File (hereafter cited as Family Affairs File), Truman Papers; [Mary Martha Truman] to Nancy Bentley, 10 May 1883, Bentley Papers; Martha Truman quotation in Margaret Truman, *Harry S. Truman* (New York: William Morrow, 1973), 47–48, 51, 540; *Christian Advocate*, n.d. "Mother Truman's Life Spanned a Rich Period in U.S. History," [27 July 1947], both in Truman, Martha Ellen Young folder, Vertical File, Truman Library.

3. First quotation in Merle Miller, *Plain Speaking: An Oral Biography of Harry S. Truman* (New York: Berkley Publishing, 1974), 67; second quotation in Bela Kornitzer, *American Fathers and Sons* (New York: Hermitage House, 1952), 14–16, 25; third quotation in Truman interview, 14 December 1951, PSF:*Mr. President*, Truman Papers; William Hillman, *Mr. President* (New York: Farrar, Straus and Young, 1952), 153; James D. Barber, *The Presidential Character: Predicting Performance in the White House* (Englewood Cliffs, N.J.: Prentice-Hall, 1972), 261.

4. First quotation in Harry S. Truman, *Year of Decisions* (Garden City, N.Y.: Doubleday, 1955), 113–15, 118–19, 121–23; Truman, "Early 1900's & late 1890's," n.d., longhand note by Truman, n.d., Personal Notes folder, Post Pres.:Desk, Truman Papers; second quotation in Miller, *Plain Speaking*, 63; for an assessment of the high quality of Truman's school work, see Monte M. Poen comment in Harry S. Truman, *Strictly Personal and Confidential: The Letters*

Harry Truman Never Mailed, ed. Monte M. Poen (Boston: Little, Brown, 1982), 139–40.

5. Quotations in Miller, *Plain Speaking,* 23–24, 34–35; Kirkendall, "Harry S. Truman," 468–69; Richard S. Kirkendall, "Truman's Path to Power," *Social Science* 43 (April 1968): 68.

6. Truman to Bess Wallace, 1 November 1911, Family Affairs File.

7. Truman to Bess Wallace, 10 January [1911], 3 May 1911, [26 May 1913], Family Affairs File, Pickwick Note, 14 May 1934, Longhand Notes County Judge folder, Truman, "Public Service," [July 1954], PSF:Longhand Notes, longhand note by Truman, n.d., President's Handwritten Notes folder, Confidential File:White House Central File, Truman interview, 1 October 1951, PSF:Mr. *President,* Truman Papers; Richard L. Miller, *Truman: The Rise to Power* (New York: McGraw-Hill, 1986), 30–33; Charles F. Horne, ed., *Great Men and Famous Women* (New York: Selmar Hess, 1894).

8. Jonathan W. Daniels, oral history interview, Truman Library; George E. Mowry, "The Uses of History by Recent Presidents," *Journal of American History* 53 (June 1966): 6–7, 14–16; Margaret Truman, *Letters from Father: The Truman Family's Personal Correspondence* (New York: Arbor House, 1981), 33; Harry S. Truman, *Years of Trial and Hope* (Garden City, N.Y.: Doubleday, 1956), 1; Harry S. Truman, *Mr. Citizen* (New York: Bernard Geis, 1960), 209.

9. Miller, *Truman,* 33–34; Truman to Bess Truman, 11 December 1935, Truman to Margaret Truman, 24 November 1937, Family Affairs File; Miller, *Plain Speaking,* 101.

10. Truman, *Year of Decisions,* [64], 124–25. See also Robert Griffith, "Harry S. Truman and the Burden of Modernity," *Reviews in American History* 9 (September 1981): 295–306.

11. Longhand note by Truman, [early 1945], Autobiographical Sketch folder, PSF:Biographical, Truman Papers; Truman application for employment, 3 April 1905, A. D. Flintom to [C. H.] Moore, 14 April 1904, Misc. Hist. Doc. 308, Truman Library.

12. First quotation in Truman, "My Impressions of the Senate, the House, Washington, etc.," n.d., Biographical Material folder, Senatorial File, second quotation in Truman to Bess Wallace, 31 December 1910, Family Affairs File, third quotation in longhand note by Truman, n.d., PSF:Longhand Notes, longhand note by Truman, [early 1945], Autobiographical Sketch folder, PSF:Biographical; Kirkendall, "Harry S. Truman," 473–76; Miller, *Truman,* 60–65.

13. First quotation in longhand note by Truman, [early 1945], Autobiographical Sketch folder, PSF:Biographical, second quotation in 2 February 1955, third quotation in 13 April 1952, fourth quotation in 1 June 1945, Truman, "My Masonic History," [1953], longhand note by Truman, n.d., PSF:Longhand Notes; Miller, *Truman,* 68–74.

14. Quotation in Truman to Bess Wallace, [postmark illegible, July or Au-

gust 1913], Family Affairs File, [Truman] to Waynce C. Williams, 25 May 1945, PSF:Appointments, Truman, "Public Service," [July 1954], PSF:Longhand Notes, longhand note by Truman, [early 1945], Autobiographical Sketch folder, PSF:Biographical, "Swearing In Ceremonies," n.d., Senate-Swearing-in-Ceremonies and Funerals folder, Post Pres.:*Memoirs,* longhand note by Truman, 12 July 1960, Personal Notes folder, Post Pres.:Desk.

15. Margaret Truman, *Bess W. Truman* (New York: Macmillan, 1986), 1–3, 6–9, 12–17, 19–22, 56, 119, 162–63.

16. First quotation in Truman, "The Ideals I've Tried to Make Work and Perhaps Haven't," May 1931, Truman, County Judge folder, PSF:Longhand Notes, Truman to Bess Wallace, second quotation in 28 July 1916, third quotation in 3 June 1916, Family Affairs File; Miller, *Truman,* [91]–102, [149]–53, 427n, 428n, Truman, *Bess W. Truman,* 10–11.

17. First quotation in Truman, "The Military Career of a Missourian," n.d., Biographical Material folder, Senatorial File, second quotation in Truman to Bess Wallace, 27 January 1918, third quotation in Truman to Bess Wallace, [27 March 1918], Family Affairs File, Truman, Pickwick note, May 1931, County Judge folder, PSF:Longhand Notes.

18. First quotation in Truman to Bess Wallace, 6 October 1918, second quotation in 20 October 1918, third quotation in 21 January 1919, Family Affairs File, fourth quotation in Truman, Pickwick note, 14 May 1934, County Judge folder, PSF:Longhand Notes.

19. Jonathan Daniels, *The Man of Independence* (Philadelphia: J. B. Lippincott, 1950), 90–91.

2. TRUMAN FINDS HIS CALLING

1. Truman, Pickwick note, 14 May 1934, County Judge folder, PSF:Longhand Notes.

2. Miller, *Truman,* 110, 167–74; Truman, Pickwick note, 14 May 1934, County Judge folder, longhand note by Truman, 10 January 1952, PSF:Longhand Notes, longhand note by Truman, [early 1945], Autobiographical Sketch folder, PSF:Biographical, Truman interview, 9 January 1952, PSF:*Mr. President.*

3. Miller, *Truman,* 181–85, 196–202; Jackson County Court Election 1924 folder, Family Affairs File, Truman, "My Impressions of the Senate, the House, Washington, etc."

4. Truman, *Bess W. Truman,* 90–91, 95, 98, 132.

5. *Examiner* (Independence), 3 January [1927]; Miller, *Truman,* [164]–67, 252–56; Lyle W. Dorsett, *The Pendergast Machine* (New York: Oxford University Press, 1968), 81.

6. Miller, *Truman,* 194–96, 247; Daniels, *Man of Independence,* 152; Dorsett, *Pendergast Machine,* 69–73; Walter Matscheck, oral history interview,

Truman Library; Andrew J. Dunar, *The Truman Scandals and the Politics of Morality* (Columbia: University of Missouri Press, 1984), 8–11; Pendergast quotation in longhand note by Truman, 10 January 1952, PSF:Longhand Notes, last quotation in Truman, Pickwick note, n.d., County Judge folder.

7. There are several Pickwick notes written from late 1930 or early 1931 to 14 May 1934. They are located in County Judge folder, PSF:Longhand Notes; Wallace quotation in Truman interview, 12 November 1949, Daniels Papers.

8. Nathan T. Veatch, oral history interview, Truman Library; Truman, "My Impressions of the Senate, the House, Washington, etc.," Truman, Pickwick note, n.d., County Judge folder, PSF:Longhand Notes; William E. Pemberton, *Bureaucratic Politics: Executive Reorganization during the Truman Administration* (Columbia: University of Missouri Press, 1979), 22–23; Larry Grothuas, "Kansas City Blacks, Harry Truman and the Pendergast Machine," *Missouri Historical Review* 69 (October 1974): 65–82.

9. Alonzo L. Hamby, *Beyond the New Deal: Harry S. Truman and American Liberalism* (New York: Columbia University Press, 1973), 41–42; Miller, *Truman,* 238–42.

10. Truman, Pickwick note, 14 May 1934, County Judge folder, PSF:Longhand Notes.

11. Truman, "My Impressions of the Senate, the House, Washington, etc."; notes of Jonathan Daniels, first quotation in 15 June 1934, second quotation in 28 May 1934, "*Star Morgue,*" Daniels Papers.

12. Hamby, *Beyond the New Deal,* 41–51; Truman Interview, 22 January 1954, Post Pres.:*Memoirs,* Truman to Charles E. Wilson, 18 December 1948, W folder, Truman to Henry Wallace, 18 February 1946, Small Business folder, PSF:General, Truman Papers.

13. Gary M. Fink and James W. Hilty, "Prologue: The Senate Voting Record of Harry S. Truman," *Journal of Interdisciplinary History* 4 (Autumn 1973): 211–31; Truman to Bess Truman, 13 February 1937, Family Affairs File.

14. Daniels note, 18 June 1936, "*Star Morgue*"; Pendergast Correspondence folder, Senatorial File; Miller, *Truman,* 296–314, 320–30, 357–58; Dorsett, *Pendergast Machine,* 118–37; Truman to Bess Truman, 1 August 1939, 3 January [1942], Family Affairs File.

15. First quotation in Truman to William A. Kitchen, 9 October 1941, Political File folder, Senatorial File, Truman to Bess Truman, second quotation in 15 September [1940], fourth quotation in 1 May 1942, Family Affairs File; third quotation in Miller, *Plain Speaking,* 238; fifth quotation in Dean Acheson, *Present at the Creation: My Years in the State Department* (New York: W. W. Norton, 1969), 136; Truman, *Letters from Father,* 85.

16. Fink and Hilty, "Prologue," 224–28; Truman, *Year of Decisions,* 164–67; Truman, *Harry S. Truman,* 138; Donald H. Riddle, *The Truman Committee* (New Brunswick, N.J.: Rutgers University Press, 1964), 12; John W. Snyder,

oral history interview, Truman Library; James F. Byrnes, *All in One Lifetime* (New York: Harper & Brothers, 1958), 91–92.

17. Pemberton, *Bureaucratic Politics*, 24–25.

18. Leon Friedman, "Election of 1944," in *History of American Presidential Elections, 1789–1968*, ed. Arthur M. Schlesinger, Jr., and Fred L. Israel (New York: Chelsea House, 1971), 4:3023–24, 3028; Henry A. Wallace, *The Price of Vision: The Diary of Henry A. Wallace, 1942–1946*, ed. John M. Blum (Boston: Houghton Mifflin, 1973), 380; Henry Morgenthau, *From the Morgenthau Diaries: Years of War, 1941–1945*, ed. John M. Blum (Boston: Houghton Mifflin, 1967), 425; James Boylan, *The New Deal Coalition and the Election of 1946* (New York: Garland, 1981).

19. Friedman, "Election of 1944," 4:3024–28; Wallace, *Price of Vision*, 295, 308–9, 334–67, 370–71; first quotation in unsigned memo, n.d., by [Edwin Pauley], attached to Matthew J. Connelly to Jonathan Daniels, 27 January 1950, President folder, Confidential File:White House Central File, Truman Papers; Byrnes, *All in One Lifetime*, 219–31; Morgenthau, *From the Morgenthau Diaries*, 280–81; second quotation in Roosevelt notes to Hannegan, [Truman] memo on talk with Frank Walker, 12 January 1950, [Truman] to Charlie [Ross], 22 January 1950, Truman to Samuel I. Rosenman, 25 January 1950, Political-Vice Presidential Nomination folder, PSF:Personal; [Robert Sherwood interview with Robert E. Hannegan], 25 May 1946, 6 MS. Am 1947 (1888), Houghton Library, Harvard University; Robert L. Messer, "'Et Tu Brute!' James Byrnes, Harry Truman and the Origins of the Cold War," in *James F. Byrnes and the Origins of the Cold War*, ed. Kendrick A. Clements (Durham, N.C.: Carolina Academic Press, 1982), 25–28; Wilson W. Wyatt, Sr., *Whistle Stops: Adventures in Public Life* (Lexington: University Press of Kentucky, 1985), 38–41; Clinton P. Anderson and Milton Viorst, *Outsider in the Senate: Senator Clinton Anderson's Memoirs* (New York: World Publishing, 1970), 53–54.

20. Longhand note by Truman, [early 1945], Autobiographical Sketch folder, PSF:Biographical, longhand note by Truman, n.d., PSF:Longhand Notes.

21. Truman, *Letters from Father*, 56; Truman, *Year of Decisions*, 193–95.

3. "IT HARDLY SEEMS REAL"

1. Truman diary note, 12 April 1945, PSF:Appointments; Edward R. Stettinius, Jr., *The Diaries of Edward R. Stettinius, Jr., 1943–1946*, ed. Thomas M. Campbell and George C. Herring (New York: New Viewpoints/Franklin Watts, 1975), 316.

2. First quotation in Truman diary note, 13 April 1945, PSF:Appointments, second quotation in Truman to Bess Truman 12 June 1945, Family Affairs File, Harry Truman to Martha and Mary Truman, 8 May 1945,

Post Pres.:*Memoirs;* U.S., Harry S. Truman, *Public Papers of the Presidents of the United States, Harry S. Truman, 1945* (Washington, D.C.: Government Printing Office, 1961), 1–6, 8–15.

3. Truman, *Mr. Citizen,* 221–22; Truman, *Year of Decisions,* 12–13, 119–20, 545–46.

4. Wallace, *Price of Vision,* 437, 458, 528; Samuel Lubell, *The Future of American Politics* (New York: Harper & Brothers, 1952), 10–12, 22, 24–25.

5. Charles S. Murphy, oral history interview, Truman Library; Ken Hechler, *Working with Truman: A Personal Memoir of the White House Years* (New York: G. P. Putnam's, 1982), 27.

6. Wallace, *Price of Vision,* 514; Matthew J. Connelly, Eben A. Ayers, George M. Elsey, Joseph G. Feeney, Harry H. Vaughan, David E. Bell, John W. Snyder, and Jonathan W. Daniels, oral history interviews, Truman Library; David E. Lilienthal, *The Atomic Energy Years, 1945–1950* (New York: Harper & Row, 1964), 7.

7. Quotation in Truman interview, 12 November 1949, Daniels Papers; notation on appointment calendar, 18 May 1945, PSF:Appointments, Truman to Jonathan Daniels, 26 February 1950, not sent, Daniels folder, PSF:Personal, Truman interview, [1953], Cabinet folder, Truman Papers.

8. Nikita Khrushchev, *Khrushchev Remembers,* ed. Strobe Talbott (Boston: Little, Brown, 1970), 223–24; Richard Rhodes, *The Making of the Atomic Bomb* (New York: Simon and Schuster, 1986), 676.

9. Wilson D. Miscamble, "The Evolution of an Internationalist: Harry S. Truman and American Foreign Policy," *Australian Journal of Politics and History* 23 (August 1977): 268–83.

10. *New York Times,* 24 June 1941; Harry Truman to T. J. Pendergast, 16 February 1935, Misc. Hist. Doc. 457, Truman Library; Adam B. Ulam, *The Rivals: America and Russia since World War II* (New York: Viking, 1971), 63; Truman to Bess Truman, 30 April 1942, Family Affairs File.

11. First quotation in Richard E. Neustadt, "Truman in Action: A Retrospect," in *Modern Presidents and the Presidency,* ed. Marc Landy (Lexington, Mass.: D. C. Heath, 1985), 4–5; second quotation in Truman interview, [26 May 1954], The Beginnings folder, Post Pres.:*Memoirs;* third quotation in Hamby, *Beyond the New Deal,* 114; Stettinius, *Diaries of Edward Stettinius,* 318.

12. Daniel Yergin, *Shattered Peace: The Origins of the Cold War and the National Security State* (Boston: Houghton Mifflin, 1977), 70–73; John L. Gaddis, *The United States and the Origins of the Cold War, 1941–1947* (New York: Columbia University Press, 1972), 198–200, 273–76.

13. Roy Douglas, *From War to Cold War, 1942–48* (New York: St. Martin's, 1981), 13–19, 62–71, 75–78, 87, 90–92; U.S., Department of State, *Foreign Relations of the United States, 1945* (Washington, D.C.: Government Printing Office, 1967), 5:147–50, 157–60, 194–96, 210.

14. U.S., Department of State, *Foreign Relations of the United States, 1944* (Washington, D.C.: Government Printing Office, 1966), 4:993; James Forrestal, *the Forrestal Diaries,* ed. Walter Millis (New York: Viking, 1951), 47; W. Averell Harriman and Elie Abel, *Special Envoy to Churchill and Stalin, 1941–1946* (New York: Random House, 1975), 317.

15. Department of State, *Foreign Relations, 1945,* 5:231–34, 252–55.

16. Ibid., 256–58; Truman, *Year of Decisions,* 80–82; Charles E. Bohlen, *Witness to History, 1929–1969* (New York: W. W. Norton, 1973), 213; Robert J. Donovan, *Conflict and Crisis: The Presidency of Harry S. Truman, 1945–1948* (New York: W. W. Norton, 1977), 445 n. 33; Harriman and Abel, *Special Envoy.* 453–54.

17. Truman, *Year of Decisions,* 85–86, 228–29.

18. First two quotations in Truman diary note, 19 May 1945, PSF:Appointments, third quotation in longhand note by Truman, 23 May 1945, PSF:Longhand Notes; Gaddis, *United States and the Origins of the Cold War,* 233–35; Eben Ayers diary, 1 June, 6–7 June, [1945], Eben A. Ayers Papers, Truman Library.

19. Quotation in longhand note by Truman, 7 July 1945; PSF:Longhand Notes, Truman to Margaret Truman, 29 July 1945, Truman to Bess Truman, 29 July 1945, Family Affairs File, Truman interviews, 4 October 1951, 9 January 1952, PSF: *Mr. President;* Charles M. W. Moran, *Churchill: Taken from the Diaries of Lord Moran, the Struggle for Survival, 1940–1965* (Boston: Houghton Mifflin, 1966), 293, 306, 454; Clement R. Attlee, *As It Happened* (New York: Viking, 1954), 205; Anthony Eden, *Full Circle: The Memoirs of the Rt. Hon. Sir Anthony Eden* (London: Cassell, 1960), 5; Edgar Snow, *Journey to the Beginning* (New York: Random House, 1958), 358.

20. Anthony Eden, *The Reckoning* (Boston: Houghton Mifflin, 1965), 621; quotations in Truman, *Year of Decisions,* 349, 351–61.

21. Quotation in longhand note by Truman, 17 July 1945, Ross folder, PSF:Personal; Gaddis, *United States and the Origins of the Cold War,* 238–43; Robert Murphy, *Diplomat among Warriors* (Garden City, N.Y.: Doubleday, 1964), 279; Yergin, *Shattered Peace,* 113–18; Gabriel Kolko, *The Politics of War: The World and United States Foreign Policy, 1943–1945* (New York: Random House, 1968), 570–75.

22. Gar Alperovitz, *Atomic Diplomacy: Hiroshima and Potsdam, the Use of the Atomic Bomb and the American Confrontation with Soviet Power* (New York: Elisabeth Sifton/Penguin, 1985); Barton J. Bernstein, "Roosevelt, Truman, and the Atomic Bomb, 1941–1945: A Reinterpretation," *Political Science Quarterly* 90 (Spring 1975): 24.

23. Martin J. Sherwin, *A World Destroyed: The Atomic Bomb and the Grand Alliance* (New York: Alfred A. Knopf, 1975), 6–8, 14–22, 26–39, 41–44, 47–53, 56–63, 67–68, 71–114, 284.

24. Gerald H. Clarfield and William M. Wiecek, *Nuclear America: Military and Civilian Nuclear Power in the United States, 1940–1980* (New York: Harper & Row, 1984), 80; Bernstein, "Roosevelt, Truman, and the Atomic Bomb," 23–24, 32–37, 35n, 49; Sherwin, *World Destroyed*, xi, 5, 8–9, 115–16, 122–31, 143–49, 152–60, 137–39, 160–64, 286–88, 291–92; quotation in Truman, *Year of Decisions*, 10–11, 85, 87.

25. Sherwin, *World Destroyed*, xi, 194–97, 200–17, 296–302, 304–8; Ferenc M. Szasz, *The Day the Sun Rose Twice: The Story of the Trinity Site Nuclear Explosion, July 16, 1945* (Albuquerque: University of New Mexico Press, 1984), 155; Dan Kurzman, *Day of the Bomb: Countdown to Hiroshima* (New York: McGraw-Hill, 1986), 12–34, 319; Bernstein, "Roosevelt, Truman, and the Atomic Bomb," 38–41; Peter Wyden, *Day One: Before Hiroshima and After* (New York: Simon and Schuster, 1984), 179–80.

26. Barton J. Bernstein, "A Postwar Myth: 500,000 U.S. Lives Saved," *Bulletin of the Atomic Scientists* 42 (June–July 1986): 38–40; Kurzman, *Day of the Bomb*, 242–46, 256; Richard F. Haynes, *The Awesome Power: Harry S. Truman as Commander in Chief* (Baton Rouge: Louisiana State University Press, 1973), 45, 57–58; Truman, *Year of Decisions*, 265, 314–15, 417; Hillman, *Mr. President*, 248; William D. Leahy, *I Was There* (New York: Whittlesey/McGraw-Hill, 1950), 384–85; Clarfield and Wiecek, *Nuclear America*, 64–65.

27. Moran, *Churchill*, 301–2; Wyden, *Day One*, 224; Sherwin, *World Destroyed*, 221–23, 308–12; Truman, *Year of Decisions*, 415; Kurzman, *Day of the Bomb*, 253–54; Truman, *Harry S. Truman*, 272–73; Murphy, *Diplomat among Warriors*, 273; Truman to Bess Truman, 31 July 1945, Family Affairs File, Harry Truman to Martha and Mary Truman, 18 July 1945, Post Pres.:*Memoirs*.

28. Quotation in Truman, *Year of Decisions*, 265–70, 415–16; Sherwin, *World Destroyed*, 188–94, 225–27; Forrestal, *Forrestal Diaries*, 78; [G. K. Zhukov], *The Memoirs of Marshal Zhukov* (New York: Seymour Lawrence/Delacorte, 1971), 674–75; Bernstein, "Roosevelt, Truman, and the Atomic Bomb," 41–49, 62–69; Szasz, *Day the Sun Rose Twice*, 147; Kurzman, *Day of the Bomb*, 257–60; Clarfield and Wiecek, *Nuclear America*, 74–75, 80; Ayers diary, 9 August [1945]; Gaddis, *United States and the Origins of the Cold War*, 211–15, 244–46; Byrnes, *All in One Lifetime*, 291, 297; Truman, *Harry S. Truman*, 273; Truman, *Year of Decisions*, 423–25; Sherwin, *World Destroyed*, 186–87, 198–200, 237–38; Wyden, *Day One*, 225; Michael Schaller, *The American Occupation of Japan: The Origins of the Cold War in Asia* (New York: Oxford University Press, 1985), 14–18; longhand note by Truman, 18 July 1945, Ross folder, PSF:Personal; Truman, *Letters from Father*, 107.

29. Akira Iriye, *Power and Culture: The Japanese-American War, 1941–1945* (Cambridge: Harvard University Press, 1981), 176–83, 212–13, 234–45, 248–65; Forrestal, *Forrestal Diaries*, 74, 76, 277; Acheson, *Present at the Creation*, 113; Truman, *Year of Decisions*, 208–10, 390–92, 396–97, 416–17, 420–21.

30. Eden, *Reckoning,* 634; Truman, *Year of Decisions,* 419–21, 426–36; longhand note by Truman, 25 July 1945, Ross folder, PSF:Personal; Clarfield and Wiecek, *Nuclear America,* 55, 65–66; Sherwin, *World Destroyed,* 232–34, 237; Haynes, *Awesome Power,* 56–57; Rhodes, *Making of the Atomic Bomb,* 734, 741–42.

31. First quotation in Truman, *Year of Decisions,* 421–43; second quotation in Marie Pottsmith to Truman, 11 August 1945, OF692-Misc., Truman Papers.

4. THE TRUMAN MERRY-GO-ROUND

1. Truman, *Public Papers, 1945,* 225.

2. William E. Leuchtenburg, *In the Shadow of FDR: From Harry Truman to Ronald Reagan* (Ithaca: Cornell University Press, 1983), 18–23; Francis H. Heller, ed., *The Truman White House: The Administration of the Presidency, 1945–1953* (Lawrence: Regents Press of Kansas, 1980), 21; Hechler, *Working with Truman,* 45–48; Ed Lockett to David Hulburd, Jr., 5 October 1945, Frank McNaughton Papers, Truman Library; Andrew H. Bartels, "The Office of Price Administration and the Legacy of the New Deal, 1939–1946," *Public Historian* 5 (Summer 1983): 6–23.

3. Barton J. Bernstein, "America In War and Peace: The Test of Liberalism," in *Towards a New Past: Dissenting Essays in American History,* ed. Barton J. Bernstein (New York: Pantheon, 1968), 300–301; Barton J. Bernstein, "The Truman Administration and Its Reconversion Wage Policy," *Labor History* 6 (Fall 1965): 231; Donovan, *Conflict and Crisis,* 107–10, 117; Bartels, "Office of Price Administration," 6–23.

4. R. Alton Lee, *Truman and Taft-Hartley: A Question of Mandate* (Lexington: University of Kentucky Press, 1966), 7–18, 28–31; William Issel, *Social Change in the United States, 1945–1983* (New York: Schocken, 1985), 36–52; Joseph C. Goulden, *The Best Years, 1945–1950* (New York: Atheneum, 1976), 111.

5. Bernstein, "Truman Administration and Its Reconversion Wage Policy," 214–15, 218–24, 226–31; Miller, *Truman,* 359–63; Truman to John J. Dempsey, 26 January 1946, OF552, Truman Papers.

6. Barton J. Bernstein, "The Truman Administration and the Steel Strike of 1946," *Journal of American History* 52 (March 1966): 791–92, 801–3; Chester Bowles to Truman, 18 January 1946, 24 January 1946, Bowles folder, PSF:General.

7. Truman, speech draft, n.d., Railroad speech, Pres. Truman's Notes folder, Clark Clifford Papers, Truman Library; U.S., Harry S. Truman, *Public Papers of the Presidents of the United States, Harry S. Truman, 1946* (Washington D.C.: Government Printing Office, 1962), 274–80, 322–29.

8. Allen J. Matusow, *Farm Policies and Politics in the Truman Years* (Cambridge: Harvard University Press, 1967), 1–32, 35–47, 50–61; Chester Bowles,

Promises to Keep: My Years in Public Life, 1941–1969 (New York: Harper & Row, 1971), 132–37, 148–57; Barton J. Bernstein, "Clash of Interests: The Postwar Battle between the Office of Price Administration and the Department of Agriculture," *Agricultural History* 41 (January 1967): 45–57; quotation in Herman P. Kopplemann to Truman, 8 October 1946, Meat folder, PSF:General.

9. Richard O. Davies, *Housing Reform during the Truman Administration* (Columbia: University of Missouri Press, 1966), x–xiv, 1–22, 25–27, 29–58, 142; Barton J. Bernstein, "Reluctance and Resistance: Wilson Wyatt and Veterans' Housing in the Truman Administration," *Register of the Kentucky Historical Society* 65 (January 1967): 47–65; Wyatt, *Whistle Stops*, 59–61, 63–70, 75–86.

10. Arthur H. Vandenberg, *The Private Papers of Senator Vandenberg* (Boston: Houghton Mifflin, 1952), 167; David W. Reinhard, *The Republican Right since 1945* (Lexington: University Press of Kentucky, 1983), 12; Robert L. Pritchard, "Southern Politics and the Truman Administration: Georgia as a Test Case" (Ph.D. diss., University of California, Los Angeles, 1970), 19.

11. Snyder, Samuel I. Rosenman, oral history interviews, Truman Library; Truman, *Public Papers, 1945*, 263–309, 359–62, 362–66, 475–91, 516–21, 546–60; quotation in Truman interview, 12 November 1949, Daniels Papers; longhand note by Truman, n.d., PSF:Longhand Notes; Richard E. Neustadt, "Congress and the Fair Deal: A Legislative Balance Sheet," *Public Policy* 5 (1954): 357–59.

12. First quotation in Truman to Mary Truman, 31 July 1946, Post Pres.:*Memoirs*; second quotation in Frank McNaughton to Don Bermingham, 29 June 1946, McNaughton Papers; Robert A. Garson, *The Democratic Party and the Politics of Sectionalism, 1941–1948* (Baton Rouge: Louisiana State University Press, 1974), xi, 133–61; Donovan, *Conflict and Crisis*, 122–24, 169–70; Monte M. Poen, *Harry S. Truman versus the Medical Lobby: The Genesis of Medicare* (Columbia: University of Missouri Press, 1979), ix–x, 51–85, 87–92, 222–30; Otis L. Graham, Jr., *Toward a Planned Society: From Roosevelt to Nixon* (New York: Oxford University Press, 1976), 86–91.

13. Hamby, *Beyond the New Deal*, xix–xx, 55–59, 82–85; Pepper quotation in Leuchtenburg, *In the Shadow of FDR*, 12–18, 26; Lilienthal, *Atomic Energy Years*, 433–34; Heller, *Truman White House*, 53; Robert J. Williams, "Harry S. Truman and the American Presidency," *Journal of American Studies* 13 (December 1979): 395; Mellon Gallery quotation in Truman diary, 4 April 1948, Post Pres.:*Memoirs*.

14. Truman, [1946], PSF:Longhand Notes.

15. Wallace, *Price of Vision*, 31–35, 38–45, 502–3, 516, 523–24, 551, 558, 589–603, 617–26, 629, first quotation at 661–67, second quotation at 612–15; Truman *Year of Decisions*, 555–60, third quotation at 557; press conference quotations in Truman, *Public Papers, 1946*, 426–27; Acheson quotation in Acheson, *Present at the Creation*, 192; Forrestal, *Forrestal Diary*, 207–9; Bernard

Gladieux, "Conversations with Secretary Wallace," 12 September 1946, 18 September 1946, Gladieux 1946 folder, Bernard L. Gladieux Papers, Truman Library; "blunder" quotation in Charles Ross Diary, 21 September 1946, PSF:Personal, Truman to Bess Truman, 16, 17, 19, 20 September 1946, Family Affairs File, Truman to Martha and Mary Truman, 18, 20 September 1946, Post Pres.:*Memoirs*, longhand notes by Truman, 17 September 1946, fourth quotation in 16 September 1946, "Commie-Jesuit" quotation in 19 September 1946, PSF:Longhand Notes, James Byrnes to Donald Russell for delivery to president [18 September 1946], unsigned memo, [19 September 1946], Byrnes and Truman, teletype conference, 19 September 1946, PSF:Appointments.

16. Donovan, *Conflict and Crisis*, 229–34, 237; Matusow, *Farm Policies and Politics*, 63–68; Boylan, *New Deal Coalition*, 132–43, 152–54; Athan G. Theoharis, "The Truman Presidency: Trial and Error," *Wisconsin Magazine of History* 55 (Autumn 1971): 53.

5. THE RUSSIANS ARE COMING

1. Thomas G. Paterson, *On Every Front: The Making of the Cold War* (New York: W. W. Norton, 1979), 12–18, 22–32; A. W. DePorte, *Europe between the Superpowers: The Enduring Balance* (New Haven: Yale University Press, 1979), 115–17; Joyce Kolko and Gabriel Kolko, *The Limits of Power: The World and United States Foreign Policy, 1945–1954* (New York: Harper & Row, 1972), 111, 329–32; Yergin, *Shattered Peace*, 7–8; Acheson, *Present at the Creation*, xvi; Walter Lippmann, *Public Philosopher: Selected Letters of Walter Lippmann* (New York: Ticknor and Fields, 1985), 477.

2. Lloyd C. Gardner, *A Covenant with Power: America and World Order from Wilson to Reagan* (London: Macmillan, 1984), xii–xiii, 4–6, 12–16; Thomas G. Paterson, *Soviet-American Confrontation: Postwar Reconstruction and the Origins of the Cold War* (Baltimore: Johns Hopkins University Press, 1973), ix–x, 1–14, 263–64; David P. Calleo and Benjamin M. Rowland, *America and the World Political Economy: Atlantic Dreams and National Realities* (Bloomington: Indiana University Press, 1973), 3–4, 7, 25–37; Loren Baritz, *Backfire: A History of How American Culture Led Us into Vietnam and Made Us Fight the Way We Did* (New York: William Morrow, 1985), 19–44; Edward Weisband, *The Ideology of American Foreign Policy: Paradigm of Lockian Liberalism* (Beverly Hills: Sage, 1973), 8–10, 48–50; Truman, *Public Papers, 1945*, 6, 431–38.

3. Yergin, *Shattered Peace*, 35–39, 43–46; Stanley M. Max, *The United States, Great Britain, and the Sovietization of Hungary, 1945–1948* (Boulder, Colo.: East European Monographs, 1985), 55–57, 133–34; Paterson, *On Every Front*, 74–77; Ernest R. May, *"Lessons" of the Past: The Use and Misuse of History in American Foreign Policy* (New York: Oxford University Press, 1973), ix–xii, 31–53; Gaddis, *United States and the Origins of the Cold War*, 1–3.

4. Paterson, *On Every Front*, 113–37, quotation at 137; Walter LaFeber, "American Policy-Makers, Public Opinion, and the Outbreak of the Cold War, 1945–50," in *The Origins of the Cold War in Asia*, ed. Yonosuke Nagai and Akira Iriye (New York: Columbia University Press, 1977), 43–62.

5. Marshall quotation in Forrestal, *Forrestal Diaries*, 459; Yergin, *Shattered Peace*, 5–6, 12–13, 193–201, 219–20; Dean Acheson, *Among Friends: Personal Letters of Dean Acheson*, ed. David S. McLellan and David C. Acheson (New York: Dodd, Mead, 1980), 86–87; Bernard A. Weisberger, *Cold War Cold Peace: The United States and Russia since 1945* (New York: American Heritage, 1984), 68–71; Melvyn P. Leffler, "The American Conception of National Security and the Beginnings of the Cold War, 1945–48," *American Historical Review* 89 (April 1984): 348–80.

6. Yergin, *Shattered Peace*, 79–82; Sherwin, *World Destroyed*, 170–74, 176–84; Joseph E. Davies, "Deterioration in Relations between the Soviets and Britain and the United States and Its Serious Threat to Peace," 29 September 1945, Davies to Truman, 30 September 1945, Davies folder, PSF:General; Wallace, *Price of Vision*, 556–57.

7. Robert L. Ivie, "Literalizing the Metaphor of Soviet Savagery: President Truman's Plain Style," *Southern Speech Communication Journal* 51 (Winter 1986): 94–105; Truman, *Public Papers, 1945*, 380–81; U.S., Harry S. Truman, *Public Papers of the Presidents of the United States, Harry S. Truman, 1947* (Washington, D.C.: Government Printing Office, 1963), 167–72; Truman interviews, 1, 4 October 1951, 14, 17 December 1951, PSF:Mr. *President;* Anatol Rapoport, *The Big Two: Soviet-American Perceptions of Foreign Policy* (Indianapolis: Pegasus, 1971), 91–92.

8. Truman, *Letters from Father*, 107–8; Deborah W. Larson, *Origins of Containment: A Psychological Explanation* (Princeton: Princeton University Press, 1985), 146–49, 151–57, 191–92; Cyrus L. Sulzberger, *A Long Row of Candles: Memoirs and Diaries, 1934–1954* (New York: Macmillan, 1969), 363–64.

9. Nikolai V. Sivachev and Nikolai N. Yakovlev, *Russia and the United States* (Chicago: University of Chicago Press, 1979), 165, 171–75, 179–96; Kolko, *Politics of War*, 344–48, 350–69; Gaddis, *United States and the Origins of the Cold War*, 157–65, 171–73; Lynn E. Davis, *The Cold War Begins: Soviet-American Conflict over Eastern Europe* (Princeton: Princeton University Press, 1974) 179–83; Isaac Deutscher, *Ironies of History: Essays on Contemporary Communism* (London: Oxford University Press, 1966), 148–56, 158–60; Kolko and Kolko, *Limits of Power*, 53–57; Rapoport, *Big Two*, 76–77; Paterson, *On Every Front*, 142–45, 148–57; Robert V. Daniels, *Russia: The Roots of Confrontation* (Cambridge: Harvard University Press, 1985) 218–20; DePorte, *Europe between the Superpowers*, 62–74; William Zimmerman, "Choices in the Postwar World: Containment and the Soviet Union," in *Caging the Bear: Containment and the Cold War*, ed. Charles Gati (Indianapolis: Bobbs-Merrill Co., 1974), 100–108; Paolo Spriano, *Stalin and the European Communists* (London: Verso, 1985), 270–

79; Timothy Dunmore, *Soviet Politics, 1945–53* (New York: St. Martin's, 1984), 1–2, 12–18, 100–106, 124–25; William O. McCagg, Jr., *Stalin Embattled, 1943–1948* (Detroit: Wayne State University Press, 1978), 32–40, 75–76, 149–73, 184–90; quotation in Charles Ross diary, 25 March [1946], PSF:Personal; Diane S. Clemens, *Yalta* (New York: Oxford University Press, 1970), 268–74.

10. Acheson, *Present at the Creation*, 113; Henry L. Stimson to Truman, 11 September 1945, Atomic Bomb folder, PSF:General.

11. Anderson, *Outsider in the Senate*, 68–69; Acheson, *Present at the Creation*, 123–24; Wallace, *Price of Vision*, 481–85, 492; Truman, *Year of Decisions*, 525–28; cabinet minutes, 21 September 1945, Atomic Bomb folder, PSF:General, see various letters to Truman on international control of atomic energy in this folder and in NSC–Atomic Bomb–Cabinet folder, PSF-Subject, Truman Papers; Ayers diary, 24 September [1945].

12. Truman, *Public Papers, 1945*, 365–66, 381–83, 437; Gaddis, *United States and the Origins of the Cold War*, 253–54, 268–73; Clarfield and Wiecek, *Nuclear America*, 87–97; Acheson, *Present at the Creation*, 131–32; Vannevar Bush, *Pieces of the Action* (New York: William Morrow, 1970), 296; U.S., Department of State, *Foreign Relations of the United States, 1945* (Washington, D.C.: Government Printing Office, 1967), 2:55–56, 59–62, 70–73; Lilienthal, *Atomic Energy Years*, 10–11, 123; Walter Isaacson and Evan Thomas, *The Wise Men: Six Friends and the World They Made, Acheson, Bohlen, Harriman, Kennan, Lovett, McCloy* (New York: Simon and Schuster, 1986), 356–60; Kolko and Kolko, *Limits of Power*, 102–3.

13. Acheson, *Present at the Creation*, 154–55; Truman, *Harry S. Truman*, 348; Lilienthal, *Atomic Energy Years*, 31–32, 42–43, 59–61, 69–70, 73, 76–77, 125; Kolko and Kolko, *Limits of Power*, 103–10; Clarfield and Wiecek, *Nuclear America*, 97–98, 81–83; Baruch to Truman, 26 March 1946, Atomic Energy Control Commission folder, Baruch to Truman, 2 July 1946, Truman to Baruch, 10 July 1946, Baruch folder, PSF:General, Truman and Acheson interview, 16 February 1955, Acheson folder, Post Pres.:*Memoirs*; Sherwin, *World Destroyed*, 3.

14. Robert A. Pollard, *Economic Security and the Origins of the Cold War, 1945–1950* (New York: Columbia University Press, 1985), 8–18, 22–23, 33–40, 67–71, 73–79, 82–84, 86–89; Kenneth W. Dam, *The Rules of the Game: Reform and Evolution in the International Monetary System* (Chicago: University of Chicago Press, 1982), 71–76; Paterson, *Soviet-American Confrontation*, 147–57; Fred L. Block, *The Origins of International Economic Disorder: A Study of United States International Monetary Policy from World War II to the Present* (Berkeley: University of California Press, 1977), 10, 36, 38–69; Kolko and Kolko, *Limits of Power*, 60–66.

15. Paterson, *On Every Front*, 1–12; Paterson, *Soviet-American Confrontation*, 33–43, 57–74; Kolko, *Politics of War*, 3–4; Truman, *Year of Decisions*, 464–80; George C. Herring, Jr., *Aid to Russia, 1941–1946: Strategy, Diplomacy,*

the Origins of the Cold War (New York: Columbia University Press, 1973), 240–75, 289–92; minutes, cabinet meeting, 19 April 1946, Matthew J. Connelly Papers, Truman Library; Harriman and Abel, *Special Envoy*, 533.

16. Paterson, *Soviet-American Confrontation*, 10–11, 77–89; quotation in Wallace, *Price of Vision*, 439–40; Kolko, *Politics of War*, 457–61, 467–74, 477–78; Trygve Lie, *In the Cause of Peace: Seven Years with the United Nations* (New York: Macmillan, 1954), 22–106.

17. Department of State, *Foreign Relations, 1945*, 2:194–200, 243–47; Walter LaFeber, "Comment on Professor Herken's Paper," in Clements, *James F. Byrnes and the Origins of the Cold War*, 99–104; Gregg F. Herken, "'Stubborn, Obstinate, and They Don't Scare': The Russians, the Bomb, and James F. Byrnes," in Clements, *James F. Byrnes and the Origins of the Cold War*, 50–56; Acheson quotation in Acheson interview, 18 February 1955, Acheson folder, Post Pres.:*Memoirs*, Truman quotation in Truman to Byrnes, 5 January 1946, PSF:Longhand Notes; Messer, "Et Tu Brute!" 36–43; Byrnes, *All in One Lifetime*, 343, 346–47, 400–404; Truman, *Year of Decisions*, 546–52; Clark Clifford interview, 26 October 1949, Daniels Papers.

6. CONTAINING THE SOVIETS

1. Quotation in Acheson, *Among Friends*, 84; Messer, "Et Tu Brute!" 36–39, 44–45; Ayers diary, 28 February [1946]; Patricia D. Ward, *The Threat of Peace: James F. Byrnes and the Council of Foreign Ministers, 1945–1946* (Kent, Ohio: Kent State University Press, 1979), 175–76, 178–79; U.S., Department of State, *Foreign Relations of the United States, 1946* (Washington, D.C.: Government Printing Office, 1970), 2:204.

2. Paterson, *On Every Front*, 52–57; David S. Painter, *Oil and the American Century: The Political Economy of U.S. Foreign Oil Policy* (Baltimore: Johns Hopkins University Press, 1986), 75–81; Yergin, *Shattered Peace*, 179–82; Kolko and Kolko, *Limits of Power*, 70–73, 235–42; Bruce R. Kuniholm, *The Origins of the Cold War in the Near East* (Princeton, N.J.: Princeton University Press, 1980), xvii–xviii, 140–48, 154–60, 177–89, 212, 236–44, 270–340, 342–59, 383–97; Paterson, *Soviet-American Confrontation*, 182–83.

3. First quotation in Acheson, *Present at the Creation*, 196; second quotation in Charles Robbins and Bradley Smith, *Last of His Kind: An Informal Portrait of Harry S. Truman* (New York: William Morrow, 1979), 15, 18–20; Fraser J. Harbutt, *The Iron Curtain: Churchill, America, and the Origins of the Cold War* (New York: Oxford University Press, 1986), 159–75; Hugh DeSantis, *The Diplomacy of Silence: The American Foreign Service, the Soviet Union, and the Cold War, 1933–1947* (Chicago: University of Chicago Press, 1980), 176–79; John L. Gaddis, *Strategies of Containment: A Critical Appraisal of Postwar American National Security Policy* (New York: Oxford University Press, 1982), 19–23, 25–

47, 54–55, 83–84; George F. Kennan, *Memoirs, 1925–1950* (Boston: Little, Brown, 1967), 1:8, 28–33, 48–49, 57, 68–70, 253–56, 292–95, 298, 354–60, 364–67, third quotation at 293; Barton Gellman, *Contending with Kennan: Toward a Philosophy of American Power* (New York: Praeger, 1984), 4–5; Paterson, *On Every Front*, 145–48; McCagg, *Stalin Embattled*, 190–209, 217–22, 227–37, 241–43, 257–58, 260; Long Telegram in U.S., Department of State, *Foreign Relations of the United States, 1946* (Washington, D.C.: Government Printing Office, 1969), 6:696–709; Kennan to Acheson, 3 January 1949, Memoirs of Conversation folder, Acheson Papers; Clifford, "American Relations with the Soviet Union," September 1946, in Arthur Krock, *Memoirs: Sixty Years on the Firing Line* (New York: Funk and Wagnalls, 1968), 419, 425–80.

4. Quotation in Paterson, *Soviet-American Confrontation*, 99–100; Michael M. Boll, *Cold War in the Balkans: American Foreign Policy and the Emergence of Communist Bulgaria, 1943–1947* (Lexington: University Press of Kentucky, 1984), 2, 189–92; Kolko and Kolko, *Limits of Power*, 112–24, 128–37, 140–44, 177–79, 196–97, 199–201, 215–17, 403–7, 422–26; Kolko, *Politics of War*, 504–6; Davis, *Cold War Begins*, 202–23, 226–27, 332, 369–88, 392–95; Max, *United States, Great Britain, and the Sovietization of Hungary*, 49, 135–39; Yergin, *Shattered Peace*, 366–67; Douglas, *From War to Cold War*, 135–36; Lucius D. Clay, oral history interview, Truman Library.

5. Donovan, *Conflict and Crisis*, 104; Russell D. Buhite, *Soviet-American Relations in Asia, 1945–1954* (Norman: University of Oklahoma Press, 1981), xi–xii; Lisle A. Rose, *Roots of Tragedy: The United States and the Struggle for Asia, 1945–1953* (Westport, Conn.: Greenwood Press, 1976), 1–8, 39, 244–48; Truman, Acheson, and Nehru, memorandum of conversation, 13 October 1949, India–Pandat Jawaharlal Nehru folder, PSF:Subject; Charles M. Dobbs, *The Unwanted Symbol: American Foreign Policy, the Cold War, and Korea, 1945–1950* (Kent, Ohio: Kent State University Press, 1981), x–xi, 196; Iriye, *Cold War in Asia*, 9–49, 53–59, 64–84, 93–96.

6. Acheson interview, 17 February 1955, *Memoirs* Acheson folder, Post Pres.:Memoirs; Robert J. Donovan, *Tumultuous Years: The Presidency of Harry S. Truman, 1949–1953* (New York: W. W. Norton, 1982), 67–69; quotations in Truman to Harry Vaughan, 12 August 1950, Ba–Bh folder, PSF:General and Truman interview, 10 November 1951, PSF: *Mr. President*; Iriye, *Cold War in Asia*, 108–24, 143–46; Donald S. Zagoria, "Choices in the Postwar World: Containment and China," in Gati, *Caging the Bear*, 116–17, 119–25.

7. U.S., Department of State, *Foreign Relations of the United States, 1945* (Washington, D.C.: Government Printing Office, 1969), 7:767–68, 770; U.S., Department of State, *Foreign Relations of the United States, 1946* (Washington, D.C.: Government Printing Office, 1972), 9:1–2; U.S., Department of State, *Foreign Relations of the United States, 1946* (Washington, D.C.: Government Printing Office, 1972), 10:53–54, 109–11, 267–68, 271–74, 289–92, 651–52,

661–65; Acheson, *Present at the Creation*, 140, 144–47; William W. Stueck, *The Road to Confrontation: American Policy toward China and Korea, 1947–1950* (Chapel Hill: University of North Carolina Press, 1981), 11–12, 18–19.

8. U.S., Department of State, *Foreign Relations of the United States, 1946* (Washington, D.C.: Government Printing Office, 1969), 7:223–24.

9. Larson, *Origins of Containment*, 279–84.

10. Lawrence S. Wittner, *American Intervention in Greece, 1943–1949* (New York: Columbia University Press, 1982), 60–64, 254–82; Byrnes to Truman, 20 December 1946, PSF:Appointments; Mark F. Ethridge, oral history interview, Truman Library; Department of State, *Foreign Relations, 1946*, 7:240–45, 840–42, 857–58; U.S., Department of State, *Foreign Relations of the United States, 1947* (Washington, D.C.: Government Printing Office, 1971), 5:23–25, 28–31, quotation on 2–3.

11. Department of State, *Foreign Relations, 1947*, 5:32–37, 44–45, 58, 58n, 60–62; Clark Clifford and Loy W. Henderson, oral history interviews, Truman Library; quotations in Acheson, *Present at the Creation*, 218–19.

12. Yergin, *Shattered Peace*, 282–84; Donovan, *Conflict and Crisis*, 281–83; Acheson, *Present at the Creation*, 220–21; Gaddis, *United States and the Origins of the Cold War*, 349–51; Bohlen, *Witness to History*, 261; Kennan, *Memoirs*, 1:319–21; Lilienthal, *Atomic Energy Years*, 159; Elsey to Clifford, 7 March 1947, Marx Leva to [Forrestal], 8 March 1947, Presidential Speech File, 1947, March 12, 1947, Speech to Congress on Greece folder, Clifford Papers; Comment by CMC [Clifford], noted by [George Elsey], 9 March 1947, March 12 Truman Doctrine Speech folder, George Elsey Papers, Truman Library; Truman, *Public Papers, 1947*, 176–80.

13. Quotation in Truman, *Harry S. Truman*, 343; John Foster Dulles to Arthur Vandenberg, 21 July 1947, Correspondence folder, Arthur Vandenberg Papers, Bentley Historical Library, University of Michigan; Richard M. Freeland, *The Truman Doctrine and the Origins of McCarthyism: Foreign Policy, Domestic Politics, and Internal Security, 1946–1948* (New York: Alfred A. Knopf, 1972), 76–79, 82–101, 102–14; U.S., Congress, Senate, Committee on Foreign Relations, *Hearings, Legislative Origins of the Truman Doctrine*, 80th Congress, first session, 1947, 5, 17, 20–22, 32, 39, 40, 47–51, 66, 124–29, 160.

14. Baritz, *Backfire*, 66; quotation in Senate, *Legislative Origins of the Truman Doctrine*, 95; Cecil V. Crabb, Jr., *The Doctrines of American Foreign Policy: Their Meaning, Role, and Future* (Baton Rouge: Louisiana State University Press, 1982), 108; Clifford to William Southern, 9 September 1949, Southern folder, PSF:Personal; U.S., Department of State, *Foreign Relations of the United States, 1949* (Washington, D.C.: Government Printing Office, 1974), 3:174–75; Kuniholm, *Origins of the Cold War*, 415–18; Freeland, *Truman Doctrine*, 115–34; Yergin, *Shattered Peace*, 275–76.

15. Wittner, *American Intervention in Greece*, 103–52, 260–77, 283–312.

16. Pollard, *Economic Security,* ix–x, 2, 9, 63–66, 103–6, 133–36, 148–52, 164–67; Paterson, *Soviet-American Confrontation,* 207, 231–34; Joseph M. Jones to Mr. Russell, 18 July 1947, Truman Doctrine:Important Relevant Papers folder, Joseph M. Jones Papers, Truman Library; Truman interview, [1953 or 1954], Foreign Policy–History of folder, Post Pres.:*Memoirs,* Truman to Martha and Mary Truman, 23 August 1947, Post Pres.:*Memoirs;* Yergin, *Shattered Peace,* 297–301, 303–9, 317–20, 329-34; Imanuel Wexler, *The Marshall Plan Revisited: The European Recovery Program in Economic Perspective* (Westport, Conn.: Greenwood Press, 1983), 4–5, 9, 26–40, 69, 249, 251–55; William S. Borden, *The Pacific Alliance: United States Foreign Economic Policy and Japanese Trade Recovery, 1947–1955* (Madison: University of Wisconsin Press, 1984), 12–15, 19–28, 29–42, 60, 152–53; Block, *Origins of International Economic Disorder,* 9–10, 70–92; John Gimbel, *The American Occupation of Germany: Politics and the Military, 1945–1949* (Stanford: Stanford University Press, 1968), 1–5, 8–16, 34–36, 53–54, 127–40, 247–74, 279–80; Alfred E. Eckes, Jr., *A Search for Solvency: Bretton Woods and the International Monetary System, 1941–1971* (Austin: University of Texas Press, 1975), 217–19; U.S., Harry S. Truman, *Public Papers of the Presidents of the United States, Harry S. Truman, 1948* (Washington, D.C.: Government Printing Office, 1964), 182–86; Freeland, *Truman Doctrine,* 154–55, 187–200, 246–64, 269–86; Yergin, *Shattered Peace,* 326–29; Alan R. Raucher, *Paul G. Hoffman: Architect of Foreign Aid* (Lexington: University Press of Kentucky, 1985), 63; Lawrence S. Wittner, *Cold War America: From Hiroshima to Watergate* (New York: Praeger, 1974), 66.

17. Dunmore, *Soviet Politics,* 108–11; McCagg, *Stalin Embattled,* 261–62; Yergin, *Shattered Peace,* 310–14, 324–26, 343–50; Kennan, *Memoirs,* 1:378–79.

18. Truman, *Letters from Father,* 107–8; Yergin, *Shattered Peace,* 351–60, 364–65; Ayers diary, 16 March [1948]; Kennan, *Memoirs,* 1:400–403; Lilienthal, *Atomic Energy Years,* 351.

19. First quotation in U.S., Department of State, *Foreign Relations of the United States, 1948* (Washington, D.C.: Government Printing Office, 1973), 2:919–21; second quotation in Forrestal, *Forrestal Diaries,* 454; Kolko and Kolko, *Limits of Power,* 488–97; Yergin, *Shattered Peace,* 366–72, 376–80, 390, 395–97; Paterson, *Soviet-American Confrontation,* 258–59; Truman diary, 19 July, 13 September 1948, Post Pres.:*Memoirs;* Lilienthal, *Atomic Energy Years,* 406.

20. Yergin, *Shattered Peace,* 264–71, 336–43, 360–62, 408; U.S., Department of State, *Foreign Relations of the United States, 1948* (Washington, D.C.: Government Printing Office, 1976), 1, pt. 2:663–69; U.S., Department of State, *Foreign Relations of the United States, 1948* (Washington, D.C.: Government Printing Office, 1974), 3:4–12, 48; Lawrence S. Kaplan, *The United States and NATO: The Formative Years* (Lexington: University Press of Kentucky, 1984), 1–5, 21, 27, 49–64, 66–71, 120; Gardner, *Covenant with Power,* 80–81,

83–84; Steven L. Rearden, *The Formative Years, 1947–1950* (Washington, D.C.: Office of Secretary of Defense, 1984), 457–75; 481; Kennan, *Memoirs,* 1:407–13; Wittner, *Cold War America,* 67–68.

21. Truman, *Years of Trial and Hope,* 250–61; Acheson, *Present at the Creation,* 21–22, 88, 249–50, 378–79; Barry Rubin, *Secrets of State: The State Department and the Struggle over U.S. Foreign Policy* (New York: Oxford University Press, 1985), 64–65; Acheson interview, 16, 18 February 1955, Acheson folder, Post Pres.:*Memoirs.*

22. Iriye, *Cold War in Asia,* 96–101, 103–8, 124–29, 132–42, 156–60; Lilienthal, *Atomic Energy Years,* 525; Ayers diary, 3 February [1948]; [Matthew Connelly], cabinet meeting, 26 November 1948, Connelly Papers; Stueck, *Road to Confrontation,* 31, 36–63, 70–74, 120–26.

23. William Manchester, *American Caesar: Douglas MacArthur, 1880–1964* (Boston: Little, Brown, 1978), 459–60, 464–66, 472, 474–83; Stettinius, *Diaries of Stettinius,* 427; D. Clayton James, *Triumph and Disaster, 1945–1964,* vol. 3, *The Years of MacArthur* (Boston: Houghton Mifflin, 1985), 7–17, 53–54, 110–35, 139–48, 154–57, 174–91, 222–35, 247, 254–60, 281–86, 295–301, 326–35; Toshio Nishi, *Unconditional Democracy: Education and Politics in Occupied Japan, 1945–1952* (Stanford: Hoover Institution Press, 1982), 286–302; Schaller, *American Occupation of Japan,* viii–ix, 24–26, 28–47, 51, 77–83, 85–97, 101–63, 212–20, 233; Borden, *Pacific Alliance,* 3–5, 61–86, 144–47, 159–64, 167–68, 191–202, 214–18, 222.

24. Freeland, *Truman Doctrine,* 9–11, 201–34, 299–306, 360.

7. POLITICAL PRESSURES, POLITICAL VICTORIES

1. Longhand note by Truman, 11 December 1946, PSF:Longhand Notes.

2. Donovan, *Conflict and Crisis,* 271–72; Oscar R. Ewing, Leon H. Keyserling, and Clark Clifford, oral history interviews, Truman Library; quotation in Hamby, *Beyond the New Deal,* xviii–xix, 3–9, 13–22, 53–54, 59–79, 88–102, 113, 147–54, 168, 170–94, 194–204.

3. Theoharis, "Truman Presidency," 49–50; Boylan, *New Deal Coalition,* introduction, 19–28, 167–72; Bernstein, "America in War and Peace," 301–2, 308; Graham, *Toward a Planned Society,* 113–14.

4. Susan M. Hartmann, *Truman and the 80th Congress* (Columbia: University of Missouri Press, 1971), 1–2, 8–17, 19–26, 29–59, 69, 79–90, 100–101, 107–12, 116–20, 128–54, 157–85, 211–16; Boylan, *New Deal Coalition,* 74–75, 85, 106–16; Reinhard, *Republican Right since 1945,* 17, 20–24, 36; Lee, *Truman and Taft-Hartley,* v–vi, 1–4, 52–53, 67–68, 71, 75–78, 81–101, 131–53, 231–37; Truman, *Public Papers, 1947,* 288–97; Truman interview, 12 November 1949, Daniels Papers.

5. Charles Sawyer, *Concerns of a Conservative Democrat* (Carbondale: Southern Illinois University Press, 1968), 175–76, 301; Steelman and Truman

interview, 9 December 1954, Steelman folder, Post Pres.:*Memoirs;* Heller, *Truman White House,* 57–58, 95–98; Steelman interview, 20 May 1959, Misc. Hist. Doc. 226, Truman Library; Bell, Elsey, Keyserling, Clifford, and Connelly, oral history interviews; Michael Medved, *The Shadow Presidents: The Secret History of the Chief Executives and Their Top Aides* (New York: Times Books, 1979), 219.

6. Richard S. Kirkendall, "Truman and the South" (paper delivered at Southern Historical Association, October 1969), 1–5; Daniels, oral history interview; [Truman], "Early 1900's & Late 1890's," Harry S. Truman's Personal Notes papers, Post. Pres.:Desk; Truman, *Harry S. Truman,* 392; first quotation in Truman, *Years of Trial and Hope,* 269; Truman to Bess Wallace Truman, second quotation at 22 June 1911, third quotation at 30 June 1935, fourth quotation at 7 July 1941, Family Affairs File; fifth quotation at [Truman] to Vivian [Truman], 8 April 1949, Vivian Truman folder, PSF:Family Correspondence; Donald R. McCoy and Richard T. Ruetten, *Quest and Response: Minority Rights and the Truman Administration* (Lawrence: University Press of Kansas, 1973), 13–16, 352–53; William C. Berman, *The Politics of Civil Rights in the Truman Administration* (Columbus: Ohio State University Press, 1970), 237–38; Richard M. Dalfiume, *Desegregation of the U.S. Armed Forces: Fighting on Two Fronts, 1939–1953* (Columbia: University of Missouri Press, 1969), 134–44.

7. Quotation in Truman interview, 30 August 1949, Daniels Papers; Truman, *Years of Trial and Hope,* 183; Monroe Billington, "Civil Rights, President Truman and the South," *Journal of Negro History* 58 (April 1973): 127–31.

8. Berman, *Politics of Civil Rights,* ix–x, 29–39, 44–53, 55–71, 79–83; McCoy and Ruetten, *Quest and Response,* 43–53, 67, 69–74, 80–83; first quotation in Truman, *Public Papers, 1947,* 311–13; second quotation in Truman to Mary Truman, 28 June 1947, Philleo Nash, "Memorandum for Mr. Truman," 21 October 1953, Security-Loyalty, Espionage folder, Post Pres.:*Memoirs,* Channing Tobias et al. to Truman, 19 September 1946, Truman to Tom C. Clark, 20 September 1946, Negro folder, PSF:General; Truman to David K. Niles, 20 September 1946, Walter White, "The President Means It," press release, 12 February 1948, Civil Rights/Negro Affairs folder, David K. Niles Papers, Truman Library.

9. Truman diary note, 2 February 1948, Post Pres.:*Memoirs;* Truman, *Public Papers, 1948,* 121–26; Bernstein, "America in War and Peace," 305–6; Truman, *Public Papers, 1948,* 179; Garson, *Democratic Party,* 170–87, 203–13, 232–35, 238–39, 241–80.

10. First quotation in Truman to Bess Wallace Truman, [4 November 1913], fourth quotation in 22 September 1947, Family Affairs File, second quotation in Truman, Recording, 6 January 1961, HST Recording Transcripts folder, Truman Papers; third quotation in Truman, *Harry S. Truman,* 304; on Mary Jane Truman's embitterment, see comment by Monte Poen, in Truman, *Letters Home by Harry Truman,* 10–11; India Edwards, Samuel Rosenman, and Matthew Connelly, oral history interviews, Truman Library; Eleanor Roosevelt

to Truman, 30 June 1946, [Eleanor Roosevelt] to Robert Hannegan, 3 June 1945, Roosevelt folder, PSF:Personal, unsigned, "List of Ambassadors and Ministers" and "List of Major Presidential Appointments," n.d. [late 1952 or 1953], Appointments, Presidential folder, PSF:General; Medved, *Shadow Presidents*, 222; Ayers diary, 14 September [1945].

11. Franklin D. Mitchell, "Harry S. Truman and the Politics of the Equal Rights Amendment, 1944–1953" (paper delivered at the American Historical Association meeting, 30 December 1984), 1–15, 17; first quotation in Truman to Emma Guffey Miller,, 20 April 1944, David Niles to William Hassett, 18 February 1946, second quotation in Truman to Miller, 12 August 1950, OF120-A, Truman Papers; Miller to India Edwards, 17 August 1950, Truman Correspondence folder, India Edwards Papers, Truman Library.

12. Edward W. Said, *Orientalism* (New York: Pantheon, 1978), 286, 307; see also the statement by Azzam Pasha in Evan M. Wilson, *Decision on Palestine: How the U.S. Came to Recognize Israel* (Stanford: Hoover Institution Press, 1979), 73–74; first two quotations in Truman, *Years of Trial and Hope*, 132–33, 135; last quotation in Miller, *Plain Speaking*, 215.

13. William R. Polk, *The Arab World* (Cambridge: Harvard University Press, 1980), 161–79; Kenneth R. Bain, *The March to Zion: United States Policy and the Founding of Israel* (College Station: Texas A&M University Press, 1979), 5–6, 9–11, 33–45, 59–60, 85–91; John Snetsinger, *Truman, the Jewish Vote, and the Creation of Israel* (Stanford: Hoover Institution Press, 1974), 1, 3–5, 9–10, 144n; Joseph B. Schechtman, *The United States and the Jewish State Movement: The Crucial Decade, 1939–1949* (New York: Herzl Press, 1966), 19–44, 59–63, 65–84; Robert W. Stookey, *America and the Arab States: An Uneasy Encounter* (New York: John Wiley, 1975), 108–9; Wilson, *Decision on Palestine*, 55–59; Michael J. Cohen, *Palestine and the Great Powers, 1945–1948* (Princeton, N.J.: Princeton University Press, 1982), 43–44; Niles to Truman, 27 May 1946, OF204, "Memorandum of Conversation between the President and Amir Faisal," 13 December 1946, PSF:Appointments.

14. Quotation in Wallace, *Price of Vision*, 607; Acheson, *Present at the Creation*, 169–71, 259; Francis Williams, *A Prime Minister Remembers: The War and Post-War Memoirs of the Rt. Hon. Earl Attlee* (London: Heinemann, 1961), 181; Bain, *March to Zion*, 61–85, 105–13, 115–34, 200–202; Wilson, *Decision on Palestine*, 7–9, 62–63, 89; Snetsinger, *Truman, the Jewish Vote*, 11–24, 26–29, 32–33, 39–44; Schechtman, *United States and the Jewish State Movement*, 13–17, 118–27, 133–45, 147–48, 152–61, 180–85; Cohen, *Palestine and the Great Powers*, 55–66.

15. Schechtman, *United States and the Jewish State Movement*, 197–207, 213–23, 250–69, 269–307; Snetsinger, *Truman, the Jewish Vote*, 12, 35–38, 45–49, 56–59, 72–93, 95–97, 99–114, 183n; Lie, *In the Cause of Peace*, 158–73; Bain, *March to Zion*, 138–58, 165–92, 192–97; Stookey, *America and the Arab*

States, 111–16; Clark Clifford interview, 26 October 1949, Daniels Papers; Cohen, *Palestine and the Great Powers,* 45–48, 295–99; Ayers diary, 20 March [1948]; Truman to Mary Truman, 21, 26 March 1948, Truman diary note, 19–21 March 1948, Post Pres.:*Memoirs,* longhand note by Truman, n.d., cabinet meetings folder, PSF:Subject, Eleanor Roosevelt to George Marshall, 16 May 1948, Truman to Mrs. Franklin Roosevelt, 20 May 1948, Roosevelt folder, PSF:Personal; Wallace, *Price of Vision,* 606; Forrestal, *Forrestal Diaries,* 309; Henderson, Connelly, and Clifford, oral history interviews; Wilson, *Decision on Palestine,* 148–49; Robert Lovett to Arthur Vandenberg, 15 July 1948, Correspondence folder, Vandenberg Papers.

16. Richard S. Kirkendall, "Election of 1948," in Schlesinger and Israel, *History of American Presidential Elections,* 4:3099–3108; Garson, *Democratic Party,* 263–64.

17. First quotation in Truman diary note, 9, 12, 13, 14 July 1948, Post Pres.:*Memoirs;* Ayers diary, 13 July [1948]; second quotation in Truman, *Public Papers, 1948,* 406–10.

18. Kirkendall, "Election of 1948," 4:3099, 3101–2, 3108–10, 3112, 3119–23, 3126–27, 3130–32, 3137–44; Truman diary note, 15 July 1948, Post Pres.:*Memoirs,* longhand note by Truman, 12 July 1960, Post Pres.:Desk, Truman to Bennett Clark, 4 August 1948, Clark folder, PSF:Personal; Garson, *Democratic Party,* 284–93, 303–10, 315–20; Matusow, *Farm Policies and Politics,* 172–84; Hartmann, *Truman and the 80th Congress,* 186–210; Ayers diary, 17 March [1948]; quotation in Truman, *Public Papers, 1948,* 189; Kirkendall, "Truman and the South," 24–29; Allen Yarnell, *Democrats and Progressives: The 1948 Presidential Election as a Test of Postwar Liberalism* (Berkeley: University of California Press, 1974), x, 2, 14–26, 60–63, 88–107, 114; Donovan, *Conflict and Crisis,* 417–18, 436–37; Snetsinger, *Truman, the Jewish Vote,* 133–35.

8. THE NATIONAL SECURITY STATE IN ACTION

1. Ayers diary, 23 March [1948].

2. Aruga Tadashi, "The United States and the Cold War: The Cold War Era in American History," in Nagai and Iriye, *Origins of the Cold War in Asia,* 66–67, 71; Carl Solberg, *Riding High: America in the Cold War* (New York: Mason & Lipscomb, 1973), 42–45; Georgi A. Arbatov and Willem Oltmans, *The Soviet Viewpoint* (New York: Dodd, Mead & Co., 1983), 15–16, 31–33, 41, 48–55; Sivachev and Yakovlev, *Russia and the United States,* 34-37, 208–9, 214–17, 220–33; Urie Bronfenbrenner, "The Mirror Image in Soviet-American Relations: A Social Psychologist's Report," *Journal of Social Issues* 17 (1961): 46–48; Ralph K. White, *Fearful Warriors: A Psychological Profile of U.S.-Soviet Relations* (New York: Free Press, 1984), ix, 2–5, 10–13, 113–22.

3. Rearden, *Formative Years*, 309–10, 422, 548–50; Cristann L. Gibson, "Patterns of Demobilization: The US and USSR after World War Two" (Ph.D. diss., University of Denver, 1983), 2–3, 11–12, 107–14, 116–18, 177–78, 191, 212–14, 285–97, 303; Alan Wolfe, *The Rise and Fall of the "Soviet Threat": Domestic Sources of the Cold War Consensus* (Washington, D.C.: Institute for Policy Studies, 1979), 2, 6–13.

4. First quotation in Truman diary note, 7 May 1948, Post. Pres.:*Memoirs*, longhand note by Truman, 11 September 1950, PSF:Longhand Notes, longhand note by Truman, 14 September 1950, J folder, PSF:Personal, Louis Johnson to Truman, 7 December 1950, Cabinet, Defense, Secy folder, PSF:Subject; Dwight D. Eisenhower, *The Eisenhower Diaries*, ed. Robert H. Ferrell (New York: W. W. Norton, 1981), 1; Rearden, *Formative Years*, 32–36, 43–50, 128, 311–30, 335–84, 388–90, 392–422, 538–39, 541; Forrestal, *Forrestal Diaries*, 350; Rosemary Foot, *The Wrong War: American Policy and the Dimensions of the Korean Conflict, 1950–1953* (Ithaca: Cornell University Press, 1985), 41; Forrestal diary, Conversation–The President, 5 October 1948, James Forrestal Papers, Princeton University Library; Acheson, *Present at the Creation*, 374.

5. Lilienthal, *Atomic Energy Years*, 464; Clarfield and Wiecek, *Nuclear America*, 101–15, 121–23; Haynes, *Awesome Power*, 70–74, 78; [Truman] to Patterson and Forrestal, 23 January 1946, NSC-Atomic, Atomic Bomb–Cabinet folder, PSF:Subject; Paul Boyer, *By the Bomb's Early Light: American Thought and Culture at the Dawn of the Atomic Age* (New York: Pantheon, 1985), 50–52; Richard G. Hewlett and Francis Duncan, *Atomic Shield, 1947–1952* (University Park: Pennsylvania State University Press, 1969), George T. Mazuzan and J. Samuel Walker, *Controlling the Atom: The Beginnings of Nuclear Regulation, 1946–1962* (Berkeley: University of California Press, 1984), 1–4, 13–20; U.S., Department of State, *Foreign Relations of the United States, 1949* (Washington, D.C.: Government Printing Office, 1976), 1:481–82; Gibson, "Patterns of Demobilization," 227–29; Kennan, *Memoirs*, 1:471–73; Rearden, *Formative Years*, 423–25, 432–46.

6. Rearden, *Formative Years*, 446–53, 455–56; Hewlett and Duncan, *Atomic Shield*, 362–409, 593; Clarfield and Wiecek, *Nuclear America*, 133; Lilienthal, *Atomic Energy Years*, 580–91, 623–32; Jonathan B. Stein, *From H-Bomb to Star Wars: The Politics of Strategic Decision Making* (Lexington, Mass.: D. C. Heath, 1984), 1–2, 41–47; Ayers diary, 4 February [1950]; longhand note by Truman, [2 March 1952], PSF:Longhand Notes, Sidney Souers interview, 16 December 1954, Souers folder, Post Pres.:*Memoirs*; U.S., Department of State, *Foreign Relations of the United States, 1950* (Washington, D.C.: Government Printing Office, 1977), 1:503–17, 541–42, 570–71.

7. First quotation in Acheson interview, 16 February 1955, Acheson folder, Post Pres.:*Memoirs*; Yergin, *Shattered Peace*, 398–401; second quotation in Gaddis, *Strategies of Containment*, 90–110; see NSC-68 in Department of States, *Foreign Relations, 1950* 1:234–92.

8. Lloyd E. Eastman, *Seeds of Destruction: Nationalist China in War and Revolution, 1937–1949* (Stanford: Stanford University Press, 1984), 216–26; Akira Iriye, *The Cold War in Asia: A Historical Introduction* (Englewood Cliffs, N.J.: Prentice-Hall, 1974), 169–76; first quotation in [Matthew Connelly], cabinet meeting, 19 January 1949, Connelly Papers; second quotation in Truman interview, 14 December 1951, Interviews folder, PSF:Mr. *President*; summary of conversation of Acheson, Ernest Bevin, and Robert Schuman, 13–15 September 1944, Acheson meeting with Ernest Bevin and Robert Schuman folder, PSF:General; David A. Mayers, *Cracking the Monolith: U.S. Policy against the Sino-Soviet Alliance, 1949–1955* (Baton Rouge: Louisiana State University Press, 1986), 16–31; Nancy B. Tucker, *Patterns in the Dust: Chinese-American Relations and the Recognition Controversy, 1949–1950* (New York: Columbia University Press, 1983), 1–3, 17–18, 38–58, 99, 111, 133, 152–53, 161–68, 173–207.

9. Bruce Cumings, "Introduction: The Course of Korean-American Relations, 1943–1953," in *Child of Conflict: The Korean-American Relationship, 1943–1953*, ed. Bruce Cumings (Seattle: University of Washington Press, 1983), 3–8; Bruce Cumings, *The Origins of the Korean War: Liberation and the Emergence of Separate Regimes, 1945–1947* (Princeton, N.J.: Princeton University Press, 1981), 47–61, 66–80, 82–108; James I. Matray, *The Reluctant Crusade: American Foreign Policy in Korea, 1941–1950* (Honolulu: University of Hawaii Press, 1985), 28–44; Gregory Henderson, *Korea: The Politics of the Vortex* (Cambridge: Harvard University Press, 1968), 120–27; Dobbs, *Unwanted Symbol*, 15–28; Soon Heung Kang, "The Problem of Autonomy for Korea Amid Rivalries of Great Powers: The Search for a New Order" (Ph.D. diss., University of Iowa, 1974), chaps. 4–5.

10. Cumings, *Origins of Korean War*, xix–xxi, 111–29, 135–50, 153–56, 158–77, 179–209, 214–27, 238–46, 267–76, 293–95, 350–82, 396–412, 414–22, 428–29, 440, 443; Kolko and Kolko, *Limits of Power*, 293–99; Dobbs, *Unwanted Symbol*, 37–48, 76–78; Stueck, *Road to Confrontation*, 76–95; Matray, *Reluctant Crusade*, 52, 73–79, 86–115, 123–26, 151–64; Khrushchev, *Khrushchev Remembers*, 367–70; Robert R. Simmons, "The Communist Side: An Exploratory Sketch," in *The Korean War: A 25-Year Perspective*, ed. Francis H. Heller (Lawrence: Regents Press of Kansas, 1977), 197–207.

11. Truman to [Vandenberg], 6 July 1950, Correspondence folder, Vandenberg Papers; Truman, *Years of Trial and Hope*, 339–41, 437, 463–64; Stephen Pelz, "U.S. Decisions on Korean Policy, 1943–1950: Some Hypotheses," in Cumings, *Child of Conflict*, 103, 105–6, 111–27, 132.

12. Quotations in Donovan, *Tumultuous Years*, 193–99, 202–3; Glenn D. Paige, *The Korean Decision: June 24–30, 1950* (New York: Free Press, 1968), 81–94, 97–100, 114, 116–41, 282–86, 299; Foot, *Wrong War*, 32–36; Pelz, "U.S. Decisions on Korean Policy," 127–31; Acheson, *Among Friends*, 100; James F. Schnabel, *Policy and Direction: The First Year* (Washington, D.C.: Office of the Chief of Military History, U.S. Army, 1972), 61, 65–66; James F. Schnabel and

Robert J. Watson, *The Korean War* (Wilmington, Del.: Michael Glazier, 1979), 72–73; Joseph C. Goulden, *Korea: The Untold Story of the War* (New York: Times Books, 1982), xix–xx, 38–41, 55–58, 107–8; last quotation in U.S., Department of State, *Foreign Relations of the United States, 1950* (Washington, D.C.: Government Printing Office, 1976), 7:157–61.

13. Paige, *Korean Decision*, 148–49, 161–79, 253–56, 276–77; Schnabel and Watson, *Korean War*, 117, 123–25; George Elsey, notes on conversation with Truman, 26 June 1950, Korea folder, Elsey Papers; Department of State, *Foreign Relations, 1950*, 7:178–83, 200–202, 240–41, 248–53; Schnabel, *Policy and Direction*, 76–77, 77n; Goulden, *Korea*, 96–106; longhand note by Truman, 30 June 1950, MacArthur folder, PSF:General, Acheson interview, 18 February 1955, Post. Pres.:*Memoirs*; Department of State, *Foreign Relations, 1950*, 7:286–91.

14. Goulden, *Korea*, 114–29, 140–44; Donovan, *Tumultuous Years*, 218, 248–53, 255–57; Jon Halliday, "The United Nations and Korea," in *Without Parallel: The American-Korean Relationship since 1945*, ed. Frank Baldwin (New York: Pantheon, 1974), 109–24; Schnabel and Watson, *Korean War*, 137–38; Schnabel, *Policy and Direction*, 137–54.

15. Department of State, *Foreign Relations, 1950*, 7:449–54, 558–61, 600–603, 623–28; quotation in Robert J. Donovan, *Nemesis: Truman and Johnson in the Coils of War in Asia* (New York: St. Martin's, 1984), 84–86; Truman interview, 15 November 1954, Korea-MacArthur Dismissal folder, Post. Pres.:*Memoirs*.

16. Walter LaFeber, "Crossing the 38th: The Cold War in Microcosm," in *Reflections on the Cold War: A Quarter Century of American Foreign Policy*, ed. Lynn H. Miller and Ronald W. Pruessen (Philadelphia: Temple University Press, 1974), 71–90; Department of State, *Foreign Relations, 1950*, 7:502–10, 712–21, 792–93; John J. Muccio, oral history interview, Truman Library; Douglas MacArthur, *Reminiscences* (New York: McGraw-Hill, 1964), 362; Stueck, *Road to Confrontation*, 238–41; Goulden, *Korea*, 240–41, 248–54; James, *Triumph and Disaster*, 492–93, 499–500.

17. Goulden, *Korea*, 274–301, 307–17; Ulam, *Rivals*, 181; Donovan, *Nemesis*, 87–89; Schnabel, *Policy and Direction*, 233–56, 277–78; James, *Triumph and Disaster*, 518–24; Stueck, *Road to Confrontation*, 250, 257–58; Schnabel and Watson, *Korean War*, 300–32; Department of State, *Foreign Relations, 1950*, 7:790–92, 795–96, 839, 848; D. A. [Dean Acheson], untitled memo, 9 October 1950, Cabinet, State, Secy of, folder, PSF:Subject; Irving L. Janis, *Victims of Groupthink: A Psychological Study of Foreign-Policy Decisions and Fiascoes* (Boston: Houghton Mifflin, 1972), 13, 57–74, 197–98; Irving L. Janis and Leon Mann, *Decision Making: A Psychological Analysis of Conflict, Choice, and Commitment* (New York: Free Press, 1977), 78, 82, 107–8, 129–32, 172.

18. MacArthur to Joint Chiefs, 28 November 1950, in Department of State, *Foreign Relations, 1950*, 7:1237–38; Acheson, *Among Friends*, 103; John

Hersey, *Aspects of the Presidency* (New Haven: Ticknor & Fields, 1980), 27–29, 54–63; Williams, *A Prime Minister Remembers,* 233–40.

19. Joe Martin with Robert J. Donovan, *My First Fifty Years in Politics* (New York: McGraw-Hill, 1960), 204–7; James, *Triumph and Disaster,* 438, 556–59; Manchester, *American Caesar,* 641–44; Roger W. Tubby, oral history interview, Truman Library; Truman, *Years of Trial and Hope,* 415–17, 440–50; Ayers diary, 1 July [1950]; [Truman], "The MacArthur Dismissal," 28 April 1951, "Text of General MacArthur's Korean Statement," 25 March 1951, MacArthur Dismissal folder, Joint Chiefs to MacArthur, 20 March 1951, MacArthur Message folder, PSF:General, Omar Bradley interview, 30 March 1955, Bradley folder, Post Pres.:*Memoirs,* Truman diary notes, 6–9 April 1951, PSF:Diaries, Truman Papers.

20. First quotation in Truman, *Harry S. Truman,* 516; second quotation in Ronald J. Caridi, *The Korean War and American Politics: The Republican Party as a Case Study* (Philadelphia: University of Pennsylvania Press, 1968), 148; Manchester, *American Caesar,* 645–64; Martin, *My First Years in Politics,* 208–9; John E. Wiltz, "The Korean War and American Society," in Heller, *Korean War,* 143, 145; Goulden, *Korea,* 509–11.

9. FIGHTING COMMUNISM AT HOME AND ABROAD

1. Harry S. Truman, *Public Papers of the Presidents of the United States, Harry S. Truman, 1949* (Washington, D.C.: Government Printing Office, 1964), 1–7, 208–13, 226–30; quotation in longhand note by Truman, 30 November 1950, PSF:Longhand Notes; Poen, *Harry S. Truman versus the Medical Lobby,* 140–68, 187–209; Truman, *Years of Trial and Hope,* 264–68; Matusow, *Farm Policies and Politics,* 110–25, 138–44, 171–72, 192–221; Davies, *Housing Reform during the Truman Administration,* 101–14, 116–32, 134–41.

2. McCoy and Ruetten, *Quest and Response,* 154–57, 171–87, 190–200, 247–50, 284–90, 298–302, 346–50; Dalfiume, *Desegregation of the U.S. Armed Forces,* 1–63, 82–131, 158–219; Kenneth C. Royall to Truman, 17 September 1948, Agencies-Military-Comm. on Equality of Treatment and Opportunity in the Armed Services folder, PSF:Subject, Philip Perlman interview, 16 December 1954, Perlman folder, Post. Pres.:*Memoirs;* Tom C. Clark, oral history interview, Truman Library.

3. Truman, *Mr. Citizen,* 175; quotation in Clayton R. Koppes, "From New Deal to Termination: Liberalism and Indian Policy, 1933–1953," *Pacific Historical Review* 46 (November 1977): 543–46, 552–66.

4. Richard Funston, "Great Presidents, Great Justices?" *Presidential Studies Quarterly* 7 (Fall 1977): 191–99; Thomas K. McCraw, *Prophets of Regulation: Charles Francis Adams, Louis D. Brandeis, James M. Landis, Alfred E. Kahn* (Cambridge: Harvard University Press, 1984), 217.

5. Pemberton, *Bureaucratic Politics.*

6. Yergin, *Shattered Peace*, 196, 216–17; Athan G. Theoharis, *The Truman Presidency: The Origins of the Imperial Presidency and the National Security State* (Stanfordville, N.Y.: Earl M. Coleman, 1979), iii–v, [10]; Theoharis, "Truman Presidency," 54–55, William M. Leary, ed., *The Central Intelligence Agency: History and Documents* (University, Ala.: University of Alabama Press, 1984), 16–18, 20–28, 37–46, NSC-10/2 at 131–33; Sidney Souers interview, 15 December 1954, Souers folder, Post Pres.:*Memoirs*.

7. Robert Griffith, *The Politics of Fear: Joseph R. McCarthy and the Senate* (Lexington: University Press of Kentucky, 1970), ix–x, 15–26, 28–35, 37–45, 52–100, 116–17; Robert Griffith and Athan Theoharis, Introduction to *The Specter: Original Essays on the Cold War and the Origins of McCarthyism*, ed. Robert Griffith and Athan Theoharis (New York: Franklin Watts, 1974), x–xi; first quotation in Acheson interview, 17 February 1955, Acheson folder, Post Pres.:*Memoirs*; second quotation in Donovan, *Tumultuous Years*, 133.

8. Truman, *Years of Trial and Hope*, 171; Truman interview, 15 January 1952, PSF:Mr. *President*, unsigned, "Truman Record on Communism," n.d., Desk Files folder, PSF:Personal; Bernstein, "America in War and Peace," 309–12; Peter L. Steinberg, *The Great "Red Menace": United States Prosecution of American Communists, 1947–1952* (Westport, Conn.: Greenwood Press, 1984), xi–xiv, 185–88, Connelly, notes on cabinet meetings, 31 October 1947, Connelly Papers; Alan D. Harper, *The Politics of Loyalty: The White House and the Communist Issue, 1946–1952* (Westport, Conn.: Greenwood Press, 1969), 1–2, 25–45, 48–52; Weisberger, *Cold War Cold Peace*, 73–75; John Lord O'Brian, *National Security and Individual Freedom* (Cambridge: Harvard University Press, 1955), 21–30.

9. Quotation in Truman to Bess Truman, 3 June 1945, 27 September 1947, Family Affairs File, longhand note by Truman, 12 May 1945, PSF:Longhand Notes, for wiretaps, see PSF:Summaries of Conversations (Cochran), Truman Papers; Connelly, cabinet meeting, 15 September 1950, Connelly Papers; for Hoover reports, see FBI folder, PSF:Subject; Miller, *Plain Speaking*, 16n; Kenneth O'Reilly, *Hoover and the Un-Americans: The FBI, HUAC, and the Red Menace* (Philadelphia: Temple University Press, 1983), 75–77, 79–86, 91–96, 101–18, 149–67; Athan G. Theoharis, *Spying on Americans: Political Surveillance from Hoover to the Huston Plan* (Philadelphia: Temple University Press, 1978), 40–54, 67–81, 99–107, 160–63.

10. Maeva Marcus, *Truman and the Steel Seizure Case: The Limits of Presidential Power* (New York: Columbia University Press, 1977), 248; Truman to William O. Douglas, 9 July 1952, not sent, Douglas folder, PSF:General, John R. Steelman interview, 8 December 1954, Steelman folder, Post Pres.:*Memoirs*.

11. First quotation in Truman to Will Durant, 7 November 1951, D Folder, PSF:General, longhand notes by Truman, 21 June 1951, second quotation in 27 January 1952, third quotation in 18 May 1952, PSF:Longhand Notes, Truman interview, 2 January 1952, PSF:Mr. *President*, [Truman] to Acheson, 14

October 1958, Correspondence General folder, Post Pres.:Desk; Gaddis, *Strategies of Containment*, 111–15; Goulden, *Korea*, 549–55; Foot, *Wrong War*, 9, 26–28, 174–88, 194–215; Matray, *Reluctant Crusade*, 1–4, 253–58; Hamby, *Beyond the New Deal*, 441; Dobbs, *Unwanted Symbol*, 191, 194–96; Gardner, *Covenant with Power*, 117–18; Callum A. MacDonald, *Korea: The War before Vietnam* (New York: Free Press, 1986), 259.

12. Kennan quotation in Walter LaFeber, *Inevitable Revolutions: The United States in Central America* (New York: W. W. Norton, 1983), 85–97, 106–10; U.S., Department of State, *Foreign Relations of the United States, 1949* (Washington, D.C.: Government Printing Office, 1976), 5:42–54; 198–207; Pollard, *Economic Security*, 107–13, 197–98, 203–5, 209–18, 221; Kolko and Kolko, *Limits of Power*, 412–13, 620–30; Thomas M. Leonard, *The United States and Central America, 1944-1949: Perceptions of Political Dynamics* (University, Ala.: University of Alabama Press, 1984), 1–11, 13; David Green, *The Containment of Latin America: A History of the Myths and Realities of the Good Neighbor Policy* (Chicago: Quadrangle, 1971), 255–73, 291–96; 81; Thomas J. Noer, *Cold War and Black Liberation: The United States and White Rule in Africa, 1948–1968* (Columbia: University of Missouri Press, 1985), 1, 15–32, 253–55; Stookey, *America and the Arab States*, xiii, 87–93, 132–34, 136, 264.

13. Roosevelt quotation in Rose, *Roots of Tragedy*, 20–31, 47–52, 55–63, 65–68, 71, 78–94; Borden, *Pacific Alliance*, 16, 120–21, 140–1, 186; Schaller, *American Occupation of Japan*, 234–45, 278–79, 290–98; Robert J. McMahon, *Colonialism and Cold War: The United States and the Struggle for Indonesian Independence, 1945–49* (Ithaca: Cornell University Press, 1981), 304–15; Ronald H. Spector, *Advice and Support: The Early Years, 1941–1960* (Washington, D.C.: Center of Military History, U.S. Army, 1983), 90–104, 106–7, 123, 148–65; Evelyn Colbert, *Southeast Asia in International Politics, 1941–1956* (Ithaca: Cornell University Press, 1977), 13–20, 54–55, 86–89, 125–27, 137–43, 197–98, 202–4, 215; Robert M. Blum, *Drawing the Line: The Origin of the American Containment Policy in East Asia* (New York: W. W. Norton, 1982), 5, 214–19; Baritz, *Backfire*, 66–73; James P. Harrison, *The Endless War: Fifty Years of Struggle in Vietnam* (New York: Free Press, 1982), 91–92, 98–122; Ronald E. Irving, *The First Indochina War: French and American Policy, 1945–54* (London: Croom Helm, 1975), 55–58, 99–107, 133–37; Buhite, *Soviet-American Relations in Asia*, 191–209; Acheson quotation in Acheson, *Present at the Creation*, 671–77; Connelly, cabinet meeting, 20 October 1950, Connelly papers; Truman, *Years of Trial and Hope*, 518–19; "Notes on the President's Meeting with Undersecretary of State James Webb," 26 March 1950, Webb folder, Charles G. Ross Papers, Truman Library. For important documents on Vietnam in the *Foreign Relations* series, see: Department of State, *Foreign Relations, 1945*, 5:843, *Foreign Relations of the United States, 1945* (Washington, D.C.: Government Printing Office, 1969), 6:1404, *Foreign Relations of the United States, 1946* (Washington, D.C.: Government Printing Office, 1971), 8:76, *Foreign Relations of the United*

States, 1949 (Washington, D.C.: Government Printing Office, 7:23–25, 101–2, "overripe apples" quotation at 105–10, 114, *Foreign Relations of the United States, 1950* (Washington, D.C.: Government Printing Office, 1976), 6:698–700, State Department working group quotation at 711–15, 717, 719, 722–23, 730–33, 812, *Foreign Relations, 1950,* 7:624–25 contains Kennan quotation.

10. THE MERRY-GO-ROUND SLOWS

1. Truman to Bess Truman, 29 June 1949, 7 June 1950, Family Affairs File.

2. First quotation in John Tebbel and Sarah M. Watts, *The Press and the Presidency: From George Washington to Ronald Reagan* (New York: Oxford University Press, 1985), 457–63; Truman, *Harry S. Truman,* 427; Truman, *Year of Decisions,* 47; Hersey, *Aspects of the Presidency,* 42–43; Truman, *Strictly Personal and Confidential,* 9–10, 21–22; Truman to Bess Truman, 26 July 1942, Family Affairs File, Truman to Martha and Mary Truman, 16 October 1946, Family Correspondence folder, PSF, second quotation in Truman to Martha and Mary Truman, 12 October 1946, Post Pres.:*Memoirs,* longhand note by Truman, 18 January 1952, PSF:Longhand Notes.

3. Dunar, *Truman Scandals,* 21–30, 33, 37–76, 78–121, 127–34, 136–47, 158–59; Chicago newspaper quotation in Siskind and Parks to William Boyle, 12 April 1951, Boyle folder, PSF:General.

4. Longhand notes by Truman, 16 April, 8 May 1950, 9, 18 February 1952, n.d. [probably 1952], PSF:Longhand Notes, Truman interview, 19 October 1953, Politics–1952 Campaign Activities folder, Post Pres.:*Memoirs;* Barton J. Bernstein, "Election of 1952," in Schlesinger and Israel, *History of American Presidential Elections,* 4:3215–336; George W. Ball, *The Past Has Another Pattern: Memoirs* (New York: W. W. Norton, 1982), 115–17; Truman, *Bess W. Truman,* 380–81, 383; Matthew Connelly and Charles Murphy, oral history interviews; Charles Murphy to Robert L. Dennison, 18 August 1952, President Harry S. Truman, Decision Not to Run folder, Robert L. Dennison Papers, Truman Library.

5. Longhand notes by Truman, 4 March, 7, 24 July, 22, 25 December 1952, n.d. [probably 1952], PSF:Longhand Notes.

6. Eisenhower, *Eisenhower Diaries,* 195; William B. Ewald, Jr., *Eisenhower the President: Crucial Days, 1951–1960* (Englewood Cliffs, N.J.: Prentice-Hall, 1981), 31–37; Hechler, *Working with Truman,* 245; Donovan, *Tumultuous Years,* 392–94; Bernstein, "Election of 1952," 3264–65; Truman to [John] Sparkman, not sent, longhand notes by Truman, 7 July, 15, 20 November, 22 December 1952, Truman to [Stevenson], not sent, n.d., Truman to Stevenson, not sent, n.d., Truman to Stevenson, not sent, n.d., [1953 folder], PSF:Longhand Notes, Truman to Bryce B. Smith, 23 May 1950, Smith folder, PSF:Person-

al, Truman to Eisenhower, 6 April 1952, North Atlantic Treaty folder, PSF:General, Truman interview, 6 November 1951, PSF:Mr. *President.*

7. Miller, *Plain Speaking,* 15–16, 20; Richard Rose, *The Capacity of the President: A Comparative Analysis* (Glasgow, Scotland: University of Strathclyde, Center for the Study of Public Policy, 1984), 64–71; Franklin D. Mitchell, "Harry S Truman and the Verdict of History," *South Atlantic Quarterly* 85 (Summer 1986): 261, 265–68; Gary M. Maranell, "The Evaluation of Presidents: An Extension of the Schlesinger Polls," *Journal of American History* 57 (June 1970): 105–13; Robert K. Murray and Tim H. Blessing, "The Presidential Performance Study: A Progress Report," *Journal of American History* 70 (December 1983): 537–45; comment by Robert H. Ferrell in Harry S. Truman, *Dear Bess: The Letters from Harry to Bess Truman, 1910–1959* (New York: W. W. Norton, 1983), 452–53; William E. Leuchtenburg, untitled address (speech delivered in New York, New York, 2 October 1984).

8. Churchill quotation in Truman, *Harry S. Truman,* 556; Barber, *Presidential Character,* 13, 246, 263–64, 271–72, 276–78, 280–82, 285, 453–54; Truman interview, 3 October 1951, PSF:Mr. *President.*

9. Lilienthal, *Atomic Energy Years,* 430; Haynes, *Awesome Power,* 21–22; Solberg, *Riding High,* 74–76.

10. Solberg, *Riding High,* 79–87, 248–53, 491–97; Deutscher, *Ironies of History,* 148; Allen J. Matusow, *The Unraveling of America: A History of Liberalism in the 1960s* (New York: Harper & Row, 1984), 3–7; Hamby, *Beyond the New Deal,* 353–54; Weisberger, *Cold War Cold Peace,* 81–82; Robert Griffith, "Old Progressives and the Cold War," *Journal of American History* 66 (September 1979): 334–479.

11. Joseph Kennedy quotation in Alfred Steinberg, *The Man from Missouri: The Life and Times of Harry S. Truman* (New York: G. P. Putnam's 1962), 428; Acheson, *Among Friends,* 120–21, 184–85, 192; Robbins and Smith, *Last of His Kind,* 14, 16–18, 105; Truman, *Mr. Citizen,* 26, 78–82; Tom L. Evans, oral history interview, Truman Library; Truman, *Bess W. Truman,* 411–12; Ron Cockrell, *The Trumans of Independence: Historic Resource Study, Harry S. Truman National Historic Site, Independence, Missouri* (Washington, D.C.: National Park Service 1985), 284, 329–35, 345, 360–61, 363, 369–70, 394; [Truman] to [Acheson], 7 July [1961], 22 August 1959, Correspondence Acheson folder, Truman to Harriman, [November 1958], Correspondence General folder, Post Pres.:Desk, Truman to Margaret Truman, 20 August 1955, Family Affairs File, Truman diary note, 21 January 1953, PSF:Diaries; last quotation in Richard Rhodes, "Harry's Last Hurrah," *Harper's Magazine* 240 (January 1970): 56.

BIBLIOGRAPHIC ESSAY

The Truman Library holds over four hundred manuscript collections, including the massive body of White House files, papers of cabinet officers and staff members, and those of Truman friends and associates. It also holds over four hundred oral history interviews, which are available on interlibrary loan. For the biographer, the essential manuscript records are the twelve hundred letters that Truman wrote to Bess Truman, Truman "Diary" jottings that provide immediate, usually pointed, comments on events, and longhand notes in which Truman often reflected on the events of his life.

Bibliographies on the Truman administration include: Richard S. Kirkendall, ed., *The Truman Period as a Research Field* (Columbia: University of Missouri Press, 1967); Richard S. Kirkendall, ed., *The Truman Period as a Research Field: A Reappraisal, 1972* (Columbia: University of Missouri Press, 1974); and Richard D. Burns, ed., *Harry S. Truman: A Bibliography of His Times and Presidency* (Wilmington, Del.: Scholarly Resources, 1984). The Truman years continue to call forth major work on foreign policy by many of the nation's best scholars. Much of that material is found annotated in several chapters in Richard D. Burns, ed., *Guide to American Foreign Relations since 1700* (Santa Barbara: ABC-Clio, 1983).

Truman's published writings provide the starting place for a study of his life. The first volume of his *Memoirs* traces his first year in office, with an extended account of his prepresidential years, and the second volume covers the rest of his presidency: *Year of Decisions* (Garden City, N.Y.: Doubleday, 1955); *Years of Trial and Hope* (Garden City, N.Y.: Doubleday, 1956). In a later book, *Mr. Citizen* (New York: Bernard Geis, 1960), Truman discusses his return to Independence and his reflections on government, history, and life. Truman letters have been published in several edited volumes: Margaret Truman, *Letters from Father: The Truman Family's Personal Correspondence* (New York: Arbor House, 1981); Robert H. Ferrell, *Dear Bess: The Letters from Harry to Bess Truman, 1910–1959* (New York: W. W. Norton, 1983); Monte M. Poen, *Strictly*

Personal and Confidential: The Letters Harry Truman Never Mailed (Boston: Little, Brown, 1982); and Monte M. Poen, *Letters Home by Harry Truman* (New York: G. P. Putnam's 1984); Ferrell also edited a collection of Truman's letters, diary entries, and memoranda in *Off the Record: The Private Papers of Harry S. Truman* (New York: Harper & Row, 1980).

Truman's speeches, press conferences, veto messages, and other official documents can be found in *Public Papers of the Presidents of the United States, Harry S. Truman,* 8 vols. (Washington, D.C.: Government Printing Office, 1961–66). Thousands of pages of important diplomatic records of the Truman years can be found in U.S., Department of State, *Foreign Relations of the United States* (Washington, D.C.: Government Printing Office, 1967–84). Other collections of documents include: Thomas H. Etzold and John L. Gaddis, eds., *Containment: Documents on American Policy and Strategy, 1945–1950* (New York: Columbia University Press, 1978); Robert C. Williams and Philip L. Cantelon, eds., *The American Atom: A Documentary History of Nuclear Policies from the Discovery of Fission to the Present, 1939–1984* (Philadelphia: University of Pennsylvania Press, 1984); and Athan G. Theoharis, ed., *The Truman Presidency: The Origins of the Imperial Presidency and the National Security State* (Stanfordville, N.Y.: Earl M. Coleman, 1979); *The State Department Policy Planning Staff Papers, 1947–1949,* 3 vols. (New York: Garland, 1983); Gareth Porter, ed., *Vietnam: The Definitive Documentation of Human Decisions,* vol. 1 (Stanfordville, N.Y.: Earl M. Coleman, 1979).

Early biographers had an opportunity to draw on interviews of Truman friends and associates. One of these books stands up very well: Jonathan Daniels, *The Man of Independence* (Philadelphia: J. B. Lippincott, 1950). Another journalist-biographer more recently provided a basic chronicle of the Truman presidency, Robert J. Donovan, *Conflict and Crisis: The Presidency of Harry S. Truman, 1945–1948* (New York: W. W. Norton, 1977), and *Tumultuous Years: The Presidency of Harry S. Truman, 1949–1953* (New York: W. W. Norton, 1982). Other biographies include those by Truman scholar Donald R. McCoy, *The Presidency of Harry S. Truman* (Lawrence: University Press of Kansas, 1984), and Britisher Roy Jenkins, *Truman* (New York: Harper & Row, 1986). An admiring biography is Robert H. Ferrell, *Harry S. Truman and the Modern American Presidency* (Boston: Little, Brown, 1983), and a critical one is Bert Cochran, *Harry Truman and the Crisis Presidency* (New York: Funk and Wagnalls, 1973). Margaret Truman wrote a biography of her father, *Harry S. Truman* (New York: William Morrow, 1973), and a valuable biography of her mother, *Bess W. Truman* (New York: Macmillan, 1986). Alonzo L. Hamby is now writing an extended biography, which will soon be available.

My note citations indicate the sources that I used most frequently. A few were especially important in shaping my thinking. Richard S. Kirkendall directed my graduate research at the University of Missouri, as he did many other Truman scholars. I especially drew heavily from his articles: "Truman's Path to

Power," *Social Science* 43 (April 1968): 67–73, and "Harry S. Truman: A Missouri Farmer in the Golden Age," *Agricultural History* 48 (October 1974): 467–83. Citations to many of Barton J. Bernstein's articles on Truman can be found in my notes, and more can be found in Richard D. Burns's bibliography, *Harry S. Truman: A Bibliography of His Times and Presidency*. Two that I found especially useful are "Roosevelt, Truman, and the Atomic Bomb, 1941–1945: A Reinterpretation," *Political Science Quarterly* 90 (Spring 1975): 23–69, and "America in War and Peace: The Test of Liberalism," in *Towards a New Past: Dissenting Essays in American History*, ed. Barton J. Bernstein (New York: Pantheon, 1968).

Richard L. Miller has written provocatively and in detail on Truman's early career: *Truman: The Rise to Power* (New York: McGraw-Hill, 1986). An important book on Truman's domestic policy and on his political thought is Alonzo L. Hamby, *Beyond the New Deal: Harry S. Truman and American Liberalism* (New York: Columbia University Press, 1973). Excellent works on Truman's domestic administration include: Richard M. Dalfiume, *Desegregation of the U.S. Armed Forces: Fighting on Two Fronts, 1939–1953* (Columbia: University of Missouri Press, 1969); Richard O. Davies, *Housing Reform during the Truman Administration* (Columbia: University of Missouri Press, 1966); Andrew J. Dunar, *The Truman Scandals and the Politics of Morality* (Columbia: University of Missouri Press, 1984); Susan M. Hartmann, *Truman and the Eightieth Congress* (Columbia: University of Missouri Press, 1971); R. Alton Lee, *Truman and Taft-Hartley: A Question of Mandate* (Lexington: University of Kentucky Press, 1966); Donald R. McCoy and Richard T. Ruetten, *Quest and Response: Minority Rights and the Truman Administration* (Lawrence: University Press of Kansas, 1973); Allen J. Matusow, *Farm Policies and Politics in the Truman Years* (Cambridge: Harvard University Press, 1967); and Monte M. Poen, *Harry S. Truman versus the Medical Lobby: The Genesis of Medicare* (Columbia: University of Missouri Press, 1979). Rounding off books on the Fair Deal is my *Bureaucratic Politics: Executive Reorganization during the Truman Administration* (Columbia: University of Missouri Press, 1979).

In chapter 9, I cited many of the important sources on McCarthyism and related subjects. The works of Robert Griffith and Athan G. Theoharis were very important to me: Griffith, *The Politics of Fear: Joseph R. McCarthy and the Senate* (Amherst: University of Massachusetts Press, 1987); Griffith and Theoharis, eds., *The Specter: Original Essays on the Cold War and the Origins of McCarthyism* (New York: Franklin Watts, 1974); Theoharis, *Spying on Americans: Political Surveillance from Hoover to the Huston Plan* (Philadelphia: Temple University Press, 1978); Theoharis, ed., *The Truman Presidency: The Origins of the Imperial Presidency and the National Security State* (Stanfordville, N.Y.: Earl M. Coleman, 1979); Theoharis, *Seeds of Repression: Harry S. Truman and the Origins of McCarthyism* (Chicago: Quadrangle, 1971); and Theoharis, ed., *Beyond the Hiss Case: The FBI, Congress, and the Cold War* (Philadelphia: Temple University Press, 1982). I also drew heavily from Richard M. Freeland, *The Truman Doc-*

trine and the Origins of McCarthyism: Foreign Policy, Domestic Politics, and Internal Security, 1946–1948 (New York: Alfred A. Knopf, 1972). Additional important books include Walter Goodman, *The Committee: The Extraordinary Career of the House Committee on Un-American Activities* (New York: Farrar, Straus & Giroux, 1968); David Caute, *The Great Fear: The Anti-Communist Purge under Truman and Eisenhower* (New York: Simon and Schuster, 1978); David M. Oshinsky, *A Conspiracy So Immense: The World of Joe McCarthy* (New York: Free Press, 1983); Richard M. Fried, *Men against McCarthy* (New York: Columbia University Press, 1976); Ronald Radosh and Joyce Milton, *The Rosenberg File: A Search for the Truth* (New York: Holt, Rinehart and Winston, 1983); Allen Weinstein, *Perjury: The Hiss-Chambers Case* (New York: Alfred A. Knopf, 1978); and Ellen W. Schrecker, *No Ivory Tower: McCarthyism and the Universities* (New York: Oxford University Press, 1986).

The history profession can take pride in the outpouring of high-quality work, often with conflicting interpretations, on the cold war. Overviews of the origins of the cold war include Thomas G. Paterson, *Soviet-American Confrontation: Postwar Reconstruction and the Origins of the Cold War* (Baltimore: Johns Hopkins University Press, 1973), and his *On Every Front: The Making of the Cold War* (New York: W. W. Norton, 1979); Daniel Yergin, *Shattered Peace: The Origins of the Cold War and the National Security State* (Boston: Houghton Mifflin, 1977); Melvyn P. Leffler, "The American Conception of National Security and the Beginnings of the Cold War, 1945–48," *American Historical Review* 89 (April 1984): 346–81; John L. Gaddis, *The United States and the Origins of the Cold War, 1941–1947* (New York: Columbia University Press, 1972) and his *Strategies of Containment: A Critical Appraisal of Postwar American National Security Policy* (New York: Oxford University Press, 1982); Gabriel Kolko, *The Politics of War: The World and United States Foreign Policy, 1943–1945* (New York: Random House, 1968); and Joyce Kolko and Gabriel Kolko, *The Limits of Power: The World and United States Foreign Policy, 1945–1954* (New York: Harper & Row, 1972).

Books I often turned to on aspects of military and foreign policy include: Martin J. Sherwin, *A World Destroyed: The Atomic Bomb and the Grand Alliance* (New York: Alfred A. Knopf, 1975); Steven L. Rearden, *The Formative Years, 1947–1950* (Washington, D.C.: Office of Secretary of Defense, 1984); Robert A. Pollard, *Economic Security and the Origins of the Cold War, 1945–1950* (New York: Columbia University Press, 1985); Lawrence S. Wittner, *American Intervention in Greece, 1943–1949* (New York: Columbia University Press, 1982); Bruce R. Kuniholm, *The Origins of the Cold War in the New East* (Princeton, N.J.: Princeton University Press, 1980); William S. Borden, *The Pacific Alliance: United States Foreign Economic Policy and Japanese Trade Recovery, 1947–1955* (Madison: University of Wisconsin Press, 1984); Bruce Cumings, *The Origins of the Korean War: Liberation and the Emergence of Separate Regimes, 1945–1947* (Princeton, N.J.: Princeton University Press, 1981); Rosemary Foot, *The Wrong*

War: American Policy and the Dimensions of the Korean Conflict, 1950–1953 (Ithaca: Cornell University Press, 1985); and Michael Schaller, *The American Occupation of Japan: The Origins of the Cold War in Asia* (New York: Oxford University Press, 1985).

Recent books on the cold war include James L. Gormly, *The Collapse of the Grand Alliance, 1945–1948* (Baton Rouge: Louisiana State University Press, 1987); John L. Harper, *America and the Reconstruction of Italy, 1945–1948* (New York: Cambridge University Press, 1986); Hugh Thomas, *Armed Truce: The Beginnings of the Cold War, 1945–46* (New York: Atheneum, 1987); Gordon E. Dean, *Forging the Atomic Shield: Excerpts from the Office Diary of Gordon E. Dean,* ed. Roger M. Anders (Chapel Hill: University of North Carolina Press, 1987); June M. Grasso, *Truman's Two-China Policy: 1948–1950* (Armonk, N.Y.: M. E. Sharpe, 1987; Gary R. Hess, *The United States' Emergence as a Southeast Asian Power, 1940–1950* (New York: Columbia University Press, 1987); Michael J. Hogan, *The Marshall Plan: America, Britain, and the Reconstruction of Western Europe, 1947–1952* (New York: Cambridge University Press, 1987); and Thomas G. Paterson, *Meeting the Communist Threat: Truman to Reagan* (New York: Oxford University Press, 1988).

INDEX

217

ABOUT THE AUTHOR

William Erwin Pemberton was born in Duncan, Oklahoma, in 1940. He attended the University of Oklahoma and University of Missouri, where he received his Ph.D. in 1974. He has taught at the University of Wisconsin–La Crosse since 1966 and is the author of *Bureaucratic Politics: Executive Reorganization during the Truman Administration* (Columbia: University of Missouri Press, 1979). He lives in Galesville, Wisconsin, with his wife, Martha. He has two sons, Gregory Alan and David Gregory, and a dog, Sage.